Fort Worth Characters

by

Richard F. Selcer

University of North Texas Press
Denton, Texas

Printed in the United States of America.

10 9 8 7 6 5 4 3 2 1

Permissions:
University of North Texas Press
1155 Union Circle #311336
Denton, TX 76203-5017

The paper used in this book meets the minimum requirements of the American National Standard for Permanence of Paper for Printed Library Materials, z39.48.1984. Binding materials have been chosen for durability.

Library of Congress Cataloging-in-Publication Data

Selcer, Richard F.
Fort Worth characters / by Richard Selcer. -- 1st ed.
p. cm.
Includes bibliographical references and index.
ISBN 978-1-57441-274-1 (cloth : alk. paper)
ISBN 978-1-57441-275-8 (pbk. : alk. paper)
1. Fort Worth (Tex.)--History--19th century--Biography--Anecdotes.
2. Fort Worth (Tex.)--History--20th century--Biography--Anecdotes.
I. Title.
F394.F7S4484 2009
976.4'5315050922--dc22
[B]
2009019433

Design by Angela Schmitt

Cover art: "Independence Day (Tarrant County Courthouse)"
by Randy Souders

Contents

ACKNOWLEDGMENTS

This book would not have happened without some very important people. At the top of the list must be Shirley Apley, "the Goddess" of the Genealogy, Local History, and Archives Unit of the Fort Worth Public Library. More than a goddess, Shirley is a wizard at genealogical research. Other members of the library's Genealogy, Local History, and Archives Unit who proved invaluable include Betty Shankle, Tom Kellam, and Donna Kruse, and in an emeritus capacity, Max Hill. In an age of Internet research and Google searches, old-fashioned human reference librarians and archivists are still important; in fact, we who call ourselves historians and authors couldn't function without 'em. Thank you one and all from the bottom of my heart.

The following people contributed their knowledge of Fort Worth history and generously shared the fruits of their own labors with me, often throwing juicy tidbits my way that they found in the course of their own research: Jan Jones, Scott Barker, Quentin McGown, Dalton Hoffman, J'Nell Pate, and Ruth Karbach. The fraternity of Fort Worth historians is a close one and generous when it comes to supporting each other in ways both large and small. Special thanks in this regard to Donna Donnell, a Fort Worth genealogist and historian who is doing groundbreaking work on Fort Worth's bawds and madams of the early days. Donna was an invaluable fellow traveler on Mary Porter.

Sergeant Kevin Foster, my good friend and collaborator on another project (*Cops and Cowboys*), is my go-to source for any and all information related to law enforcement. Kevin is a naturally curious researcher who keeps my e-mail box full of historical nuggets he finds without any quid pro quo.

My unpaid research assistant and one-woman fan club, Clara Ruddell, was always there to go picture hunting, proofread, and run interference when necessary. Clara is best known to most of historical-minded Fort Worth as the Fort Worth Convention and Visitors Bureau lady who has put together more historic events than anyone—maybe ever! But to me, she'll always be a dear friend and collaborator.

Paula Oates at the University of North Texas Press has been after me for years to bring a manuscript to them. Thanks, Paula, for being the matchmaker who finally succeeded in putting me and UNT together. It is editors like Paula whose kindness and professionalism attract authors to one press instead of another.

Much thanks to informal readers who perused the manuscript at various critical points in the process and offered their advice to help keep me from making dunderheaded mistakes of fact and language. Specifically, heartfelt thanks to Bill Voelker, *aka* Wahathuweeka, of SIA: The Comanche Nation Ethno-Ornithological Initiative in Oklahoma for straightening me out on all things Comanche, and to Gayle Hanson for graciously correcting me in some matters of African American culture. Bill's perspective as a German-Comanche-American was refreshing!

Thanks to Randy Souders, my longtime friend and the only celebrity artist I know. Randy graciously allowed me to use one of his distinctive paintings as the cover of this book. I only hope what's between the covers of this book can live up to the promise of the excellent cover art!

Thanks to Bob Smith, architect par excellence, who has allowed me to dragoon him for several books now to do map work, floor plans, and the like, which allow readers to get a clear picture of things where words are insufficient. Bob, you're a charter member of my stock company of artists, historians, archivists, and librarians. The pay is lousy, but you have my undying gratitude!

Finally, I can't quit without recognizing family members who have supported and encouraged me in this crazy writing profession for too many years to count. Here's to Mother who is looking down on me smiling, and to my sister Janet Lee who praises my every literary endeavor as if I'm the second coming of David McCullough.

This acknowledgment is long, but so is the list of people who have made this book possible.

Richard Selcer
February 2009

INTRODUCTION

The twelve people in this book are not counted among Fort Worth's Finest. But neither are they all scoundrels and ne'er-do-wells. They are mostly people who slipped through the cracks of Fort Worth history. Our city has more than its share of larger-than-life figures, although for some odd reason we have never put up statues to them: Amon Carter, Buckley B. Paddock, John Peter Smith (a bust but not a statue), Ephraim M. Daggett. Still, they have their names attached to buildings, streets, and other prominent landmarks dotting the city. There is no possibility they will ever be forgotten. This book is not about them. It is about the people who do not fit the mold of First Citizens of Fort Worth. Jeff Daggett, Hagar Tucker, and Quanah Parker were not part of what was once called "the great Anglo-Saxon race." Maggie Tewmey and Mary Porter were women of shady reputations. Jim Courtright, Sam Farmer, and Thomas Finch all tarnished the badges they wore in one way or another. Only Ripley Arnold, Al Hayne, and James Swayne are conventional heroic figures. What all of these folks have in common, aside from being characters in every sense of the word, is that they are all part of our city's history but dropped from the pages of the history books after their passing. It is time we resurrected them through the miracle of historical research. If, as F. Scott Fitzgerald said, there are no second acts in American history, these twelve people at least deserve a curtain call.

Why these particular characters? Some were minor players who cast large shadows in Fort Worth history. Others were major players in their day who dropped out of our collective memory somewhere along the way. There was no attempt to be politically correct with representatives from all major groups or time periods. The choice of the twelve people discussed in this book was based on a purely arbitrary standard: they appeal to me! There is no attempt to whitewash their sins. They are what they are.

Three, Jim Courtright, Jeff Daggett, and Thomas Finch, were outcasts from another literary project of mine, *Cops and Cowboys: The Stories behind the Badges*. The men in *Cops and Cowboys* were all representatives of the law who died in the line of duty. Courtright, Daggett, and Finch may have worn badges, but their deaths had nothing to do with duty; they were victims of personal feuds and their own bad decisions.

I have always been more interested in sinners than saints, but I was attracted by Judge Swayne's sturdy integrity and complete fearlessness. On the other end of the scale is Sam Farmer. When I first discovered Sam, I was ready to nominate him for sainthood, or at least a statue in some local park. After digging into his life, I decided ol' Sam was a cowboy-booted Jekyll and Hyde. There was Marshal Farmer who drew up the first comprehensive set of rules for the Fort Worth Police Department, then there was Sam the Jayhawker and despicable husband. Neither one was half as interesting as the two together.

Mary Porter is something of a mystery woman. I have been fascinated by Mary for a quarter century, ever since I discovered she was not a pal of Butch Cassidy and the Sundance Kid. Fort Worth's most famous madam did not even qualify as a "person of interest" to the Pinkertons at the time they were chasing Butch and Sundance all over the West. A serious historical blunder has been perpetrated over the years by several Western authors who confuse Mary Porter with her contemporary, San Antonio's Fannie Porter. In Civil War history, it would be an unpardonable sin to confuse the various General Johnstons, General Jacksons, or General Hills, but in Western history, two Madam Porters seem to be an alien concept to many chroniclers of the Wild Bunch.

As I write this I find myself referring to these people by their first names as if they were personal friends. After spending so much time with them, I do feel like I know each and every one of them personally. I only wish I could meet them personally in some otherworldly interview room, if only for a few minutes, to ask them the burning questions that are not revealed in the skimpy historical records of their lives. Sam Farmer, did you really go to Central America, and if so, where did you end up? Mary Porter, did you meet Butch and Sundance when they passed through Fort Worth in 1901? Jim Courtright, how did Luke Short manage to get the drop on you that night?

The lives of these twelve people provide snapshots of various moments in Fort Worth history, mostly in the nineteenth century. There is no single thread running through their lives or through their stories. Their stories don't fit together like the pieces of a jigsaw puzzle. In this regard I find comfort in the words of novelist Anne Lamott: "I say don't worry about plot; worry about characters."[1]

The eponymous old TV series used to open by saying, "There are a million stories in the Naked City . . . ," and every week told a different one of those stories. There are probably *not* a million stories in Fort Worth history, but there are plenty that are waiting to be discovered by new generations of Fort Worthers. Let's hope this is just the beginning of bringing those stories to light and ensuring that they never recede into the shadows of history again. I am proud to say Fort Worth has more actively working historians than any other city I know of. I challenge my historical friends and colleagues to continue to dig into our city's wonderful history and publish, publish, publish. Only by publishing can we truly share our knowledge and the fruits of our research.

Ripley and Catherine Arnold, daguerreotype taken in a studio sometime after the Mexican War, probably not at Fort Worth. The only known image of Fort Worth's founder. (Courtesy Applewhite-Clark Historical Collection, W. O. Clark.)

CHAPTER 1

The Curious Story of Brevet Major Ripley Arnold

As the American frontier marched westward in the nineteenth century, a number of obscure, even junior-grade Army officers would make their marks on history. For instance, Fort Worth, Texas, was named for Major General William Jenkins Worth; Dodge City, Kansas, for Major General Grenville Dodge; and Pike's Peak, Colorado, for Lieutenant Zebulon Pike. None of these men were what might be called giants in history, yet all are remembered today because their names are attached to important landmarks.

Then there was Major Ripley A. Arnold who founded three different posts on the Texas frontier: Camp Inge, Camp Thornton, and Fort Worth. No monument marks the first two sites because they are under water (Lakes Waco and Whitney respectively), while the third site, his crowning achievement, is not even identified with its founder because Arnold graciously named it for his department commander. Thus, one of the most vibrant and booming cities in the Southwest today is named Fort Worth not Fort Arnold. Four years after founding Fort Worth, Ripley Arnold had the unique distinction of being gunned down at Fort Graham, Texas, by his own post surgeon, the only time such a thing happened in the entire history of the U.S. Army. Doctors are supposed to be healers, not killers. Arnold's untimely demise left a wife and three daughters destitute because they were not pension-eligible under the circumstances. Those same dubious circumstances also kept the Army from honoring Arnold by naming a frontier fort after him in the years following.

Ripley Allen Arnold's story begins on January 17, 1817, in Pearlington, Mississippi, where he was born to Willis H. and Nancy Chinn Arnold. On his mother's side he was related to Daniel Boone, and the blood of French Huguenots also coursed through his veins.[1] His life was unremarkable until he got caught up in Manifest Destiny, the driving force behind westward expansion in the nineteenth century, which held it was the divine mission of this great English-speaking nation to "overspread the continent allotted [them] by Providence." [2]

As a specimen of manhood, Ripley Arnold reportedly stood about six feet tall, with gray eyes and a pleasant face. His most notable feature was his hair, said by some sources to be auburn and by others to be red. His reddish hair has often been cited as the key to his fiery temperament, which is well documented. Throughout his life he was impulsive, proud, and had a short fuse. That combination got him in serious trouble more than once.[3]

Unlike most Americans in the nineteenth century, Ripley Arnold had the benefits of an excellent education growing up. His father was principal of the Pearlington Academy and a big believer in schooling. He saw to it that Ripley learned more than the traditional three Rs, first at Pearlington, then at the Oxford Academy in Ohio, and finally at the U.S. Military Academy at West Point. Seventeen-year-old Ripley entered West Point as a member of the class of 1838.[4] Willis Arnold was a contrarian whose Whig sympathies made him "the only man in Hancock County, Mississippi who dared to vote against General [Andrew] Jackson." Papa's well-known Whig sympathies in a Democratic-dominated state during a Democratic administration in Washington made securing one of the prized appointments to West Point for Ripley all the more remarkable.

The young man found the picky discipline and lofty academic standards of West Point onerous. He spent most of his four years among the "Immortals," those hovering near the bottom of the class academically, and piling up demerits for disciplinary infractions. During his freshman year he got into a brawl with two sophomores that escalated from fists to chairs and then knives. Arnold bested the two older boys and successfully argued his innocence on grounds of self-defense at the subsequent court-martial proceedings. Like many other cadets after 1825, he often sneaked out at night to visit nearby Benny Havens' tavern. According to legend, he shared credit with Lucius O'Brien for composing the lyrics of the famous "Benny Havens, Oh!" drinking song in 1838.[5]

West Point cadets could receive up to 200 demerits per school year (100 per semester) before facing dismissal, and Cadet Ripley came dangerously close every year. During his senior year he was caught off post, court-martialed, and sentenced to three months' room arrest, meaning he could only leave his room for classes and official functions. Even before he had completed that punishment he was slipping away to attend an off-post birthday party in his honor. Upon returning, he found his roommate and some friends having a party in his room, so he bunked in another cadet's room that night only to be brought up on charges for the third time for being out of his room after taps, violating room arrest, and buying the jug that the others were enjoying when they were caught. He was found guilty of all charges and threatened with expulsion, but got another chance, which he also blew. Before the first month of 1838 was out, he was back in the dock yet again, this time charged with loudly quarrelling with the same cadet he blamed for telling lies about him at the last court-martial. To that charge was added leaving the grounds on the previous occasion. Young Ripley Arnold, it seemed, could not follow the rules or fit into the Academy's regimen. Once again he was found guilty and faced expulsion. To avoid that humiliation, he tendered his letter of resignation, then had a change of heart and appealed to the commandant, who chose to disregard the letter and sentence him to yet another stretch of room arrest.[6]

Yet young Ripley's most troubling breaches of Academy discipline were not for missing curfew or slipping off post but for being unable to control his temper. He had a notoriously short fuse. According to West Point lore, he fought a duel with another, unnamed cadet at Benny Havens' tavern. The outcome of the duel is not recorded, nor is there any record of disciplinary action being taken. If no harm was done, it could have been hushed up by his fellow cadets or simply dismissed as one of those "affairs of honor" between Southern gentlemen, of whom West Point had more than its fair share during the antebellum years.[7]

Ripley Arnold is Exhibit A against the argument that U.S. Military Academy discipline has always been exceedingly strict and unforgiving. Cadet Arnold managed to graduate with his class on July 1, 1838, after finishing his senior year with 199 demerits, one short of the fatal number. He did much better in the classroom, ranking twenty-fifth out of forty-four graduates in the class of '38, twenty-three spots behind future star of the class, noted Confederate General Pierre Gustav Toutant Beauregard. Arnold's middling ranking earned him assignment to the infantry, not as good as the engineers but better than the mounted branch. If he were going to make a career in the military, it would have to be in combat or the supply branches (quartermaster and commissary). His relatively low standing secured him a spot in the infantry, since the engineer and cavalry arms were reserved for higher-ranking graduates.[8]

As a newly minted second lieutenant, effective July 1, 1838, he was ordered to Florida to join the Second Seminole War in progress. Before reporting for duty, however, he went home to Mississippi where he conducted a whirlwind courtship of fourteen-year-old Catherine Bryant, a soldier's daughter. When her father refused to give his blessing to the union, they eloped in the middle of the night. Thomas Bryant, who had been an Army surgeon, never completely forgave Arnold for whisking away his daughter, but in time he gave up thoughts of plugging his son-in-law.

After reporting to his command in Florida, Arnold requested and was granted a transfer to the Second Dragoons, a regiment authorized by Congress barely two years before. He arrived in the middle of the Second Seminole War, which had erupted in 1835 when the U.S. government tried to move the Seminoles en masse across the Mississippi to the Indian Territory. Many of the Indians retreated into the Florida Everglades where they held out for the next seven years, although they were eventually defeated by the merciless operations of Colonel William Jenkins Worth. It was the first time, but it would not be the last, that Ripley Arnold's path crossed Worth's, and it was always fortuitous for him.

The Seminole Wars were not fought by large units fighting set-piece battles. Rather, they were fought by small, semi-independent units scattered across a sprawling war zone. It required a lot of self-reliance and initiative on the part of junior officers who might spend weeks out in the field on "detached service." Arnold was attached to Company K of the Second Dragoons, and his exemplary conduct caught the eye of his superiors. He led by example and drove his men hard. A career that had gotten off to a very rocky start at West Point was looking up. As a freshly minted lieutenant, he was already leading troops in combat and winning the approval of his superiors. True, the Florida swamps were a miserable place to live, but such was a soldier's life, and Catherine was living close enough, right across the state line in Georgia, that he could visit her on leave occasionally. It was while she was living there that their first child was born before the end of 1838, a boy whom they named Willis after his father. The timing of Willis' birth, only a few months after Ripley and Catherine were married, suggests another reason why they chose to elope rather than have a traditional ceremony.[9]

The Second Dragoons pulled out of Florida in June 1839 and nobody was happier to leave than Lieutenant Arnold. Despite his relative youth and junior rank, the Army considered him a comer. He was placed on detached service and sent to a number of northern cities to recruit while the rest of the regiment rested and refitted. The cushy urban postings meant he could bring Catherine to live with him—at least until he was ordered back to Florida with the regiment in the late fall. On his return to the war, he found himself serving under Colonel David Twiggs, a well-regarded combat officer at this point in his career, later to be remembered as the biggest traitor to the U.S. Army since Benedict Arnold (no relation to Ripley). Second in command was Lieutenant Colonel William S. Harney, destined for fame in the Mexican and Mormon wars and infamy in the Civil War. Lieutenant Arnold's fellow company officers were Hamilton Merrill and William J. Hardee, former West Point classmates. While dozens of soldiers, including Twiggs himself, fell sick in the malarial swamps, Arnold's health bore up remarkably well. Apparently he fortified himself with alcohol, beginning a heavy drinking habit that followed him the rest of his life but made him, if anything, less sympathetic of others with the same problem.[10]

The dragoons found themselves chasing elusive Indians through the swamps fruitlessly trying to catch phantoms. After weeks of this, they staggered back to camp to rest and regroup. Ripley Arnold would remain in this war zone for two miserable years. He grew so lonely that he brought Catherine and Willis to join him, and the couple was in Florida when their second child, a daughter whom they named Florida Belle, was born there in 1840.[11] Catherine Arnold was also getting a crash course in Army life. Having hitched her star to a shavetail lieutenant, she was forced to grow up fast. Barely seventeen, she already had two infant children. Following her husband from post to post for the next thirteen years would test not just the bonds of marriage but her mental toughness and physical stamina as well. Meanwhile, Ripley Arnold's career was progressing nicely. On February 1, 1841, less than three years removed from West Point, he was promoted to first lieutenant. It was a small but significant step in his career because it was the first rank he had earned in the field.

In the spring of 1842 the war climaxed when Colonel Worth launched a major offensive against the last remaining Seminole chief, Halleck Tustenuggee, who led a band of 114 followers. Company K was part of the attacking force when they cornered Tustenuggee's band on April 19 on one of the high grounds that dotted the Everglades known as the Big Hummock of Pilaklikaha. The fact that the foe was faceless, the engagements small-scale, and the battles fought in obscure places whose names did not exactly roll off the tongue made the Seminole War a forgotten conflict even while it was going on. The Battle of Big Hummock of Pilaklikaha was typical. The numbers on the two sides did not number more than a couple of hundred with Tustenuggee probably not commanding more than fifty or sixty. The fighting in the jungle-like conditions was close and personal, the sort of battle where colonels led charges. William Worth placed himself at the head of Company K before they charged and was in the thick of the fighting. The dragoons comported themselves well, helping to rout the enemy after some fierce hand-to-hand fighting. Arnold at one point was cut off from the rest of the company with nine of his men, but they held on until help arrived. Colonel Worth was impressed enough with Arnold's performance to cite him for "gallant conduct" in his report and promote the shavetail lieutenant to brevet captain on the spot. Tustenuggee surrendered and was shipped off to the Indian Territory, and General Worth declared the war over on August 14, 1842. Unlike seventy-four of his fellow officers, including thirteen West Point graduates, Arnold was alive and well. Just as important, he had covered himself with glory. The "brevet" before his captain's

The graves of Major Ripley Arnold and two children (Sophie and Willis) are in Fort Worth's Pioneer's Rest Cemetery, marked by a boulder and two concrete slabs respectively. None of the markers are original, and no one knows how the graves were marked originally. Sophie and Willis were probably interred here in 1850, Ripley Arnold in 1855. (Author's collection.)

rank was military vernacular for a battlefield promotion, which carried no weight in the War Department but meant everything in the field. Ripley Arnold was one of only four officers from the classes of 1837–1839, eighty-two men in all, to receive a brevet promotion during the Second Seminole War.[12]

Meanwhile, back home in Pearlington, Willis Arnold was doing everything he could to boost his son's rise through the ranks. In June 1840 he wrote a letter to Senator John Henderson of Mississippi asking that Ripley be promoted to captain and reassigned to the Quartermaster's Department. Papa pointed out that not only could his son "render more service to the U.S. in the Quarter Master's [*sic*] Department," but that the increase in pay would "the better enable him to support his family." Willis concluded, "I am emboldened to ask your influence and aid in promoting to the first vacancy of Captaincy this son of mine as he has determined to devote himself entirely to the service of his country in the profession of Arms." Henderson forwarded the request to the War Department, eliciting this response from the

Secretary of War: "I have the honor to inform you that the claims of that gentleman [Willis Arnold] will be respectfully considered when a vacancy of that grade shall occur." Ripley got his coveted promotion in the next year, but it had nothing to do with his father's lobbying.[13]

Not long after the Battle of Big Hummock, Chief Halleck Tustenuggee surrendered, bringing the curtain down on the Second Seminole War, but as U.S. troops withdrew from Florida, the dragoons were the last to pull out. The regiment was broken up into small units and scattered across the West. Arnold and Company K ended up in Baton Rouge, Louisiana, where they spent the next year. Catherine and the children pulled up stakes again and joined him at his latest post. It was there that their third child, a daughter whom they named Kate, was born in January 1843. Baton Rouge was a tough frontier town, but Catherine and the children were not there long enough to put down roots. Captain Arnold was on the move again.[14]

In the spring of 1843 the Army sent him to Fort Jesup (Louisiana), twenty-two miles west of Natchitoches on the Old Spanish Road into Texas. The fort was commanded by Brigadier General Zachary Taylor, one of the Army's old-school, untrained senior officers who had come up through the ranks and put little store in book learning, but Taylor had succeeded in taming the "Neutral Strip" between Louisiana and Texas. He called his force the "Army of Observation," and (Brevet) Captain Arnold was now part of that force. Taylor was not particularly impressed with West Pointers, but he quickly took a shine to the young officer whom he made his adjutant. Meanwhile, the Army reassigned Arnold to Company F, Second Dragoons, Colonel David Twiggs commanding, and he spent the next two years at Fort Jesup, bringing Catherine and the three children to be with him as soon as he settled in. Catherine was getting very good at packing because the frontier Army was always on the move and also because her husband did not like being separated from his family for too long. Arnold was Company F's second-in-command and got along well with his immediate superior, Captain Seth B. Thornton. But he was not on good terms with other members of the command, in particular Lieutenant Stephen Dobbins, the Pennsylvanian with whom he clashed at West Point. Their differences carried over to Fort Jesup because Arnold did not let go of grudges and because both men were strongly opinionated, specifically on sectional issues.

The hard feelings boiled over unexpectedly a year after Arnold came to Fort Jesup. At the time, the two men were relaxing on the porch of the post adjutant's office. Dobbins casually demeaned the local civilian population calling them "degenerate, ignorant . . . and somewhat tinctured of Negro blood." The last point was the ultimate insult in white Southern eyes.

Although he had not kin in the area and had never expressed strong opinions about either slavery or abolitionism, Arnold took exception, comparing the locals favorably to "the voters of Pennsylvania [who are] a damned sight meaner class of people than our blacks in the South." The pot was now stirred and neither man would back down.

Said Dobbins indignantly, "I distinctly and positively say it is not so, sir."

"I don't care a damn what you say, sir," retorted Arnold. "It is my opinion, and I don't care for yours." He started to walk away, then turned on his heel and stepped close, getting in Dobbins' face. "God damn you, sir, . . . you have frequently attempted before in conversation to insult me, and God damn you . . . sir, if you ever attempt it again, I'll slap your face—I'll slap your face, sir!"

Arnold was obviously scrapping for a fight right then and there, but the lieutenant declined the unstated challenge and instead pressed charges of "conduct unbecoming an officer." Arnold's first response was typical. He sneered that a gentleman would have "demanded instant satisfaction." A court-martial was convened, and its members, after hearing from both principals as well as witnesses, came down on the side of Captain Arnold's gentleman's defense, finding him not guilty. General Taylor, a plain-talking, unpretentious commander, approved the court's finding, but urged his two hotheaded junior officers just to get along with one another. Observers could not help but wonder how many more scrapes Arnold could get into without suffering severe consequences.[15]

Ripley and Catherine were still at Fort Jesup a year later when the looming war with Mexico interrupted their idyllic life. As tension between the U.S. and its southern neighbor escalated, President Polk ordered Zachary Taylor to south Texas with his little Army of Observation. The Second Dragoons rode out of Fort Jesup in July 1845 headed for Corpus Christi to link up with Taylor who had gone ahead by ship.

Arnold remained with the main body as Colonel Twiggs' chief of staff during the march through east Texas. It was his first visit to the Lone Star State. Not long after the regiment reached Corpus Christi, Taylor ordered Arnold back to New Orleans to recruit for the undersized regiment. He did not rejoin the Army until April 1846, by which time a lot had happened that he missed out on, including trouble with the civilian population of Corpus Christi. The men of the Second Dragoons were notorious carousers and brawlers. Even the regiment's officers participated. Being on a war footing did nothing to lessen their natural combativeness. Throughout their life, the Second Dragoons would carry that reputation, challenging the leadership skills of anyone who tried to command them. They could be hell on Indians or Mexicans, or when other targets were lacking, their own officers.[16]

Arnold not only missed the mayhem caused by the dragoons, he also missed the opening of the Mexican War. General Taylor had advanced his force to the Rio Grande and begun aggressive reconnaissance-in-force patrols. On one such patrol on April 25, 1846, Captain Thornton and sixty-three dragoons of Companies C and F were ambushed by elements of General Anastasio Torrejon's cavalry at Rancho de Carrisitos, Texas. Sixteen men were killed or wounded, and the Captain was captured along with the rest of his command. It was only because Arnold had stayed behind at headquarters as a staff officer that he did not suffer the same fate as the rest of Company F that day. It was April 26; the Mexican War started two days later.[17]

In the months that followed, Taylor's army advanced into Mexico and fought sharp engagements at Palo Alto (May 8) and Resaca de la Palma (May 9). Arnold was present but in the rear areas still serving as Twiggs' chief of staff. He did carry orders from headquarters to the front during both battles, afterwards racing back to Fort Brown to fetch medical help for the wounded. Writing an account of his activities two years later to Mississippi Senator Henry Foote, Arnold was rather defensive about not being in the thick of the fight with the rest of the Second Dragoons. He went to great pains to explain what heavy fire he came under while carrying out the General's orders. Apparently, Taylor did not have any reservations about his role in the two hard-fought battles because he promoted Arnold for "gallant and meritorious conduct" immediately afterwards. Effective May 9, 1846, Ripley Arnold was a brevet major. In the field the "brevet" was dropped, and he would henceforward be addressed as "Major Arnold." Although unofficial, it was the highest rank he ever achieved.[18]

The summer of 1846 found Arnold assigned to the Quartermaster Corps of Taylor's army. It was good training for his later assignments to isolated posts on the Texas frontier, but he chafed at still bringing up the rear of the Army. Nonetheless, he played an active role in the campaign that captured Monterrey on September 28, 1846. But when most of the Second Dragoons were reassigned to Winfield Scott's army for the campaign against Mexico City, Arnold stayed behind with three dragoon companies as part of Taylor's occupation army. They defended supply lines, battled guerillas, and rode uncounted miles as scouts and messengers. One of his assignments was chasing down three deserters, a task he found distasteful but not because he felt any compassion for the runaways. He also bought a black slave named Carter to be his body servant, the ongoing expense of which was picked up by the U.S. government since Arnold was a commissioned officer.[19]

In October 1847 word came that Captain Seth Thornton had been killed in the fighting near Mexico City. Meanwhile, Arnold's own career was in the ascendancy. War had that effect on career soldiers; a man could advance rapidly through the ranks as opposed to the glacial pace of promotion during peacetime. Arnold's promotion to full captain (cf. brevet) had come through on August 18, but it was anticlimactic since he was now "Major Arnold" to everyone except the War Department. The distinction did not affect his responsibilities as he was now the regular commander of Company F, Second Dragoons. Their lives and performance in the field rested squarely on his shoulders. The rank at which he was carried on the official rolls might have been just a formality except that new rank came with a higher pay grade. He was also grateful not to be spending his time doing staff work and filling quartermaster requisitions any longer. He expected to be sent with his company to Winfield Scott's army on its way to Mexico City, but his first orders took him back to the United States for another round of recruiting, this time in the Midwest. The assignment was not without its benefits. Catherine and the children joined him, but when he got orders to rejoin his regiment as part of the preparations for a move to Texas, he left them behind in Kentucky. Catherine was pregnant again, and Texas practically the end of the world at the time. It was October 1848 when Arnold bid farewell to his family, not knowing when he would see them again. A few months later, in early 1849, Catherine gave birth to their fourth child, a daughter for whom they had already picked out the name Sophia (*aka* Sophie). Based on experience, she anticipated moving to Texas before too much time had passed.[20]

Arnold was reunited with Company F in East Pascagoula, Mississippi, a few miles from Mobile, in time to help prepare them for their upcoming move. The U.S. Army's plans for its two dragoon regiments after the Mexican War were the same as after the Seminole Wars: to break them up and scatter them across the West guarding the frontier. The longest and most dangerous stretch of that frontier was in Texas. They marched to New Orleans and boarded a steamer for Houston, Texas, where they disembarked and marched north to Austin, which was to be the permanent headquarters for the six companies of Second Dragoons in Texas. The infantry established its camp at San Antonio, which was also the headquarters for the Eighth Military Department (Texas).

The long journey from Pascagoula to Austin was the first chance Major Arnold had to get to know his men personally. They were a polyglot group, never numbering more than about fifty men, only two of whom had ever served under him, Sergeant Jacob Dearing and bugler Thomas Noland. The majority were recent immigrants, mostly German and Irish, with names like Helmerling, Kaas, and Knaar, who had enlisted fresh off the boat in New York City. Dragoon training at Carlisle Barracks, Pennsylvania, was their welcome to America. They were rough men, ill-trained and ill-disciplined, with little unit cohesiveness between the veterans and the green recruits or among the various nationalities. And their new captain could not overawe them with his combat experience in the recent war. His own service paled beside the Certificates of Merit for extraordinary bravery received by ten of his troopers during that conflict.[21]

Arnold's first assignment in Texas was founding Camp Inge on the Bosque River in December 1848, one of the harshest winters in Texas history. He named it for a fellow West Point graduate and dragoon officer who had been killed at the Battle of Resaca de la Palma.[22] Three months later, he established Camp Thornton near an abandoned Caddo Indian village, naming it for Seth Thornton, the Second Dragoon captain killed in action in the recent war.

Camp Thornton was part of a line of U.S. military forts guarding the western frontier of Texas all the way from the Rio Grande to the Red River. It was the brainchild of General Worth. A few weeks later, Colonel Harney visited the Camp and criticized the site. On his orders, the garrison moved eight miles up the Brazos River and established Fort Graham on March 27, 1849, which was named for Lieutenant Colonel William Graham, who had died at the Battle of Molino del Rey during the advance on Mexico City. The U.S. government did not secure ownership of the land on which the fort sat; it simply appropriated it for the duration of its stay. The Army would soon be moving farther west, following the frontier line. In the meantime, Fort Graham stood watch on the frontier all the way up to the Red River and beyond to Fort Washita in Indian Territory.[23]

Because there were so few dragoons in Texas, so much territory to be covered and so many duties, officers were frequently away from their commands on detached service. Arnold did not join his men at Fort Graham until April 16, at which time he relieved Lieutenant Samuel H. Starr. And since Fort Graham was considered a "permanent" post and the surrounding county so pleasant, he brought Catherine and the children up from Austin to be with him. Florida, Fort Jesup, Fort Graham, and soon Fort Worth—Catherine Arnold was truly a soldier's wife, married to the Army as much as to her husband.

A month later, Arnold took a small party of men and rode farther north toward the Trinity, scouting for another site for yet another fort. He found the perfect site near the confluence of the Clear Fork and West Fork of the Trinity River, on a bluff a hundred and fifty feet above the river with plenty of water and wood. Meanwhile, on May 7, the commander of the department, General Worth, had died of cholera at San Antonio, so when Arnold returned to the Trinity with Company F at the beginning of June to commence construction, he christened the new post Fort Worth. The name stuck. This latest post, just about eighty miles south of the Red River, was the new anchor of the First Military Frontier Line in Texas (1848–1853). On June 2, Arnold wrote the adjutant general to inform him, "I have located a new Post on the West Fork Trinity River. My address will be 'Dallas, Dallas County, Texas' a town about thirty-five miles east of me." As usual, he signed it, "R. A. Arnold, Bvt. Major," but Army clerks recorded it in the register book under his true rank as "Captain Arnold." [24]

The U.S. Army had come to the Twin Forks of the Trinity. As with Fort Graham, however, the government was not interested in purchasing the land, which had been assigned to the Peters Colony by the Republic of Texas some years before. No problem; in 1849 there were no homesteaders in the vicinity to protest the land-grab, so the dragoons settled in as virtual squatters.

As Fort Worth's commanding officer, Major Arnold had very little help carrying out the myriad duties involved in commanding a military post *and* a company of men. Ever since relieving Lieutenant Starr at Fort Graham, he had been the only officer with Company F. Typically, every company had two lieutenants, but Arnold had court-martialed his other junior officer, Lieutenant William Saunders, for drinking on duty. Therefore, his second-in-command during his first four months on the Trinity was Sergeant Jacob Dearing. He had no junior commissioned officer to share the burdens of command until Samuel Starr rejoined Company F in October. For most of his stay in north Texas, Arnold never had more than a single junior commissioned officer with him. This meant, among other things, that Arnold was forced to function as his own quartermaster and commissary officer, duties he was well acquainted with from his Mexican War service.

While he usually lacked junior commissioned officers, he always had a post physician. His first medical officer was Jesse M. Standifer, a civilian contract doctor who lived at Johnston's Station (modern-day Arlington), but regularly visited the fort, ten miles distant. Starting in 1851, Arnold had an Army doctor, Assistant Surgeon Thomas Williams. Arnold enjoyed an excellent relationship with both men. When he was at Fort Graham, his physician was Dr. Josephus Steiner.

Arnold's post on the Trinity was hardly one to inspire pride of command. It was actually an "outpost" in military parlance, i.e., an extension of Fort Graham fifty-four miles to the south. It would never be a "fort" in the popular sense of the word: that is, an enclosed garrison protected by a stockade. The dragoons spent the first two months camped in a grove of live oaks to the northeast of the chosen site while they were building the fort. They built it with their own hands, using local, green timber. Most structures were jacal-style construction, meaning vertical posts stuck in the ground and chinked with mud.[25] The only visible signs from a distance that it was a military post were the flag flying over the parade ground and the whitewashed buildings. Major Arnold's first headquarters on the windswept bluff was a tent with the rest of the camp laid out around it "according to army regulations." Some of the troops were still occupying tents when winter came. By then, however, Arnold's quarters and the hospital had been finished. In the next two years some of the buildings would be rebuilt using framing and clapboard construction, but none of the structures ever really kept out dust or rain. It was the soldiers' fate to swelter and eat dust in the summer, get soaked and shiver in the winter.[26]

The post included a parade ground, with the barracks, storehouses, officers' quarters, stable, and hospital around it. The stables were located close to the living quarters not by mistake but to cut down on threat of Indian sneak thieves slipping past the sentries at night to steal them. Fort Worth did not lose a single horse to the Indians while Arnold commanded.[27] Cookhouses and laundresses' cabins stood behind each of the two barracks. Last but not least, a one-room guardhouse was built, and Arnold kept it occupied more often than not.

In October 1849 elements of the Eighth U.S. Infantry joined the dragoons at Fort Worth, making it a combined post. Although the foot soldiers had their own officers, Major Arnold continued to act as post commander. With the infantry and the dragoons both present, he now commanded nearly 100 men, although continuous comings and goings and sickness took their toll. Catherine and the four children also joined him at Fort Worth before the year was out. The north Texas prairie was definitely a hardship post for a young mother with three small children ranging in age from one to eleven. A fifth child would be born while they were at Fort Worth. To provide for himself, his family, and two servants, Major Arnold drew $188 per month. Out of that amount he also provided generous hospitality to all travelers, military or civilian, who came through. Finances were always tight. The Army paymaster was supposed to come through every month, but sometimes that gentleman, a young Albert Sidney Johnston, did not make it.[28]

The main duty of the garrison, aside from maintaining watch on the north Texas frontier, was to regularly scout the open country all the way up to the Red River. Fort Graham continued to have responsibility for the area between the Brazos and the Trinity. The scouting parties headed out every month, covering the nearly 160 miles in about two weeks, leaving men and animals exhausted when they returned. The Comanches, Kiowas, and Wichitas, the only warlike tribes in the region, were the putative enemy. Indian campfires could be seen dotting the prairie surrounding Fort Worth in the summer, but the presumption (hope?) was that those fires belonged to the peaceable Tonkawas, Caddos, and Wacos. Fortunately for the undermanned garrison, the Comanches and their Kiowa allies preferred to keep west of Tarrant County, while the Wichitas remained mostly north of the Red River. Fort Worth never suffered an Indian attack during its four years of existence, later local legends to the contrary. The *Austin Telegraph and Texas Register* praised the dragoons, noting that when they were active they were as "efficient" as the homegrown Rangers, but adding that when they stuck close to their posts, they were as useless as "hobbled donkeys."[29]

Ripley's most serious problem at Fort Worth was his unruly troops. When they were not riding scouts, Arnold kept the men busy on fatigue details, full-dress drills on the parade ground, and keeping a vegetable garden per War Department orders. In letters to the War Department, he regularly lamented their lack of basic training and slovenliness. As soon as a sutler's store opened up near the post, soldiers beat a path there to purchase alcohol. Drunk or sober, bored young men found countless ways to get into trouble. And a few even deserted. In all these situations, Major Arnold showed himself to be a tough, albeit creative, disciplinarian. He once ordered a trooper to stand in the broiling sun for hours with a stolen hog's carcass tied around his neck. He also quarreled with the local civilian population, a handful of hardy settlers who had put down roots near the fort. After Arnold's timber-cutting parties took wood on private property, the owner demanded compensation. Arnold refused, even in the face of a lawsuit filed by the man in district court, and instead of negotiating a settlement, begged the War Department for the money to hire a lawyer.[30]

Besides having to ride herd on a bunch of misfits, Ripley Arnold had other problems. The nearby river was a source of malarial infection, which caused three serious outbreaks in just the first year. In four years, more than a thousand cases were recorded at Fort Worth. Arnold justifiably feared not only for his troops but also for his family. The mosquito was a bigger threat to the post than the Indian! That helps explain why his wife took the children every summer and fled to San Antonio, the Gulf Coast, or even New Orleans, to escape the miserable weather on the north Texas plains. Fort Worth was really the worst of two worlds: the hellish heat of the plains and the swamp-like conditions that came with living right next to a sluggish river. Catherine was not an absentee wife, however; she stayed around long enough to get pregnant for the fifth time and give birth to a daughter, Nannie Arnold, in 1851.[31] The Arnold family was now complete, but its happiness was shattered while living at Fort Worth. Arnold had dragged his wife and infant children all over the country for more than ten years. Living conditions were usually primitive, and the state of medicine in that era only multiplied the risks to which the family was exposed. Two of the children, twelve-year-old Willis and two-year-old Sophie, died at Fort Worth. It is not clear from the record just what they died of or even the exact dates of their deaths. Available evidence suggests that he died in March 1850 and she died sometime after November 1850. They may have died of typhoid fever, which struck the garrison more than once during its stay on the Trinity. Willis and Sophie were buried in the post cemetery near the live oak grove, along with eleven enlisted men who died of various non-hostile causes in four years. Their graves were marked by piled-up rocks topped by a pair of limestone slabs hewed from the nearby cliffs.[32]

During his four years in north Texas, the Army kept Major Arnold on the move, mostly between Fort Worth and Fort Graham, but also to Austin for court-martial duty. This was not to punish Arnold but because the Army was stretched too thin in Texas and had to juggle its limited human resources to cover all the bases.

In June 1851, Arnold led his dragoons back to Fort Graham, turning Fort Worth over to elements of the Eighth U.S. Infantry, commanded by Captain J. V. Bomford. In January 1852 the dragoons relieved the infantry at Fort Worth and stayed until the following August, when they rotated back to Fort Graham. Major Merrill and Company B of the Second Dragoons took over at Fort Worth and remained until the place closed the following year. Meanwhile, Arnold had been called to Washington, D.C., in October. He did not return to Texas until June 1853 when he reported to Fort Graham. In all, Ripley Arnold spent thirty-two months at the post he founded on the Trinity. Yet, it was "a favorite place with him," according to a newspaper report after his death. There is no reason to doubt that statement considering that he spent most of his career in places like the Everglades, northern Mexico, and Fort Graham. By comparison, Fort Worth must have looked like a vacation spot.[33]

By the spring of 1853 the Texas frontier had moved farther to the west, and orders came down to prepare to close Fort Worth. The buildings and property—everything that could not be carried away—would be declared surplus property and left to the locals. The troops would return to Fort Graham or be reassigned to Fort Belknap, 100 miles to the west. Major Arnold was not involved in closing Fort Worth because he was back at Fort Graham at the time. In September, the troops at Fort Worth marched out, saying their farewells to the Twin Forks, leaving only a sergeant's guard to finish shutting the place down.

Meanwhile, at Fort Graham Major Arnold was showing the effects of four hard years on the Texas frontier with no furlough, burying two children, and maintaining constant vigilance for Indians. The stress of command made the thin-skinned, hotheaded commander even more short-tempered and belligerent than usual. It came to a boil when he picked a fight with the least likely of opponents, Assistant Surgeon Josephus Steiner, a Pennsylvanian who was hardly the diffident sawbones his title suggests. The Teutonic Doctor was just as hot-tempered as the son of Erin who was his commander and just as unwilling to back down. Years earlier, he had cut a fellow "almost to pieces" with a bowie knife in a billiard-room brawl. Afterwards, however, he sewed the man up. During the Mexican War, he was recognized as one of the most skillful surgeons in the Army. He was a smallish man with quite refined manners, compassionate toward his patients but quick to take offense at perceived insults.[34]

There had been bad blood between physician and officer dating back to the spring of 1849 when Steiner first reported for duty to Fort Graham. The Doctor considered Arnold a brutal martinet who beat his son "unmercifully," but he said nothing publicly, preferring to maintain a frosty silence toward the abuser. The antipathy turned ugly in October 1852 over the matter of a government horse that Arnold sold with the intention of pocketing the money. Steiner not only reported the "misconduct" but also took delight in Arnold's subsequent discomfiture. Other officers at Fort Graham observed the growing enmity with bemusement but not any particular alarm.[35]

On September 6, the hard feelings between the Doctor and the Major came to a boil. The previous night, Steiner had been in the quarters of Lieutenant Thomas Bingham (or some reports say Lieutenant Tyler's quarters). Steiner and Bingham became so drunk and boisterous that Arnold came over personally and ordered them to call it a night. He did not threaten to arrest either man at the time, but Dr. Steiner still threatened, in front of witnesses, to kill Arnold if he should try. After sleeping on it, Arnold the next morning ordered his adjutant, Lieutenant Richard H. Anderson, to place Steiner and Bingham under arrest and wrote out the orders confining them to quarters until they could be brought before a court of inquiry. Reports differ over whether Steiner was at Bingham's or at Tyler's quarters when Anderson showed up with his orders, but whichever the case, he was obviously picking up where he left off the night before. What is not in dispute is Steiner's reaction to being placed under arrest. He flew into a rage, denying that he had been either drunk or disorderly, and announced that he was going to see Arnold personally and demand an explanation. He stormed off "in a high state of excitement" on his way to Arnold's quarters.[36]

He found the Major on his porch talking to another soldier and advanced up the steps until the two men were face to face.

"I am arrested and should like to know what for," demanded Steiner.

"For drunkenness and riotousness," Arnold shot back.

Steiner answered that he was "insulted," but Arnold cut him off before he could continue, ordering him to his quarters and shoving him to emphasize the point. Steiner backed down the steps brandishing the walking cane that he habitually carried. Not waiting to see what the other man might do next, Arnold stepped back out of range of the cane and drew a Colt Navy revolver. At almost the same instant, Steiner drew his own pistol from his waistband. Arnold got off the first shot but missed. Steiner returned fire, and both men continued shooting at a distance closer even than the traditional dueling range of twenty paces. Arnold fired at least two times, Steiner, at least three. Neither of Arnold's shots hit their intended target, but Steiner's marksmanship was perfect; he put all three shots into Arnold who fell, mortally wounded, and died fifteen minutes later. Ripley Arnold was only thirty-six years old, which, had he lived, would have made him forty-two when the Civil War came and with his rank and experience in line to get a colonel's commission (or higher) in the rapid troop buildup of 1861. Instead, he lay dead on the front porch of his quarters. Mrs. Arnold probably saw the whole thing. She had shared her soldier's life for fifteen years, seen the best and the worst of men, but she had never seen an officer assaulted by one of his officers. She was also well acquainted with her husband's temper, but she hoped he was mellowing with age and family responsibilities. Post quarters were small enough and the exchange between Arnold and Steiner was loud enough that it would have only been natural for her to come outside to see what was going on. And since she knew Dr. Steiner well, she might have hoped to intervene and defuse the situation. Instead, she watched her husband shot down in a hail of bullets. At least seven other witnesses also saw the whole thing. All of them later testified under oath that Major Arnold fired the first shot.[37]

The most troubling testimony insofar as Arnold's reputation was concerned was that of Sergeant William Slade who stated that he had been summoned to the Major's quarters prior to the shootout, although it is unclear whether that was some days earlier or the morning of the sixth. Arnold told Slade, "I shall have a difficulty with Dr. Steiner, so I wish to be in readiness for him and give him the first shot." When the Sergeant expressed misgivings about his commanding officer's attitude and advised caution, Arnold replied vehemently, "No, damn him, if he comes in my sight I will shoot him. I ought to have done so four years ago, the damned scoundrel!" The oddest part of Slade's testimony was that Arnold had wanted to borrow a "small pocket pistol" to have "in readiness."[38]

The Sergeant's testimony seems to prove that Arnold's subsequent actions were not in the heat of the moment, but a premeditated assault. Arnold certainly had a short fuse and a long memory when it came to personal slights, and it may be he just took an instant dislike to Pennsylvanians. But more to the point, this sort of vitriolic confrontation followed a pattern established at West Point of letting his emotions run away with him, consequences be damned.

For the second time that day, Dr. Steiner was placed under arrest, but his time he went meekly to his quarters. The shocking death of Ripley Arnold reverberated throughout the small antebellum Army and spread far beyond the borders of Texas. It was reported in newspapers as far away as Maryland and New York, although it took two to three weeks for the news to reach those distant places from the Texas frontier. The interest of readers across the country was not due to either Arnold's or Steiner's personal notoriety, but because of the bizarre nature of the incident. "Post Surgeon Shoots Post Commander" was big news everywhere. The *New Orleans Picayune* called the affair "a duel," putting a distinctly Southern spin on a simple gunfight that did not conform to the code duello in any way.[39] Steiner hung around to face the music but requested a civil proceeding, granted by his superiors, which meant either Brigadier General Harney in Austin or Major General Persifor Smith in San Antonio. That dropped it squarely into the lap of the district court of Hill County. The accused was released from military arrest so that he could consult with his lawyer in preparation for appearing at the next district court session in Waco. Ordinarily, the Army would not have allowed a soldier accused of murdering another soldier to have a civil proceeding, but Steiner was a civilian contract physician working for the Army, not a soldier. At least that was the opinion of department headquarters in San Antonio. When the case got back to Washington, however, the War Department reversed the Texas decision and ordered that Steiner be arrested and tried by court-martial.

By this time, Dr. Steiner had already been tried and acquitted by a jury of twelve solid Hill County citizens on grounds of "justifiable homicide." All of them apparently believed his story and none felt any particular sympathy for the dead Major. The U.S. Army spent the next eight years trying to get civil authorities in Texas to arrest Steiner and turn him over, which they adamantly refused to do, although he was living and practicing medicine openly in Austin. Such brazen defiance provoked a minor brouhaha in civil-military relations and federal-state jurisdictions both. The affair did not die until the Civil War caused both sides to address more pressing matters. The U.S. Army finally dropped Josephus Steiner from its rolls. The good Doctor spent the war years serving as a surgeon in the Confederate Army, and it was a good thing he was never captured by U.S. forces because of the outstanding warrant hanging over his head. After the war, the Army had bigger villains to pursue as part of the legacy of the war. Steiner returned to civilian life, and he died at home in Marietta, Georgia, in 1873.[40]

Ripley Arnold's story did not end so conventionally. He was initially interred at Fort Graham with minimal ceremony. After the funeral, Catherine Arnold could not get her children or her personal belongings packed up fast enough. She kicked the dust of Fort Graham off her feet, never to return. In June 1855, some eighteen months after being buried, Arnold's remains were moved to Fort Worth. This came about because brother Masons from Fort Worth, led by Middleton Tate Johnson and Adolphe Gouhenant, decided that his former home on the Trinity should be his final resting place. The Army had no objections since both Fort Graham and Fort Worth had been abandoned by that date, and the military was only interested in living soldiers, not dead ones. The Major's remains, "in excellent state of preservation" as it turned out, were re-interred in a small burial ground soon to be known as Pioneer's Rest Cemetery, about a half-mile from the site of the original post. The service was Fort Worth's very first Masonic funeral, attended by a small group of his fraternal brothers and four veterans who had settled in the area after being mustered out of the Army. No member of his family was present. Catherine Arnold and her daughters at that time were living with her father in Mississippi. The spot was marked not with a proper headstone but with a "rough pile of stones." In the years that followed, a scraggly tree managed to take root between the stones. [41]

While Fort Worth and the U.S. Army moved on, Mrs. Arnold's ordeal had just begun. As far as she was concerned, there was unfinished business. Bringing Josephus Steiner to justice was something she was willing to leave to the proper authorities, but as for her children and herself, she refused to go quietly into the night. She had lost not just a husband but a breadwinner. She applied for a military pension to support them in the years to come, seemingly a perfectly reasonable request considering her husband's long and honorable service as a career soldier, which included two wars. She found the system stacked against her, however. Military pensions at this time were only voted by Congress for particular wars, not for peacetime service, and only for disabled soldiers or their families if the soldier died as a result of wartime service. Arnold had served in two wars, but his death was not related to either, and at the time of his death, the country was not at war. Then there were the questionable circumstances surrounding his death; a civil court had found his killer innocent by reason of self-defense. For all these reasons, Catherine Arnold's petition to the War Department was turned down, so she did what many Army widows have done in the nation's history when the War Department slammed the door in their faces; she appealed directly to Congress for a private bill granting her pension relief. And as often happened in these cases, the politicians found merit where the bureaucrats found none, and granted her request on February 10, 1855: twenty-five dollars per month for the rest of her life, retroactive to September 6, 1853.[42]

However, what Congress passed and the War Department actually did were not always in agreement. The bureaucrats proceeded to bury her under paperwork for the next forty years. The fact that she moved several times made it harder for her because each time she moved she had to refile the paperwork. When the Civil War came along and she found herself on the wrong side of the lines, she received even less sympathy from the federal government. After the Civil War she finally settled with Nannie, Florida Belle, and Kate in Marlin, Texas, not far from Waco and her husband's final posting. She hired herself a lawyer, ex-Confederate General Felix Robertson, and resumed her battle. When she finally died in 1892, her last living daughter, Kate, carried on the fight for another eight years before giving up. Kate Arnold was not just fighting for her mother's memory; she herself desperately needed the money to provide for her old age. Kate fought her lonely battle clear up to the White House, writing a letter to President Theodore Roosevelt in 1902 pleading for his intervention. "Had [my father] lived I should not be making this appeal," she wrote. "He was a good man, and might have been great." She closed by saying, "Give yourself time to think this matter over before you reply." Roosevelt, famous for possessing the common touch and taking a deeply personal interest in the lives of ordinary Americans, did not reply. His office passed the letter on to the Bureau of Pensions, which filed it with all the rest.[43]

During the four-plus decades that Catherine Arnold and daughter fought for her congressionally approved widow's pension, the payments were turned on and off like a spigot. Frequently, Catherine found herself fighting for her current benefits and those in arrears at the same time. She lost more fights than she won and died a virtual pauper.[44]

Meanwhile, Ripley Arnold's memory did not fare much better. The Founder of Fort Worth faded quickly from both collective memory and official consciousness. Decades passed, and the community that he had founded and named for General Worth never got around to honoring its founder. No statues were erected to him, no streets were named for him; not even so much as a public park bore his name. The city only roused itself to action in 1901 when the U.S. Army announced it was gathering the scattered remains of its soldiers buried at countless frontier posts over the years and reburying them all in one mass grave in San Antonio. City fathers protested, and the Army left Arnold undisturbed. That was the very last time the U.S. Army took notice of Major Ripley Arnold. Two years later, however, the city was taken to task for "the parsimony and neglect with which modern Fort Worth has treated the ashes of its gallant founder." The city's leading newspaper, the *Fort Worth Telegram*, thundered "the neglected grave of Major Arnold . . . should be a source of shame to all Fort Worth." The newspaper ended its editorial with this call to arms: "BUILD A MONUMENT!"[45]

Still, the time was not yet ripe for monument building. The city finally paid modest tribute to its founder in 1936 as part of the observance of the Texas Centennial. While the city garnered the credit, the Pioneer Cemetery Association actually came up with the money to place a massive granite boulder with a bronze plaque attached over the grave. The plaque, by a local sculptor, depicted a group of dragoons planting the U.S. flag on the site of the fort, with this inscription:

> In memory of Maj. Ripley Arnold, who with a detachment of the Second Dragoons, United States Cavalry, acting under the authority of the United States Government, established on June 6, 1849, Camp Worth, later Fort Worth.

Even that brief inscription managed to contain two mistakes: It was never "Camp Worth," and the U.S. Dragoons preceded the creation of the U.S. Cavalry by decades. The accompanying ceremony was impressive, and unlike the first time, members of the Arnold family were in attendance. But the proud monument was still just a boulder; in the middle of the Great Depression, the city was still unwilling to go first class by putting up an obelisk or vault. Trying to make a silk purse out of a sow's ear, one local newspaper called it a "statue" and spoke of its "unveiling."[46]

Even the rank inscribed on the plaque was not strictly accurate. As far as the U.S. Army was concerned, be it 1853 or 1936, Ripley Arnold was a captain. That is how he was carried on the rolls and that is what his pay grade was at the time of his death. Nearly fifty years after his death, when his old comrade in arms, Abraham Harris, wrote the Quartermaster Department to inquire about moving Arnold's remains to the national cemetery at San Antonio, the reply referred to "the late Captain R. A. Arnold, 2nd U.S. Dragoons." Yet the Army's stubborn insistence on protocol has never stopped the citizens of Fort Worth from referring to their founder as "Major" with no "Brevet" to complicate things. A succession of mayors and City Councils of Fort Worth, supported by the Fourth Estate, has seen fit to commission Ripley Arnold a major, and all the bureaucrats in Washington, D.C., will never change that.[47]

Ripley Arnold faded into obscurity again until 1940, when the city finally stuck his name on something truly substantial. Fort Worth's first public housing project, a 268-unit complex overlooking the Trinity, was named for him. It was not much of an honor. The Ripley Arnold Projects became a refuge of last resort for the poor and the forgotten, much like its namesake. Even that dubious "monument" was done away with in 2001 when the city sold the prime, riverfront site to RadioShack Corporation for 20 million dollars to build a corporate campus. The 520 residents were evicted and relocated in private suburban apartment complexes while Ripley Arnold's only memorial was transformed into RadioShack's world headquarters.[48]

The founder himself continues to lie not far from his two children under the trees of Pioneer's Rest Cemetery, although the cemetery association admits the memorial boulder does not mark the exact spot where he was laid to rest, only an approximation. Catherine Arnold's final resting place is an even bigger mystery. Her last surviving child buried her at Marlin or maybe Waco; nobody knows for sure. Kate Arnold Parker asked the U.S. government to pay for a headstone for her mother's grave, but that request was never even acknowledged.[49] Catherine Arnold's gravesite today is unknown because, like her husband, in death she dropped from the historical record.

Today, the redheaded veteran of two U.S. wars and founder of Fort Worth is largely a forgotten man. Precious little remains to even mark the passage of the man through this life: a grave marker in Pioneer's Rest Cemetery, a handful of daguerreotypes in private hands, and his officer's sword, the last named on display in the 1895 Room of the Tarrant County Courthouse. It would be nice if the community he founded built a monument to him someday, to go along with existing monuments to performer Will Rogers, businessman Charles Tandy, Comanche Chief Quanah Parker, and cowboy Bill Pickett. But there is no founder's monument, nor any other suitable recognition of his personal accomplishment, not even a portrait likeness. Until recently a portraiture was not even possible because there were no known images of him for an artist to go by. So one hundred and fifty years after he made history here, Ripley Arnold remains Fort Worth's Phantom Founder, a ghostly presence barely known and dimly remembered.

CHAPTER 2

Legendary Marshal Timothy Isaiah Courtright

"[May] all his faults be forgotten and only the good deeds he has done be remembered in the hereafter."[1]

"Longhair Jim" Courtright is remembered in Fort Worth history for his tonsorial style—à la Wild Bill Hickok—and one legendary gunfight, which he lost. But there was far more to the man than the two-dimensional figure of legend. Large swaths of Courtright's personal life and career are unknown. Most people do not even know that the name "Longhair Jim" is a misnomer; his given name was Timothy, not Jim or James. He can be fairly called a mystery man who has caused more than one would-be biographer to despair.[2]

According to the best evidence, Timothy Isaiah Courtright was born in Illinois in 1846 or 1847 growing up quietly on the Illinois and Iowa frontiers until the Civil War changed everything. His only education before being swept up in the fighting came from the school of hard knocks because he had no time for proper book learning. His complete lack of education would haunt him the rest of his life in the form of subliterate spelling and grammar that was as bad, if not as notorious, as Andrew Jackson's. Unlike Jackson, however, he never managed to soar over his limitations. He was always more comfortable with a gun in his hand than a pen.

Barely in his teens when the Civil War came, he joined the Union Army as a drummer boy with an Illinois regiment, but soon traded in his drum for a musket. His courage and initiative attracted the atten-

One of two universally accepted images of Timothy Isaiah Courtright, a studio photograph taken in Fort Worth, ca. 1885–86, wearing his custom-made deputy sheriff's badge. No indication from this photo how he acquired the name "Longhair Jim." (Courtesy Fort Worth Public Library, Genealogy, Local History, and Archives Unit.)

tion of Brigadier General John A. Logan who took young Timothy under his wing. The boy had an unfortunate penchant for getting in the way of bullets, suffering three wounds in two years. But he was young and vigorous and recovered rapidly, returning to duty after each injury. The exact nature of that duty is unknown because he never drew a pension in later life.

Sometime after the war, he married fourteen-year-old Sarah Elizabeth ("Betty") Weeks of Little Rock, Arkansas. They had their first child, a daughter they named Mary Ellen, in 1872. At the time, they were living with her parents in Arkansas, and he was farming on his father-in-law's land. In the next seven years, the couple would have two more children, a son, John, born in 1877 and another son, James, born in 1879. In 1873 the Courtrights relocated to Fort Worth, which at the time was a struggling hamlet on the Twin Forks of the

A questionable photograph reputed to be of Longhair Jim, purportedly taken in Fort Worth in 1884. With a beard concealing the chin line, no badge and no background or photographer's name attached, it is impossible to say for sure. (Courtesy Sergeant Kevin Foster.)

Trinity River. Timothy bought a little homestead on the north side of the river opposite the bluff. The first thing Fort Worth residents noticed about their new neighbor was his hair length; it was the fashion favored by many frontiersmen and army scouts but unusual among farmers and townsmen.[3]

Contrary to legend, Courtright's first job in law enforcement was not wearing a badge but working as a custodian at the city lockup. He was hired as turnkey by Marshal T. P. Redding in December 1875 and only took the menial job because he was fed up with life as a dirt farmer. At the relatively advanced age of twenty-eight or twenty-nine, his only marketable skills were quick reflexes and steely nerves. He could not support a wife and child on a turnkey's wages, but the job offered more opportunities than farming did, and besides, the idea of being a lawman appealed to him. In 1879 he would tell a gullible newspaper editor that before coming to Fort Worth he had "many years experience as marshal of frontier towns"—a shameless lie.[4]

Courtright fancied himself a full-fledged member of the Fort Worth Police Department (FWPD) and on the night of December 16, 1875, he attempted to arrest a couple of inebriated young hotspurs, one of whom shot him in the stomach. His remarkable constitution saved him yet again from his fourth gunshot wound in a relatively short career. The episode had a positive outcome because it got his name mentioned prominently in the press all over Texas. The newspapers even made him a "deputy marshal," something the City Council had not done.[5]

He had his eye set on public office from the beginning, helping to pave the way by joining the volunteer fire brigade (M. T. Johnson Hook and Ladder Company) and the Odd Fellows fraternal order. He achieved his ambition when he was elected town marshal in April 1876, on the eve of the boom times sparked by the coming of the railroad that summer. He won by just three votes over a field of four other candidates. The thinness of his mandate helps explain why he was not too strict about enforcing the law when cowboys came to town during the annual cattle season. Such a laissez-faire approach was also what city fathers wanted because cattle drives were the lifeblood of the town in those early years. Courtright tolerated the cowboys' shenanigans, only ordering them out of town when they became too boisterous but not before insisting that they settle up for any damage they had done. One cowhand later recalled, "They gave us all the rein we wanted in Fort Worth. . . . Whatever we did, I do not recall anybody ever trying to arrest us—we nearly had the town to ourselves." Courtright once told another cowpuncher that he and his friends "need not fear arrest as long as they confined themselves to having fun without hurting anyone."[6]

Courtright's approach to law enforcement was the same as that followed by the man with the star in a dozen other cowtowns just like Fort Worth: keep the body counts down and the cash receipts up. *Fort Worth Democrat* Editor B. B. Paddock once commended him for "not annoying persons for frivolous misdeeds," which presumably meant such activities as getting drunk, shooting out the streetlights, and galloping up and down the town's main streets.[7]

Re-elected twice, in 1877 and 1878, by the good citizens of Fort Worth, Longhair Jim justified their faith by continuing to enforce the law selectively. His activities, both good and bad, got his name in the newspapers frequently. He was acknowledged to be "fearless," the sort of lawman who would "arrest a circular saw if necessary." While his judgment was sometimes suspect, no one ever questioned his nerve. Said the *Democrat* during one of his re-election campaigns, "six-shooters or shotguns have no terrors for Jim." He was admired for being "unassuming" and considered to be generally honest by the lenient standards of the day. While his methods left much to be desired, there were many who approved of his "free-and-easy style" of law enforcement.[8]

According to legend, Courtright wore a fancy, two-gun rig with the grips of his pistols forward, setting up an awkward cross-body draw in the event of a face-off. Still, he was not the only Western gunslinger to favor such a rig. His contemporary, "Commodore" Perry Owens, Sheriff of Apache County, Arizona, and a man also known for his long locks, wore his pistols that same way and, like Courtright, was said to be a shootist par excellence with either hand. Courtright's particular talents included mastering the classic "road-agent's spin" and the "border shift," which only the most accomplished gunslingers had in their arsenal. And like Owens, Courtright sometimes put on shooting demonstrations.[9]

Yet the popular descriptions of his ambidextrous six-gun wizardry do not jibe with one important fact: He had a crippled left hand, probably the result of one of his war wounds. Regardless of the cause, it would certainly have kept him from being a quick-draw artist with that hand. [10] Another curious fact: For a man with such impressive credentials as a shootist, there is no record that Longhair Jim ever engaged in a stand-up gunfight during his marshal's tenure, which is not to say he never drew his weapon during his time in Fort Worth. Between 1875 and 1882, he used his pistol on at least five occasions, none of them shootouts, which suggests that his legendary reputation was a concoction of later writers.[11]

As an elected officer of the law, Marshal Courtright did not keep his political fences mended, nor was he too good with details. He proved an indifferent administrator, a poor manager of subordinates, and a less-than-squeaky-clean peace officer. His flirtation with the dark side of the law grew ever more brazen as time went by. He frequented the very saloons he was supposed to police, indulging his fondness for drinking and gambling heedless of propriety. After the summer of 1876, Fort Worth's reputation as a wide-open town attracted a class of men whose behavior went far beyond boisterous, yet Courtright treated the cowboys with kid gloves, winning their friendship if not their respect. Unless the cowboys unlimbered their six-shooters and began slinging lead or openly defied "Marshal Courtright's law" he preferred not to rein them in, although he was not above abusing his authority on occasion, working over any man he took a dislike to, getting drunk on duty, and picking fights that turned into brawls. In his defense, it must be said that to all appearances he was a happily married man who stayed out of the cathouses, and that there was some disagreement about how much he drank. Editor Paddock once praised him as a man who "took his beer straight," which made him practically a teetotaler by frontier standards.[12] In the end, the negatives came to outweigh the positives. The good citizens of Fort Worth took an increasingly dim view of his personal behavior and grew tired of the gamblers and gunmen who infested the town on his watch.

Courtright did not wear out his welcome all at once; it was a series of things. The first if not the worst occurred in December 1876 when he shot saloon man N. H. Wilson after Wilson had the temerity to place a "personal advertisement" in the *Democrat* accusing the Marshal and the Mayor of being in cahoots protecting crooked gambling interests. Courtright and one of his deputies stopped Nate Wilson on Main Street in broad daylight and roughed him up, then Courtright shot him in the leg. The unrepentant Marshal was subsequently arrested and charged with assault to commit murder, but nobody except Wilson was eager to press the matter. Months went by. Witnesses proved difficult to find, and Courtright hired good lawyers who entered a plea of self-defense. In the meantime, the Marshal was re-elected to a second term in 1877 and a third term in 1878. In the summer of 1877, Paddock of the *Democrat* was still singing his praises, proclaiming, "All honor to our Marshal Courtright and his assistants." Twenty months after the Wilson shooting, Courtright was acquitted by a jury composed of his neighbors and constituents.[13]

In the span of four years, from 1877 to 1881, Courtright was charged with serious criminal behavior at least four times. His list of offenses included "assault to murder," "malfeasance in office," "challenge to fight a duel," and "theft over $20." The outcome in each case was either "no action [taken]" or the "charges dismissed." His remarkable ability to avoid prosecution is hard to fathom at this date. Either he was the victim of malicious prosecution—repeatedly—or else he managed to wiggle out of one predicament after another thanks to the badge and his reputation with a gun.[14]

Even when he was on the job, Courtright did not devote himself exclusively to his Fort Worth responsibilities. Like many lawmen of his day he wore multiple badges, three to be exact. He held a commission as a deputy U.S. marshal for the Northern District of Texas from December 4, 1877, right up to his last day as city marshal. He

Captain G. H. Schmitt's heavily armed company of Texas Rangers, called in to help the local boys maintain law and order in Fort Worth during the 1886 Railroad Strike. (Schmitt is on the far right end of the line.) They are standing outside the old T&P Railroad Station while deputized citizens look on curiously. (Courtesy Western History Collections, University of Oklahoma.)

also held a deputy sheriff's commission for the duration of Tarrant County Sheriff J. M Henderson's administration (1876–1880). There was a lively debate in legal circles whether a man could legally hold simultaneous commissions under Texas law, but points of law did not faze Longhair Jim.[15]

Courtright's biggest mistake, however, was his failure to play the political game. He was too thin-skinned for his own good, reacting violently to even the smallest criticism, and when he answered his critics his weapons of choice were not words but fists or guns. As a lawman, he thought he was above the mundane duties of his office, such as keeping the streets clean and patrolling his domain regularly. Such cavalier disdain for his constituents caused even loyal supporters such as B. B. Paddock to grumble. Perhaps Courtright felt he had paid his dues by mucking out the jail in his early days on the police force. Now he took his election to the marshal's office as a mandate to do things his own way, and the City Council be damned. He had Wyatt Earp's independent streak without Wyatt's charisma or solid record of accomplishment. Courtright did not even pick his battles wisely. He outfitted his policemen in blue uniforms even after the Council had authorized gray coats. The last straw may have come when he tried to wrest control of the police force away from the Mayor in clear violation of the city charter.[16]

By the time annual municipal elections rolled around in 1879, the voters were fed up. Five other candidates ran against Courtright for the marshal's office. Even B. B. Paddock, formerly one of his biggest boosters, chose to endorse Henry P. Shiel, formerly one of Courtright's handpicked deputies. The marshal's race was the hottest among all municipal races that year, drawing nearly 1,500 votes. When the votes were tallied, Sam Farmer was the new Marshal and Longhair Jim was out of a job, but the true measure of the public's disapproval was that he placed third out of the six candidates—behind Farmer and W. P. Thomas.[17]

Courtright did not take his comeuppance philosophically. He resented Farmer's rapid rise to the top spot, recalling that at one time the new Marshal had been his protégé, or what the Dallas newspaper called his "right-hand man." In fact, Courtright had been grooming Farmer as his successor until the protégé got tired of playing second fiddle. After the campaign and election, the Courtright-Farmer friendship was over as far as Longhair Jim was concerned.[18]

Almost as much as he disliked Sam Farmer, Courtright resented the voters' ingratitude after all he had done for Fort Worth. Without even the pretense of keeping the peace to motivate him any longer, he began a steady decline into alcoholism and criminal activity. Rather than opt for a change of scenery as other frontier lawmen usually did when turned out of office, he chose instead to hang around town making life difficult for his successor. With his marshal's salary and perks ended, Courtright made a buck any way he could. Since he still held appointments as a deputy sheriff of Tarrant County and deputy U.S. marshal for the Northern District of Texas, he could earn fees by tracking down wanted men, serving warrants, and performing other services. In between official jobs he put his six-shooter and lawman's instincts to work as a private detective, meaning a hired gun. In 1881, after the FWPD purchased two bloodhounds so it would not have to bring in outside animals when there was tracking to be done, Courtright took on the job of training "Flora" and "Sam Houston."[19]

Mostly, Courtright spent his time in saloons playing poker, faro, or any game that gave him a chance to pad his bankroll. Like

Bat Masterson, Wyatt Earp, and countless other contemporaries in the law enforcement fraternity, he segued easily into the gambling life, in spite of the fact that he was an indifferent gambler. He even found work in one of the town's middling saloons as a house dealer. His specific job was running the keno game, which required no particular skills. It also placed him on the wrong side of the law, and he could expect only so many free passes from his lawman buddies. The police arrested him at least twice for "exhibiting a keno bank," a charge which represented token law enforcement more than a serious legal matter, but was another sign of how far the mighty had fallen.[20] This lack of respect for a brother lawman got his dander up. A lot of things got his dander up these days, prompting him to lash out at the slightest perceived insult. Courtright's fellow citizens began to give him wide berth, regarding him more as a hooligan than a favorite son. There were no tears shed when he finally left town.

But first he made one more run for the city marshal's job. In 1881 he entered the race against the incumbent, Sam Farmer, and two unknowns, Benton R. Elliott and John Burford. Although the *Democrat* on the occasion of his announcement characterized him as "one of the bravest and most efficient officers that ever wore a star," voters were not impressed. On election day, April 5, he came in a poor third behind Farmer and Elliott. Only 283 citizens voted for him out of 1,418 votes cast. It was another humiliation and his last run for public office.[21]

Jim finally got his chance to leave town *and* make some respectable money at the end of June 1882. The opportunity came via the frontier lawman's network. The city fathers of Caldwell, Kansas, had heard of his exploits in Fort Worth and offered him a job cleaning up their lawless cowtown. Caldwell's latest marshal, George Davis, had just been gunned down on June 22, and they needed someone who "knows no fear and whose highest ambition is to be dreaded by man."[22] The description certainly fit Courtright, but he turned them down, perhaps because of the paltry pay—$50 per month, the same amount he had earned when he started out as Fort Worth's marshal in 1876. Or the reason may have been because he did not want to be under the thumb of the City Council. (Caldwell's marshal was appointed, not elected.)

One thing is certain; he did not pass on the job because he had lost the fire in his belly. Later that same year he accepted the marshal's job at Lake Valley, New Mexico Territory. In an unusual arrangement, the little mining town (population: 500) decided to hire two marshals, Courtright and Jim McIntire, a longtime Courtright pal.[23] Courtright needed a chance to start over and Lake Valley needed a proven marshal (or two) to keep the rowdies in line. Perhaps the biggest factor in his decision was the chance to split the $300 monthly salary that came with the job. He bid his family goodbye, and set out for New Mexico in the fall of 1882.

The Lake Valley marshal's job apparently did not pan out. After only a few months, he and McIntire traded in their marshals' badges for jobs as guards with the Sierra Grande Mining Company. The positions came with deputy U.S. marshals' commissions, but they were still "regulators" working as private security for the mining company. Their job was to eliminate rustlers, thieves, and other threats to their employer—by whatever means necessary.[24]

Courtright was in his element again. The job paid well, gave him plenty of latitude in the use of his gun, and did not require any politicking. In the spring of 1883 he and McIntire switched employers again, going to work as regulators for the American Valley Cattle Company, a job with no long-term prospects. Courtright's career seemed to be going backwards. Although the new job paid $10 per day, it was only temp work.[25] One of his assignments was to run off small homesteaders (squatters) in the valley who were taking up grazing land. On May 6, Courtright and cronies executed two homesteaders, Alexis Grossetete and Robert Elsinger. Nineteen days later they were indicted by an Albuquerque grand jury for the double murder, and the Socorro County Sheriff placed Courtright under arrest. McIntire managed to get away.[26] In the meantime, the news had spread across the territory like wildfire. On the same day as the grand jury indictment, the *Santa Fe New Mexican* called the crime, "cold-blooded, unprovoked, and wanton murder."[27]

Courtright did not spend long in custody. He escaped on May 29, hooked up with McIntire, and hightailed it back to Fort Worth. In their absence, the Albuquerque grand jury handed up indictments, charging them with a total of fourteen murders. New Mexico Governor Lionel A. Sheldon sent a request to his counterpart in Austin requesting extradition. When that did not produce the desired results, he placed a reward of $500 each on the fugitives' heads at the end of October, hoping the free enterprise system could accomplish what the legal system could not.[28]

While all this was going on, Courtright was back home, secure in the belief that his many Fort Worth friends would never deliver him up to New Mexico authorities. As the months passed, Courtright remained watchful yet tried to live a normal life with Betty and the kids. The New Mexico troubles seemed to have been a wake-up call as he curtailed his non-stop gambling and brawling in favor of starting up a private detective business, the T.I.C. Detective Agency. The firm's logo replaced the letter "I" with a human eye, an idea he stole shamelessly from the Pinkerton Detective Agency. He also rejoined the M. T. Johnson Hook and Ladder Company. Those old fraternal ties with firemen and lawmen would soon come in handy.

He was happy to be on the side of law and order again. Being a private detective gave him a chance to put his old skills back to work, and he soon got his badge back, too. In the spring of 1884, Marshal William Rea took Courtright on as his deputy marshal, persuading the City Council to give him a commission and put him on the payroll. Rea, who had been on the job just a year at this point, was taking a chance hiring the popular and more experienced ex-Marshal. This demonstration of trust made Courtright a friend for life. Unfortunately, Longhair Jim did not seem to have learned anything from being around Rea and watching him in action. Bill Rea enjoyed an enviable reputation as a straight shooter, a model of decorum and restraint when it came to the rough stuff, and an officer who always kept his fences mended with city fathers. These were the qualities that allowed his career to endure for more than three decades.

Jim Courtright appreciated his second chance, but he still resented his humbled status. Deputy was a step down for the man who had been city marshal three times over, although it was a step up from his recent work as a regulator, private detective, and keno dealer.[29] While he waited to see how the New Mexico troubles played out, Courtright behaved himself. He also refused to discuss what had happened there or why New Mexico authorities wanted him. His badge and his local network of admirers allowed him to keep informed of all strangers who came to town. He did not fear vengeance-minded friends of his victims coming for him as much as he did officers showing up with an arrest warrant and extradition papers.

His worst fears were realized in October 1884 when New Mexico Sheriff Harry Richmond and a pair of Texas Rangers, Lieutenant A. C. Grimes and Corporal H. L. Hays, arrived in town with requisition papers and a warrant for his arrest. By coincidence, Marshal Rea was out of town, having gone to Mississippi to join in the manhunt for Dock Bishop, murderer of his deputy, W. T. Wise. Left in charge of things in Fort Worth while the Marshal was away was his new deputy, Jim Courtright. What followed would never have happened if Longhair Jim had accompanied his boss to Mississippi or even gone in his place. Then he would have been safely out of reach when Sheriff Richmond and the Rangers showed up.

Socorro County Sheriff Harry Richmond had been embarrassed by Courtright's escape from his custody on May 29. Now he was determined to place Courtright under arrest and take him back to New Mexico to stand trial for the murders of Grossetete and Elsinger. Richmond carried requisition papers bearing the signature of Governor John Ireland. The complicity of the Texas Governor must have surprised several prominent local men who considered Longhair Jim both a lawman and a true son of the Lone Star State, making him untouchable. Tarrant County Judge R. E. Beckham, County Attorney W. S. Pendleton, and Sheriff Walter T. Maddox had all placed their signatures on a petition requesting the Governor to ignore any extradition request from their neighbor to the west. Initially, Ireland had gone along, influenced in equal parts by the historic antipathy between the two states and by Courtright's popularity. However, after further consideration and perhaps a little arm-twisting, he signed the requisition papers.[30] Now Richmond was in Fort Worth to collect his man, backed up by two of Texas' best. If the famous motto "One riot, one Ranger" was already true at this early date, then the fact that the Governor sent not one but *two* Rangers indicated the level of respect still accorded Jim Courtright.

In a town as small as Fort Worth three strangers wearing badges stood out like visitors from Mars. On the other hand, the visiting lawmen had no trouble finding such a local celebrity as Longhair Jim. But they had to be careful how they grabbed him. They did not want a shootout or a vigilante mob trying to rescue the hometown hero. They adopted a stratagem of luring the unsuspecting ex-Marshal to a hotel room on a fool's errand, then getting the drop on him, and slapping on the shackles. They tried to time it so that they could quickly board an Austin-bound train and be gone before the locals knew what had happened. It was a good plan that failed in the execution.

They sprang their trap on Saturday, October 18, 1884, by asking Courtright to come to their room at the Ginnocchio Hotel and look at some pictures of wanted men. As soon as the door closed behind him, they placed him under arrest. So far, so good, but when the officers attempted to board the train, they ran into trouble on the platform. Longhair Jim flashed his shackles to a friend who raised a hue and cry, getting the attention of everybody within earshot. Before the officers could hustle Courtright aboard, they found themselves surrounded by a hostile crowd. Shoving their prisoner ahead of them they beat a hasty retreat back to the hotel where they holed up in an upstairs room with the door locked and a Fort Worth police officer posted at the foot of the stairs.

While Courtright looked on in bemusement, his three guards planned their next move. They could not hole up in the hotel for twenty-four hours until the next southbound train departed. They were afraid the crowd in front of the hotel would rush them and try to free the prisoner. If that happened, they could not expect much help from either the local police or the Sheriff. Since they would not release their prisoner, and they were not expecting the crowd to part like the Red Sea so they could get back to the station, the only option left was another retreat, this time to the county jail at the other end of town. There at least they had a chance if the standoff turned into a gun battle.

When it came time to make their move, they were assisted by local attorney William Capps. While he addressed the crowd in soothing tones from the roof of the railroad ticket office, the lawmen slipped their prisoner out the back door and hustled him up the street.[31] By the time the mob back at the hotel realized they'd been had, Courtright was safely locked up in the county jail.

There was still the problem of getting the prisoner onto a southbound train. The mob from the Ginnocchio Hotel was now camped out in front of the county courthouse, if anything, in a worse disposition than before. They were convinced that letting New Mexico authorities have Courtright was tantamount to turning him over to a Mexican lynch mob. Texans had long memories when it came to Mexico. Shouts of "Remember Goliad!" and "Remember the Alamo!" could be heard even inside the courthouse. One man in the crowd with lungs like a bellows harangued his fellows shouting, "The governor has forgotten Travis and Crockett, but we haven't! Courtright shall not be murdered by the greasers, by God!"[32]

It was a tense situation, but not as tense as it was portrayed in subsequent retelling. Two years after the affair, Sheriff Maddox would regale a gullible Dallas newspaper reporter with the story of how he and Marshal Rea had been prepared to stand off the mob if it broke down the door. As Maddox recalled the scene, he sat in the cell area while Rea sat in the vestibule, a locked and barred door between them, both men with a gun in hand prepared to sell their lives dearly. Maddox swore, "I was never in such danger in my life." At the time all this was supposed to have happened, however, Rea was 569 miles away in Oxford, Mississippi. While Maddox was spinning his yarn for the gullible reporter, Rea was sitting right there at his elbow and never opened his mouth to correct the tall tale. When Maddox's tall tale subsequently appeared in the *Dallas Morning News*, the two Fort Worth lawmen must have gotten a good laugh out of putting one over on the Dallas folks.[33]

When the warmth of the Indian summer day gave way to the evening's chill, the crowd dispersed to their homes or favorite watering holes, but before leaving, they promised to be back in the morning. During the long night that followed, each side made a fateful decision. Some of the pro-Courtright mob formulated a plan to spring their hero using guile instead of force, while the officers inside the jail decided the crisis had passed and they could stand down until time to catch the next day's train. What the Rangers knew and the mob did not was that reinforcements were on the way. More Texas Rangers would be arriving the next day from Wichita Falls with Jim McIntire in tow. With a full squad of Rangers on hand, the locals would never dare start anything. The next morning, the embattled lawmen in the courthouse breathed a sigh of relief as they watched the first rays of light chase away the shadows outside.

Famished after their all-night vigil, the three jailers decided it was safe to take their man out of his cell and walk him over to Merchant's

Restaurant at 41 Main Street for a little breakfast.[34] For some unfathomable reason, they decided to remove his shackles even though they were going out on the public streets with a man whom the mob had already threatened to free. When the jail party emerged, a sullen crowd followed them, albeit at a respectful distance, to their destination, waiting outside while they ate.

Christopher Lawson's restaurant was close to the courthouse and served excellent food. When the four from the jail came in, it was almost deserted. The owner served them, and when the food came, all four men attacked their plates, but three of them also kept an eye on the crowd outside, which had grown until it was now spilling from the sidewalk onto the street.

The meal passed without incident, and Courtright was escorted back to his cell. Later that day the Rangers received a telegram that Captain George H. Schmitt, Company C, Frontier Battalion, and a squad of Rangers would be arriving on the 6:30 p.m. train from Wichita Falls.

The lawmen continued to act carelessly. When suppertime rolled around, they decided to make another foray to Lawson's restaurant. They may have even told the owner they'd be back for supper. That is the only way to explain the surprise reception awaiting them when they returned at 6:00. The previous ten hours had given Courtright's friends time to plan a little reception at the restaurant and even get word to him inside the jail. When the jail party strolled into Lawson's, the owner ushered them to an empty table in the back of the room, perhaps even the same table they had occupied that morning. The crowd waited outside again, presumably having nothing else to do except gawk at the four diners. Courtright ordered fish, perhaps appreciating the irony that the "day's catch" was about to get away. His three companions had again taken chairs facing the door, but this time their carelessness caught up with them.

Just as the food was being served, the crowd, as if on signal, surged through the front door. The Rangers jumped to their feet reaching for their six-guns. They did not notice Courtright casually drop his napkin on the floor and bend over to retrieve it. When he raised up, he was not holding a napkin but a brace of pistols that had been fastened underneath the table. Courtright had the drop on the Rangers. Sheriff Richmond was so surprised by the turn of events, he literally fell out of his chair. The Rangers hesitated for a split second, but they were in no position to argue.

"Shove out, all of you," Jim barked. "You've had your time. I'll take mine now." His friends rushed forward and pushed the lawmen back into their chairs, then covered them with drawn pistols while Courtright dashed out the back door.[35]

Behind the café, the rest of the escape plan was already in place: a fast horse tied up and waiting. Courtright mounted in one smooth motion and dug his heels into the animal's flanks. Off they went around the corner and onto Main Street. As the crowd in front of Lawson's caught sight of their hero, they gave a ragged cheer. He responded by firing one pistol into the air as he galloped up the street toward the river. It would have been a perfect, Hollywood-style getaway except that as he rounded another corner, his horse stumbled and fell, throwing Courtright to the ground. Fortunately for the future legend, an unidentified man straight out of Central Casting rode up on a white horse, jumped off and handed the reins to Courtright. A hurried thanks and the fugitive was on his way again. Longhair Jim was last seen galloping full tilt up the street toward the river.

Back at Lawson's, the three embarrassed lawmen were released by the crowd. They rushed outside to try to see which way their prisoner had gone. When they could see no sign of him, they hurried down to the station to meet the train from Wichita Falls. It was a disgusted Captain Schmitt who stood on the platform a little later and heard his officers' tale of woe. He assumed command, ordered McIntire off to jail, and mounted a search for the fugitive. Schmitt placed a heavy guard on his remaining prisoner and suspended restaurant privileges.

The Ranger Captain with help from Sheriff Maddox collected a less-than-unenthusiastic posse to search for Courtright. Not surprisingly, their search proved fruitless; the ex-Marshal had disappeared, apparently into the Trinity River bottoms.

But Courtright had not left town. He was being hidden by friends, some of whom wore badges. One of those badge-wearing friends was Ab Woody, a special officer with the Santa Fe Railroad. On the night of November 1, Woody slipped Jim into the baggage car on a Galveston-bound train. Two days later, Courtright was safely on a steamship headed for New York under an alias. Meanwhile, the

Rangers scoured the north Texas countryside for weeks looking for their fugitive.[36]

Courtright's brazen escape had serious repercussions for the Rangers. Grimes' and Hays' careers never recovered. Corporal Hays was discharged for insubordination just a month later, on November 16, 1884. Albert Grimes, who had just been promoted to lieutenant when he was sent to Fort Worth, did not keep that rank. When he re-upped the following year, he was reduced to sergeant, and that was his final rank when he mustered out of the Rangers on November 30, 1887.[37]

We can only speculate about Courtright's movements after he fled the state, but he apparently kept in touch with friends and family back in Fort Worth during a fifteen-month odyssey around the country. Eventually he received word that it was safe to come home, and on January 20, 1886, he stepped off a train from Denison accompanied by pal George Holland and police officer Jim Thompson. He was not shackled, and the crowd that greeted him on the platform burst into applause as soon as they saw him. His friends had negotiated a deal for Courtright to give himself up and face the New Mexico charges.[38]

By this time, the indictment against him was a dead letter. Jim McIntire had already gone before the district court in Albuquerque on October 15, 1885, but when the prosecution could produce neither witnesses nor evidence against him, the charges were dismissed.[39] After that, there was no possibility that Courtright would ever be prosecuted in New Mexico, so appearing in an Albuquerque court in February 1886 was a mere formality. He walked out of court a free man.[40]

In the second coming of Jim Courtright on March 6, he returned to Fort Worth the conquering hero. After a few celebratory rounds in every saloon up and down Main Street, things quieted down and Longhair Jim returned to what he knew best, putting his gun and reputation to work making money. He reopened the T.I.C. Detective Agency and was soon sporting a badge on his chest again just like in the good old days.

Less than a month after his return, Courtright was commissioned a Tarrant County deputy sheriff and played a leading role in the Great Railroad Strike of 1886. He was seven years past his glory days as city marshal, but still a magnet for trouble. This time the stakes were higher than they had been with that little range war in New Mexico. The events of April 1886 would give him one more chance to redeem himself, adding "strikebreaker" to his résumé in the process.[41]

Employees of Jay Gould's Missouri, Kansas, and Texas Railroad (the Katy) started the strike in Marshall, Texas. The shop men there had been unionized by the Knights of Labor, so when the company cut wages and began laying off workers, the union resisted. They demanded $1.50 a day minimum wage and when management refused to budge, 9,000 shop men walked off the job, paralyzing commerce all across the Southwest. Strikers in Marshall, Sherman, Waco, and Fort Worth occupied rail yards, vandalized equipment, and blockaded the tracks. Town fathers, pushed by railroad executives, responded with a show of force. They called out every man on their police rolls, including "special officers," and deputized additional men to defend railroad property. Federal and state authorities got involved. In Fort Worth, the U.S. Marshal for the Northern District deputized twenty men to help protect the U.S. mails. Texas Governor Ireland issued a proclamation calling on every peace officer in the state to be "vigilant, active and fearless in preserving the peace and giving protection to life and property." A worried Tarrant County Sheriff Walter Maddox beefed up his small force by deputizing additional men.[42]

Maddox was a member of the tight fraternity of Fort Worth lawmen, which included his brother and chief deputy Jim Maddox, City Marshal Bill Rea, and former City Marshal Jim Courtright. On occasions like this, they knew they could rely on each other. At one time or another, each one had backed the play of the others. Now Maddox pinned a deputy sheriff's badge on Jim Courtright and posted him at the Katy yards.

Fort Worth in the spring of 1886 was a powder keg. Strikers and their friends gathered on street corners to watch and be watched by deputies nervously fingering their weapons. A Knights of Labor strike committee urged their men to stand firm. Angry crowds of laborers gathered at the rail yards day after day as the stalemate continued. Marshal Rea and Sheriff Maddox had no experience in this sort of thing. Keeping the peace in a labor war was a far cry from chasing down rustlers and train robbers. The line between lawbreaker and law-abiding citizen was not clear.

Railroad officials secured an injunction from Judge R. E. Beckham, ordering the strikers to stay off "Missouri-Pacific" property and not interfere with traffic into and out of Fort Worth. Then they concocted a scheme to break the impasse by running a freight train loaded with coal and armed guards through the blockade to Alvarado. If they tried to stop it, they would be in violation of a court order to cease and desist, and that would bring the full weight of federal and state authorities down on them.

The strikebustin' train would make its run on April 3. Its escort would consist of a five-man company guard plus a contingent of sheriff's deputies. There was only one man to command that contingent—Jim Courtright. Maddox gave the ex-Marshal carte blanche in picking his team, and Courtright tapped seven men he knew well.

The morning of April 3, a Saturday, started quietly enough, although the tension in the air was thick enough to cut with a skinning knife. Word had gotten around town that some sort of a showdown was coming. The strike was now in its second month, and it was clear that management intended to break the strike rather than settle. Even before the sun peeked over the roof of Union Depot, 500 sullen unemployed men occupied the street in front of the railroad reservation, abiding by Judge Beckham's injunction but just barely. Sheriff Maddox was also up early, deploying his entire force, minus Courtright's squad, at intervals up and down the tracks facing the crowd. Knights of Labor organizers, took up a blocking position where the tracks crossed a city street, declaring that they were not on Katy property. One of them strolled over to Maddox and, in a calculated ploy, informed him that after thinking it over, they were going to call off the strike. In return, however, the union man asked the sheriff not to enforce the injunction. Maddox informed him he could not do that.

Courtright and his seven men boarded the train for its run up to Hodge to pick up the coal cars. He was the last man aboard, impatiently waving the crowd back from the tracks. The first sign of trouble came just as the engine was getting underway. A group of strike leaders was seen huddling on the street. After a brief conference, the men hurried away, obviously on some mission that did not bode well.

The union men had decided to stop the train not in the yards but outside of town. It was the same ambush stratagem that had been used by countless train and stagecoach robbers over the years. When the train came back through a couple of hours later, it stopped on the northern edge of town just long enough to pick up Courtright and his deputies. He placed three officers atop the cars with the company guards while he and the other four crowded into the engine cab with the engineer and fireman.

The train passed back through Fort Worth between 12:30 and 1:00. Two miles south of town, at a switching point called Buttermilk Junction, the strikebreaking special was ambushed by a rifle-toting bunch who had prepared a warm welcome. The train was forced to a halt after the engineer noticed the switch was turned in the wrong direction. Changing it back would only take a matter of moments, but the train would have to stop while it was done. The whole thing seemed very suspicious because two groups of men were waiting and watching nearby. No one doubted that they were up to no good, but just what they intended was not clear. As the engine stood chuffing just short of the crossing, Courtright and three of his men hopped down out of the cab and started forward to confront one group leaning against a pile of ties on the east side of the tracks. The unknown group did not appear to be armed and they made no threatening moves.

Courtright skipped the preliminaries in placing them under arrest and ordered them to walk back to the train. He had not brought any shackles with him. Next, he led his men across the tracks toward the second group who were sitting on a slight rise about a hundred yards distant. As he drew closer, he hailed them in the same tone that had given pause to many a barroom drunk in his marshal days: "Gentlemen, lay down those guns." But these men were not drunk, nor were they cowboys on a frolic. Instead of meekly following orders, they raised their rifles. For the first time, Courtright seemed to realize what a dicey situation he had gotten himself into. Switching tones, he pleaded, "For Christ's sake, don't shoot!"[43]

They ignored his plea just as they had ignored his command and opened fire. Not anticipating resistance and with no tactical plan, Courtright and his men could do nothing but drop to the ground and try to get back to the train. Courtright reached the tracks and lay down between the rails using them as cover. It soon became apparent to the other lawmen that the bushwhackers were focusing their fire on Longhair Jim. He was safe as long as he stayed where he was. His survival instincts were good, but he had effectively taken himself out of the fight, too.

The other lawmen on the train and on the ground fought back as best they could with their six-guns against Winchesters. Why nobody had thought to bring along rifles was a question that would be asked afterwards, without getting a satisfactory answer.[44]

The lawmen were battling for their lives and getting the worst of it. Officer Dick Townsend went down in the first volley, and two others were severely wounded in the next few minutes. The lawmen finally managed to drive the bushwhackers away. Then Courtright got his men back on the train and ordered the engineer to open the throttle and back it all the way to the city. He did not have to give the order twice. The forces of law and order fled the scene, but not before blooding their enemy. Nonetheless, it had obviously been a one-sided battle, and the survivors were glad to get back to the safety of the rail yards.

Under questioning, Officers Fulford and Tucker were able to identify at least two of the men who had ambushed them: Henry Henning and Thomas Nace. Both were well-known union men.[45] A sheriff's posse quickly fanned out across the countryside to search for the bushwhackers. In the next twelve hours, Sheriff Maddox's inadequate force was reinforced by state militia and Texas Rangers summoned to the scene. After April 3, local officers were no longer calling the shots.

What was quickly dubbed the "Battle of Buttermilk Junction" by the newspapers did nothing for Courtright's already-tarnished reputation. The *San Antonio Express*, no fan of Longhair Jim's, reported the engagement under the headline, "Courtright's Crew Ambushed and Out-fought." No Fort Worth editor would have dared to print such blunt criticism of the volatile ex-Marshal who had followed the ancient wisdom, "He who fights and runs away lives to fight another day." Sure enough, he was riding on the same train the next day when it made a second attempt to run the blockade. This time it made it to Alvarado unmolested.

The blockade was broken, but there was no time to celebrate. During the next few days, Courtright earned his pay putting in long hours searching for the bushwhackers. On the night of April 19–20, he was part of a scratch group of deputies assembled by Sheriff Maddox after midnight to raid a house where Frank Pierce was reported hiding. They did not find Pierce, but the manhunts continued.[46]

While the Sheriff's and Marshal's men chased their tails, Texas Rangers and uniformed soldiers took over most of the work of keeping the peace. For all practical purposes, the city was under martial law. It would remain that way for almost a week before life began returning to normal.

Reverberations of the strike and the Battle of Buttermilk Junction did not fade quickly. There were still lots of questions to be answered, guilt to be assigned, and justice to be served. Fort Worth was even in the national spotlight. The U.S. House of Representatives appointed a subcommittee to investigate the strike. Members of the subcommittee journeyed to Fort Worth to hold hearings from April 20 to May 14. They met in a dingy room of a printing office on the public square, but that did not prevent them from calling a "cloud of witnesses." It was the first time a real Congressional subcommittee had ever descended on Fort Worth.[47]

Testimony before the subcommittee caused the official version of the Buttermilk Junction ambush to begin unraveling. The deputies and train guards first said that the bushwhackers had fired first, but when closely questioned they were not so certain. Fortunately for the authorities, the Knights hurt their own cause by refusing to be completely open about their involvement in the strike. Jim Courtright was also called to testify but added little to the record.[48]

Courtright was back on the witness stand on January 15, 1887, at Henry Henning's bond hearing in Seventeenth District Court. Longhair Jim did not make much of a witness for the prosecution and did serious damage to his own public image with his testimony. He said that Dick Townsend had been back-shot from point-blank range, citing the "powder burns" on the back of the officer's coat as proof. Problem was, he was dead wrong. Other officers who participated in the battle and the attending physician all contradicted that part of his testimony. They agreed that Townsend had been shot in the back, but the shot came from some distance and the residue on the back of his coat was not powder burns but coal dust that had got there when he landed on his back beside the tracks.[49]

Things got worse from there. Other witnesses confirmed what the newspapers had already reported, namely that Courtright had spent most of the battle hugging the ground trying to keep from getting his head blown off. A witness for the State said one of the bushwhackers told him later he would have killed "his man [Courtright] if he had ever raised up." The implication was clear: Jim Courtright was not in the fight, which, if believed, meant that his days as a local hero were finished.[50]

Courtright did not get another chance on the witness stand to correct or explain his testimony because he died before any of the Buttermilk Junction defendants came to trial. But his ghost hung over all the trials. His testimony before the committee was brought up at Henning's trial and shot full of holes by the defense. And after John Hardin, the ringleader, was acquitted by a Fort Worth jury, the *Dallas Morning News* said the verdict was in a great degree attributable to the reputation of Jim Courtright.[51]

Longhair Jim Courtright emerged from the 1886 railroad strike and the Battle of Buttermilk Junction unscathed but with his reputation in tatters. What saved him from complete ruin was that the manhunt for the perpetrators took precedence over assigning blame. Still, the *San Antonio Light* blamed him personally, saying, "Jim Courtright is largely responsible for the Fort Worth massacre," and suggesting that he was a loose cannon. From the safe distance of 238 miles, the *Light* stated,

> It is a criminal act to place a man of his known antecedents in the lead when the peace of society is threatened. The man has been a terror of society [and] should not be entrusted with the delicate and very serious responsibility of keeping the public peace.[52]

How far the mighty had fallen! Longhair Jim Courtright was once "Mr. Fort Worth" and the face of local law enforcement. His is the story of a great talent misspent and of a legend with feet of clay.

The Battle of Buttermilk Junction was yet another black mark on Courtright's already tarnished reputation. The San Antonio press was particularly hard, blaming him for the "massacre" and questioning whether he had even been a duly deputized officer at the time or just a hired gun in the employee of the railroad. The *Light* of that city characterized him as a loose cannon that neither Sheriff Maddox nor Marshal Rea could control, and revived the familiar charge that he was nothing but a "bully." The *Dallas Morning News*, at the time of John Hardin's trial five years later, described him as the "local desperado in charge of the [train] guards." Even a newspaper in far-off Georgia weighed in. The *Atlanta Constitution* had picked up the original story on the wire, and showed no mercy to the notorious Longhair Jim, dismissing him as "a typical border ruffian." The newspaper's editor went on to say, "When a regular desperado enrolls himself on the side of the law there is trouble ahead if he is opposed," then in a twist of logic added, perhaps with tongue firmly planted in cheek, that the best way to "utilize our dangerous classes is to give them a badge" and put them to work on the side of the law![53]

Even a scrupulously fair evaluation of Courtright's performance that day in April 1886 finds him wanting. From start to finish, the operational decisions he made were seriously flawed, marked by hubris and lack of foresight. The string of miscalculations began with his decision to set out armed only with six-shooters. That bad decision was compounded when he detrained his men at the junction and marched them across open ground right into the gun sights of an armed and obviously hostile party of men. Finally, his ill-informed testimony at the bond hearing completed a trifecta of blunders. All things considered, Courtright's only accomplishment in the whole affair was not getting himself shot at Buttermilk Junction.

During the rest of 1886, Courtright kept a low profile, unusual behavior for him, probably because he was focusing all his energies on running his detective agency (office at Houston and Second). Still in his thirties, he should have been in the prime of life, but instead he was on the downhill side of both his life and career. A lifetime's worth of drinking and hard living had taken its toll. He had a family, but no savings and no steady job. His detective agency was actually a cover for an extortion racket he was running that collected protection money from a number of Fort Worth saloons. Even that was not going smoothly. Luke Short, the gambling kingpin of the White Elephant Saloon, refused to be intimidated and told the ex-Marshal to go jump in the river. Courtright brooded about the insult until he worked himself up to a drunken state of fury. It was not just being disrespected that galled him; it was the fear of being shown up in front of the whole town. Short's challenge had to be answered. William Rea, who knew Courtright as well as anyone, said years later that it was "money matters" that drove the fatal wedge between Courtright and Short, but it is clear in hindsight that pride and ego also played a role in what followed. Afterwards, Short started the story that Courtright was a hired assassin sent to kill him, but he never bothered to explain who had hired Courtright or why. Another equally preposterous explanation was that Courtright had his eye on Hettie Short, but nobody who knew either man put any credence in that.[54]

On the evening of February 8, Courtright, fortified with liquid courage, came looking to square things. He wasn't seeking an apology so much as he was determined to make Short pony up like his fellow gambling operators. Courtright arrived at eight o'clock in the vestibule of the White Elephant and loudly called Short outside. Short was cold sober and armed although he typically kept his pistol out of sight. He willingly accompanied his challenger outside. Courtright had brought along a pal, Charley Bull, and Short was accompanied by his former partner Jake Johnson, a mutual friend of both men, but this thing would be settled between the two principals alone. Bull and Johnson made themselves scarce when Courtright and Short moved a few steps down the sidewalk away from the saloon entrance. Stopping in front of a shooting gallery, they talked intently for just a few moments before one of them, probably Courtright, went for his gun. He was wearing a six-shooter strapped to his leg gunslinger-style. Short's little .45 caliber snub-nose was in a hip pocket, giving him easy access.[55] Remarkably, the gambler beat the gunfighter to the draw and got off the first shot. He was standing too close to miss his target, and he did not stop with one shot. In a showdown, experienced gunfighters kept shooting until either their opponent went down or they ran out of bullets. Short kept firing until he had emptied his pistol and Courtright lay sprawled on the sidewalk bleeding from four wounds, his revolver still clutched in his hand, unfired. It was a sight no one ever thought they would see. Four previous shootings and at least one narrow escape at Buttermilk Junction had used up his nine lives. Only twenty minutes had passed since he walked in the front door of the White Elephant.[56]

A couple of officers nearby, including Courtright's pal J. J. Fulford, came running to the scene. They were too late to do anything except send for the patrol wagon to remove the body, and escort Short to the city jail. Courtright's last words, whispered into Officer Fulford's ear, were dime-novel ready: "Ful, they got me." The corpse was dropped off at the undertaker's where his fifteeen-year-old daughter, Mary Ellen, first saw it. Throwing herself on the bloody form, she rained kisses on his hands and face while moaning, "Papa, Papa."[57]

News of the shooting spread quickly. Everybody had known about the bad blood between the two men. This was simply the denouement of a very public feud. According to the code governing such things, therefore, it was a fair fight, not a case of murder. Still, there were the formalities of the law to be observed. Luke Short spent the night in jail, and he had to appear before a coroner's inquest at ten o'clock the next morning, but no charges were filed. The Justice of the Peace set bond at $2,000, which was promptly paid by an odd alliance that included Sheriff Walter Maddox, gambler Jake Johnson, and attorneys Robert McCart and N. A Steadman. All four men had a long history with both principals in the shootout, and now with Courtright gone, they felt no pangs of conscience standing up for their other friend.[58] The grand jury also felt no moral qualms about no-billing Luke Short. They agreed with the judgment on the street: It was a simple case of self-defense.

In death, Longhair Jim's financial problems became public knowledge. Betty Courtright could not even afford the cost of the funeral, and there was no way the city would foot the bill. Any official gratitude felt for the legendary Marshal had long since dissipated. Fortunately, Courtright was not lacking in friends willing to pass the hat to bury him. They chipped in enough to cover the funeral expenses plus a little extra for the widow and children. If Jim Courtright had never been anything but a hired gun and a brawler, the well born of Fort Worth would never have contributed so generously to a fund in his name. It was a final gesture of respect for the man who had helped make Fort Worth a decent town to live in. Luke Short even kicked in a few dollars, telling a newspaper reporter that no one felt worse about the killing than he did.[59]

Timothy Isaiah Courtright was buried in what was almost an unseemly rush to put him in the ground. Funeral arrangements were minimal. The next day, February 9, at 1:00 p.m., the brief service commenced at the Courtright residence. This was just a couple of hours after the coroner's inquest adjourned *sine die*, so citizens who wanted to attend both events barely had time to change into their funeral garb. The simple service in the Courtright parlor was followed by a somber procession across the river to Oakwood Cemetery. Mourners lined up with the curious and morbidly minded to form a funeral cortege six blocks long. The City Council had ordered the fire bell not to be rung, but somebody, probably a member of the M. T. Johnson Hook and Ladder Company, defied the order and rang the big bell in the traditional show of respect for a fallen fireman. Whatever else Courtright had done in his life, he was still one of their own.

He was interred in Oakwood Cemetery in the same grave as his son James. Whether that decision was driven by financial considerations or simple sentiment is impossible to say. After the funeral, Mrs. Courtright kicked the dust of Fort Worth off her feet just as fast as she could pack and catch a westbound train. There was no estate to be settled. Jim had owned little more than his guns, his horse, and the clothes on his back. Betty and the two children moved to Los Angeles to live with her parents, and she never returned to Fort Worth. Nor did the city ever erect a memorial to its one-time hero.

The question that must be answered for Timothy Isaiah Courtright is this: Was he the latest in a long line of lawmen to fall in the line of duty or was he a gunslinger who got what he deserved? The answer is both yes and no—to both questions! On the character issue, Courtright was once described by a Galveston reporter who came to town to meet the legend as "fearless to a fault" and a peaceable man "when not under the influence of liquor."[60] Since he was often under the influence of liquor in his latter years, his peaceable days became fewer and further between.

At the time of his death Jim Courtright was a duly commissioned deputy sheriff of Tarrant County, a fact largely overlooked afterwards.[61] That means he died a lawman and in proper Wild West fashion with his boots on, but he was not performing any official duties when he died. He had been semi-retired for years, helping out with both the Police Department and Sheriff's Office when needed. He probably only put on the badge for the fees; otherwise, when not drinking or gambling, he devoted himself to his detective agency.

His career as a lawman gets mixed reviews. He was Fort Worth's first marshal to complete a full term in office, and he went on to serve two more terms during the town's wildest era—when it was a principal stop on the major cattle trail out of Texas—and during the boom times that followed the coming of the railroad. He brought stability and respect to the office. As an underpaid and overworked city marshal who had to learn on the job, he succeeded beyond everyone's expectations in keeping Fort Worth from falling into the same sort of lawlessness that plagued Dodge City, Caldwell, and other Kansas cowtowns. Even after the voters rejected him, Courtright had no lack of admirers in high places. County Attorney W. S. Pendleton, who drafted the petition to John Ireland in 1884 asking the Governor to refuse New Mexico's extradition request, praised the ex-Marshal for his "great service to law and order during the 'hurrah' days of Fort Worth." Around the same time, Sheriff Walter Maddox publicly praised him as "a brave man and . . . an able and efficient officer in Fort Worth when he was City Marshal here."[62]

What is also true, however, is that Courtright got into more than his share of scrapes, with the Lake Valley murders and the shootout with Luke Short being merely the most infamous. In the matter of the railroad strike he did not cross the line, but once again he showed a troubling willingness to hire out his gun. Like many of his badge-wearing contemporaries, Longhair Jim was no saint, but he got the job done under difficult circumstances, often working alone or with inadequate and untrained backup. Even after being unceremoniously booted from the marshal's job, Courtright continued to work in law enforcement in both Texas and New Mexico and could have, if he had desired, put on a badge in Kansas. At various points in his twelve-year career (1875–1887), he served as a town marshal, deputy sheriff, and deputy U.S. marshal. He helped transform the FWPD by introducing its first uniforms and serving as trainer for its first K-9 corps. And in the end, he was Fort Worth's first celebrity lawman, carving a niche for himself in Western history, in the process putting Fort Worth on the national map. At the end, the *Fort Worth Gazette* delivered the best eulogy, bidding "a farewell mingled with hope that all his faults might be forgotten and only the good deeds he has done be remembered in the hereafter."[63]

CHAPTER 3

Hagar Tucker: Fort Worth's First Black Policeman

Before I. M. Terrell and "Gooseneck Bill" McDonald there was Hagar Tucker, Fort Worth's first black citizen of note. The first two were exemplary gentlemen, Terrell as an educator and McDonald as a businessman-politician. Tucker made his mark as a lawman, or more specifically, a "special policeman" with the Fort Worth Police Department (FWPD), the only person of color on an otherwise all-white force.

Hagar Tucker was born into slavery in Kentucky bluegrass country in July 1842. His parents were the chattel of William B. Tucker, which is how he came to get his surname. (During those days, black slaves typically took the name of their master's family upon emancipation since slaves did not have last names.) Hagar had a proper, Old Testament given name, an adopted last name, and his freedom, but no education to ease his path through life. Even as an adult, he never learned to write his own name, another one of the legacies of slavery.[1] He worked as a field hand and along with other members of his family accompanied the Tucker family to Texas in the mid-1850s.[2] He was officially emancipated at the same time as other Texas slaves on June 19, 1865, after the Civil War ended. He enjoyed an extraordinarily good relationship with his former master, so he stayed on in Fort Worth after becoming a freedman. Local whites shortened his name to "Hague," and that is how he was remembered decades later.

After reaching Texas he tied the knot with another Tucker family slave known simply as Amy, whose age has been variously estimated at nine years younger to two years older than her man.[3] It was probably not a proper Christian marriage because of the circumstances of their servitude, but the marriage endured for at least thirty-two years. They started their family in Texas when their first child was born in 1857. Over the years that followed, their family grew to include at least eight children.[4]

Hagar worked hard to carve out a place for himself in the community on the Trinity. There were few blacks living in Tarrant County after the Civil War, and those who did were held down by white intolerance in general and the active presence of the Ku Klux Klan specifically. White men, many of them Confederate veterans, made sport by firing their six-guns into the ground beneath the feet of blacks to make them dance.[5] The victims of such shenanigans could do nothing but endure such insults. This is why it is all the more remarkable that a mere two years after the war Hagar Tucker owned property and registered to vote in Tarrant County on July 30, 1867, one of only a handful of blacks among the community's 1,169 registered voters.[6]

After incorporation in 1873, city fathers decided that their budding town needed an officer of color to police the black community, serving as a combination enforcer and liaison. Reconstruction was still going on in Texas, and relations between the two races were strained at best. The city had an elected white marshal, Ed Terrell, and an all-white police force, but city fathers wanted a black man that they could depend on. They cast about for someone to serve as the right arm of the law, what one white resident would later describe as "a big buck Negro" respected by whites and blacks alike.[7] Terrell was no civil rights crusader, just a public official with a job to do, and having a black officer would make that job easier. He made a formal proposal to the City Council, and after some discussion they accepted it.

Besides meeting the obvious qualifications of being black and respected in the black community, Hagar Tucker had something equally important: a powerful white patron. William B. Tucker, Sr., his former master, also happened to be a large landowner in the

As a worthy representative of Fort Worth's early black community, Hagar Tucker has always been overshadowed by his more famous contemporary, "Gooseneck" Bill McDonald. Even in death his modest grave in the Trinity section of Oakwood Cemetery is overshadowed by the massive monument to Bill McDonald. (Author's collection.)

county and an alderman, and he had complete faith in Hagar to keep within the bounds of the job and not overstep his very limited authority. Tucker, Sr., became Hagar's advocate in the white power structure, and the other five aldermen on the Council were persuaded by his endorsement. However, they did not make Hagar a full-fledged member of the police force. He was designated a "special policeman," drawing his pay outside the regular channels and restricted to policing only members of his own race. As the enabling ordinance put it, he was "to arrest all offenders . . . within the city limits . . . of his own color".[8]

Oakwood Cemetery, Fort Worth's second public cemetery, has three sections. The Old Trinity Cemetery was the segregated black section. Cf. the general cemetery and the Catholic Calvary section. (Author's collection.)

When Special Officer Hague Tucker patrolled the black section of Fort Worth in the 1870s, there was not much to the town, just a few dusty streets and wood-frame buildings between modern-day Lancaster and the bluff, as this undated photo from that era shows. Note the fire bell/school bell in center background. (Courtesy Fort Worth Public Library, Genealogy, Local History, and Archives Unit.)

This was the only time Hagar Tucker's name ever appeared in the minutes of the City Council. For the white power structure, there had been a problem duly addressed and fixed; there was no need to revisit it. Hagar was something more than a token, but way less than an equal member of the force. He performed his job capably, without making waves for his employers or being branded an "Uncle Tom" by his own people. His job required as much diplomacy as policing skills.

Ed Terrell lasted only seven months as marshal, quitting in November 1873. There is unfortunately no record of how long Hagar Tucker remained on the city payroll after that. His involvement cannot be detected in the way a couple of ugly racial incidents played out during the next two years. On November 30, 1874, a sizable number of the town's black residents gathered and started raising a ruckus. As one of Fort Worth's later chroniclers described it, "Negroes of the city had been encroaching upon the patience of the citizens by their midnight debaucheries under the guise of religious gatherings." In the face of such brazen defiance of authority, the man sent to "quell the disturbance" was not Hagar Tucker, however, but white deputy marshal Columbus Fitzgerald, who had a well-known reputation as a hard-nosed bigot. The Negro mob was not impressed by the Irishman's badge and handled him roughly. The next morning the Sheriff and City Marshal went down to the black district and confronted the ringleaders, placing one of them under arrest.[9]

That may have been the first, but it was not the last violent clash between the city's white authorities and its black residents. In 1875 Fort Worth was the scene of a lynching, the first since the early days of the Civil War. The victim was a black man, Sol Bragg, accused of assaulting a white woman, which was a virtual sentence of death for any black man regardless of the evidence or lack of same. Bragg was seized by a band of white vigilantes and taken out to the Cold Springs Road where they strung him up to a sycamore tree.[10] There was nothing Hagar Tucker could have done to prevent this miscarriage of justice. The whole affair only underscored his powerlessness. He operated on a very short leash.

What is likely is that without Hagar Tucker's presence as a liaison between white and black communities, both incidents could have been a lot worse. Progress must sometimes be measured in small increments. The Fitzgerald and Bragg incidents may have been what finally drove Hagar off the police force. He was a proud man who did not appreciate his second-class status; moreover, the City Council may have reconsidered its earlier decision to bestow a measure of authority on a man they called "free" only because the federal government had insisted in 1865.

By 1877 Hagar Tucker was out of law enforcement and working as a porter, i.e., a janitor or maintenance man, in one of Fort Worth's many saloons. He and his family lived in one of what the fire insurance maps called the "Negro tenements" on the eastern edge of town.[11] A few years later, he went into the grocery business selling locally grown foodstuffs out of a shack between Crump and Harding streets. When that did not pay enough to support his family, he hired himself out as a "room washer and cleaner." Meanwhile, he saw to it that his children learned reading and writing and a practical trade. One daughter became a teacher in the city's only colored school; another became a laundress and still another a cook. His sons included a porter, a waiter, and a laborer.[12]

Somewhere along the way, Hagar joined the Masonic fraternal order for men of color, commonly known as the Prince Hall Masons. The Grand Lodge of Texas, Free and Accepted Ancient York Masons, was organized at Brenham, Texas, in August 1875, and although Fort Worth did not have one of the charter lodges of the Negro Free and Accepted Masons, it acquired its own lodge a few years later. It is not known who sponsored Hagar's membership in the Prince Hall Masons, but his decision to join must have pleased his mentor who was himself a charter member and the first "Tiler" of Fort Worth's first Masonic lodge, no. 148.[13]

Hagar's Masonic membership was another way he benefited from maintaining a close relationship with the white Tucker family who possessed a lot of clout in the community. No black man living in an overwhelmingly white, rural Southern community could afford to be too independent or aloof. It was not only expedient but also shrewd to nurture a close relationship with his former master. Over the years, William Tucker was able to shepherd, shield, and even actively promote his former bondsman. It was a relationship that made both men better.

By 1890, after a lifetime of hard labor, forty-eight-year-old Hagar was ready to ease into retirement, which brought him back under the roof of his old master. William Tucker had built himself a baronial estate on 170 acres at the southern limits of Main Street (just south of Broadway today, in the vicinity of John Peter Smith Hospital), which he grandly dubbed "Tucker Hill." Hagar, his wife, and three daughters, Florence, Doña, and Mattie, moved into the servants' quarters at Tucker Hill, which was a huge improvement over the shotgun shacks and tenements where most the city's black citizens lived at the time. It was a reward for Hagar's years of faithful service and an altruistic gesture by a man who, like Hagar, had started with nothing and was self-educated and self-made. William B. Tucker certainly enjoyed his comfortable lifestyle, but he never forgot his humble origins.[14] While the three girls worked as domestics, Hagar and Amy enjoyed the owner's kind hospitality in their sunset years.[15]

Despite the humble circumstances at the end of his life, Hagar Tucker was hardly destitute. A decade after the war, he owned a town lot valued at $100, three horses or mules, and two cows. The following year he owned two lots plus a wagon, six horses or mules, eleven cattle, and five hogs. His wealth continued to grow over the years, as did his state and county taxes. However, more than ten years after emancipation, he was still labeled in public records a "free man of color" in a society that defined its citizens by the color of their skin.[16]

With the end approaching, Hagar Tucker decided to draw up a will to be sure he passed the fruits of his life's labors on to "my beloved wife Amy Tucker." He was probably encouraged in that course of action by two important influences in his life, William Tucker and Robert W. Cook, the latter a longtime black friend. Both men had business and legal expertise, which they were glad to share. The result was a last will and testament, which was written on September 26, 1891, and witnessed by Robert and Emma Cook and someone named Mary Gibson.[17]

Hagar Tucker died on October 2, 1892. He was buried in the Trinity section of Oakwood Cemetery, the city's segregated burial ground for African Americans.[18] An engraved marble obelisk with symbolic markings on it was placed over the grave. The markings consist of a five-pointed "Eastern Star" with an "X" inside, above a pair of swinging gates on columns, all of that above a globe. These things are all part of the arcane symbology of nineteenth century Freemasonry.[19] It seems doubtful, even with the size of the estate Hagar left, that his surviving family would have spent it on anything so extravagant as an engraved marble marker. More likely, William B. Tucker paid for it. Such a possibility is likely not just because of their friendship but because William Tucker was also a high-degreed member of a Masonic order who would have been conversant with Masonic symbology.

Hagar's will was submitted for probate on December 5, 1892, leaving an estate, before legal and burial expenses, of $500. He left it all to "my beloved wife Amy Tucker," and appointed Robert Cook as sole executor of his estate. Later, Amy Tucker moved into the home of Robert and Emma Cook. She was about the same age as Emma Cook, and the families had been close for years.[20]

Sadly, the precedent, in terms of diversity on the Fort Worth police force, set by Hagar Tucker did not endure. The city employed no more black policemen, "special" or otherwise, for the next twenty or more years after Hagar retired. In 1897 after much angry debate with the Police Department going back to 1891, the Council appointed a black officer to patrol Douglass Park, the city's only green space for African Americans, named for Frederick Douglass.[21] The city continued to assign "special policemen" to Douglass and another "Negro park" until 1910, by which time Jim Crow had hardened to the point where the old accommodations no longer worked. No black policeman was carried on the city rolls from 1910 until 1953 when the modern FWPD finally broke the color barrier once and for all.[22] How much more progress might have been achieved if Hagar Tucker had been merely the first of many officers of color on the police force over the decades that followed instead of an anomaly in the Department's history.

African Americas on the FWPD today, comprising about 14 percent of the force, should honor the memory of Hagar Tucker for the trailblazer that he was, and vow never to let his name be forgotten again. Tucker opened the door for them, and while that door was soon slammed shut, he showed doubting white officials that the world would not end nor civilization come crashing down if the two races worked together on the force. Hagar Tucker was the first Fort Worth citizen of color to serve this community as a public servant, and while his accomplishment may seem exceedingly modest by modern standards, at the time it was a giant step forward.

CHAPTER 4

Marshal Sam Farmer: Fort Worth's First Professional Peace Officer

Sam Farmer was a man of principle. Sam Farmer was a scoundrel. Sam Farmer was a dedicated lawman. Sam Farmer was a slacker. He was all of these depending on which aspect of his life and career one chooses to focus on. Like so many Western lawmen (see Jim Courtright), Sam Farmer's character had its dark side. When I first started digging into his life, I thought here was a breath of fresh air after Jim Courtright's stormy tenure in the Marshal's Office—a paragon of virtue, a pillar of law enforcement. That impression lasted until I dug into his life in Missouri before he came to Fort Worth and into the court records of his divorce. No Fort Worth marshal was re-elected more times than Sam Farmer, but he proved to be far more than just an eight-term marshal.

On April 1, 1879, Sam Farmer was elected city marshal of Fort Worth against a field of five other candidates, most of them with larger reputations and more impressive résumés. It was a bitterly fought campaign with name-calling and charges of ethical misconduct flying back and forth. His opponents were all friends and fellow officers before the election, including former marshal H. P. Shiel, veteran policeman W. P. Thomas, and incumbent marshal T. I. Courtright. When he entered the race, he had an understanding with Courtright that the three-time marshal would not run for a fourth term but instead

The only known pictures of Sam Farmer from his marshalling days are these studio portraits taken in D. L. Swartz's Fort Worth studio in the mid-1880s: *(left)* with a custom-made badge and sporting a Wyatt-Earp walrus-style mustache; and *(right)* with wife Mattie Johnson Farmer. (Courtesy J. R. Taggert of Lohman, MO.)

would throw his support to Farmer. Courtright reneged on the deal four months before the election and jumped into the race with both feet. Sam's first reaction was to drop out and not challenge the popular Marshal, but when the *Fort Worth Democrat* publicly urged him to reconsider, he jumped back in. To assist the voters, the *Fort Worth Democrat* limned the top three candidates in broad, symbolic strokes: "Farmer smokes, Courtright takes [his] beer straight, and Thomas drinks lemonade."[1] In the end, the electorate preferred the smoker over the two imbibers and the rookie over the two veterans. Farmer's margin of victory was forty-nine votes more than the total of the other five candidates, but his election represented more of a protest vote against the status quo than a ringing endorsement for the novice Marshal.

Prior to his victory, Sam's career on the Fort Worth Police Department (FWPD) almost did not get out of the gate. The police force operated on one-year appointments; it was reconstituted every year following municipal elections in April. Sam joined the force in the middle of February 1878 as a temporary replacement for Officer J. W. O'Connell, then stayed on to fill in for W. P. Thomas when that officer had to take a leave of absence. While Sam did good service, he would still have to apply for reappointment come April. When Jim Courtright won his third term in April 1878, he invited Farmer to stay on. But things got complicated after that because the prickly Marshal butted heads with the Mayor and Council over the composition of the force for the coming year, a dispute that dragged into May. Finally, Sam became one of four officers appointed by the Council at its May 21 meeting, but only after they reduced the force from six to four in a retrenchment move. He barely made the cut as number four on the list. But at least he was guaranteed a job as a Fort Worth police officer for the next eleven months.[2]

During those eleven months, Sam came to believe he would make a better marshal than Courtright, so after his false start in December, he formally filed for office in March 1879. He probably owed his subsequent victory to a change in the political winds. Decent folks were fed up with their town being taken over by the cowboys every spring and summer. There was also growing outrage over Hell's Half-acre. The city at this time was caught in the grip of vice interests who called "the Acre" home. Mayoral candidate R. E. Beckham pledged to clean out the den of thieves and prostitutes that occupied the south end of town, and Sam Farmer, the political unknown, rode into office on Beckham's reformist coattails. Following their electoral triumph, however, the honeymoon between Farmer and Beckham lasted less than a year, which is how long it took the cleanup campaign to take a back seat to their personal feud. Maybe if the Mayor had looked into the Marshal's background more carefully, he would have seen that Sam Farmer was not one to follow the path of least resistance or run with the pack.

Or maybe Beckham had the same problem that we have today: Sam Farmer's life before coming to Fort Worth is one big enigma, starting with his birth. He was born in 1847 (exact date unknown) in Cole County, Missouri, to William C. and Sarah Ann Richardson Miller. Another part of the mystery is whether his given name was "Samuel" or "Saul M.," as both names appear later in official documents. The Farmers were a large family. Sam had six siblings: an older sister, Mary, four younger sisters (Nancy, Martha, Ellen, and Anna), and two younger brothers, Joseph and Montgomery ("Gum"), all born between 1845 and 1860. William Farmer supported his brood working as a huckster, which in the vernacular of the day meant someone who sold cheap, low-quality goods, not a flimflam man. Nothing is known of his boyhood growing up in Missouri, a frontier state and a battleground between North and South. What is known is that Missouri also gave birth to the James and Younger brothers among other notorious outlaws of the era. Jesse James was in fact born the same year as Sam but chose the outlaw trail over the lawman's trail.[3]

When the war came in 1861, Missouri was a slaveholding state that did not secede from the Union. For the next four years Confederates and Unionists fought it out to the hilt for control of the state, no quarter asked or given. One later tradition says Farmer sided with the Unionists in the bitterly divided state, serving as a captain in the pro-Northern militia. However, family tradition says he rode with William Clarke Quantrill, arguably the most vicious bushwhacker and guerrilla leader on the Southern side during the war. Quantrill's band of outlaws murdered and pillaged their way through Kansas, Missouri, and Kentucky. His followers included both the James and Younger siblings, and "Bloody Bill" Anderson. According to family lore Sam came home once with the Yankees hot on his tail. He only avoided capture when his mother hid him between two feather mattresses. The family also attributed Sam's later skill with firearms to his wartime service with Quantrill.[4]

All of this is in direct contradiction to rumors that followed him to Texas after the war that he had served as a Northern spy on his fellow Missourians and had been a lackey for the state's Unionist governor, Hamilton Gamble. Sam never did satisfactorily answer all the questions about his wartime service, and the charge of being a scalawag, i.e., a Southerner who sold out, would haunt him long after he settled at Fort Worth. Such an accusation, even if unproven, could be fatal to anyone with political aspirations because unreconstructed Rebels in Texas after the war liked to brag that they voted as they had shot. He vehemently denied any connection with anything so vile as Radical Republicans and scalawags, but the rumors persisted, and he helped keep them alive by styling himself "Captain Sam" without bothering to specify just how he came by that rank.[5]

In postwar Missouri he served as a deputy U.S. marshal during the administration of Reconstruction Governor Joseph W. McClurg, who was scorned as a "chinch bug" by Southern sympathizers. Sam was piloting McClurg's militia when he was obliged to shoot an unreconstructed Rebel for resisting arrest, an act that only confirmed the suspicions of those who considered him a traitor to his people. Nonetheless, he proved adept enough at the game of politics to win election as constable for Cole County in 1868.[6]

Sam waited until he was twenty-five to marry. The war had discouraged many men from settling down, but after it was over they started trying to make normal lives for themselves. Sam married Melinda Norfleet in 1872. She was the daughter of a prominent Missouri family, which some thought too good for the likes of Sam Farmer. Sam's sister Mary also married a Norfleet. Sam's marriage did not last. Whether because she died or he divorced her, he was a single man again in 1873 when he left for Texas.[7]

We can only speculate on Sam's reasons for moving to Texas. The wartime devastation and bitter partisan feelings in Missouri persuaded many men to leave. The end of his marriage could also have played a part in his decision. Anyway, he landed in Texas in the middle of 1873 at a time when the hand of Reconstruction still lay heavily on the Lone Star State, personified by Radical Republican Governor Edmund J. Davis. Later, after Sam embarked on a political career, his supporters would assert that he had settled in Fort Worth for health reasons, specifically because he suffered from "hemorrhage of the lungs," but there had to be other reasons since Fort Worth was hardly known for its salubrious climate. Skeptics still believed that he had fled Missouri because of a different kind of threat to his health.[8]

Sam's Northern political leanings were only slightly less problematical in Texas than they had been in Missouri. New accusations arose connecting him to the detestable Davis as a member of the Governor's State Police. Still, he settled down in Fort Worth and began winning over the townspeople by serving his adopted community in a number of ways. He was not a member of the local volunteer fire company when a kitchen blaze occurred in Delmonico's Restaurant and quickly spread, threatening the business district, but he pitched in and worked right alongside the firemen. Afterwards, the newspaper commended him for his "efficient work saving property."

Subsequently, he was welcomed as a member of the M. T. Johnson Hook and Ladder Company. Being accepted by the clannish bunch of men who formed the volunteer fire company was a major step in establishing himself in the community. Like most men of his day, he was a "joiner," and when it came to a fraternal order, he was a member of the oldest and most exclusive, the Freemasons. He had joined the Hickory Hill Lodge no. 211 when he lived in Cole County, Missouri, rising through the ranks until he became a Master Mason on July 23, 1870. When he got to Texas, he continued his affiliation. Being a Mason could open many doors. In 1877 he formally transferred his membership to Lodge no. 148 of Fort Worth. He remained an active member in good standing until he completely dropped out of sight in the mid-1890s. The Fort Worth lodge expelled him in 1896 for being arrears in his dues.[9]

Sam's political ambitions were almost derailed because devastating rumors of his Missouri activities followed him to Fort Worth. Even worse than being accused of being a "Billy Yank" during the war, he was accused of being a Northern spy. Ab Woody, a fellow policeman, even swore out an affidavit saying Sam had told him he had to flee to Texas because things got too hot for him in Missouri. His political opponents in the 1879 race gleefully exploited the rumors and probably embroidered them, too. They also spread rumors that he had withdrawn from the race. His prospects began looking so bad that he asked three former Missouri neighbors now living in Wise County to swear out affidavits attesting to his wartime service, and he had these published in the *Democrat*. Then, when rumors continued to fly, he made a quick trip to Missouri to round up additional affidavits from former neighbors and acquaintances. All of this was fought out in the pages of the *Fort Worth Democrat* with B. B. Paddock refereeing the fight. The voters ultimately accepted Sam's version of events, plus having the endorsement of Tarrant County Sheriff Joseph Henderson did not hurt.[10]

Following Courtright's turbulent, three-year tenure, Sam Farmer was a refreshing dose of integrity and restraint. To the skeptical he proved himself an excellent officer of the law, as "cool and calm in the hour of uncertainty as in the time of danger." His laconic style and what the *Democrat* called his "good-natured" ways concealed a quick mind and surprising felicity with the King's English. Just one month after his election, the *Democrat* gave its stamp of approval to his job performance, saying he gave "universal satisfaction as marshal."[11] When members of the new administration addressed a town meeting on April 7, Marshal Farmer used his time to assure those

An elderly Sam Farmer, long after he left marshalling and deserted Mattie looking for greener pastures. (Note: He still wears a ring on his wedding finger.) This photograph may have been taken in Central America, sometime after the turn of the century. (Courtesy J. R. Taggert of Lohman, MO.)

present that he would do his duty as an officer of the law: "My desire is to do right," he said. "I first want to know that I am right, and then go ahead." The audience erupted in applause, the mudslinging of the recent campaign forgotten.[12]

On the job, however, Sam's performance did not always measure up to his rhetoric. In the beginning at least, he did not disappoint. Before he had been in office a month, he rounded up "all the disreputable women in the city" and hauled them into police court on charges ranging from disorderly conduct to prostitution and disturbing the peace. When twenty-two of the twenty-five refused to pay even the minimal fine of five dollars, he led them Pied-Piper-like from the courtroom back to the jail, "one of the girls hanging onto his coattail" the whole way. He did not go easy on the pimps either, rounding them up in the same sweep.[13]

As time went by, however, Sam's dedication seemed to fade, or perhaps he just discovered that there was more to be gained by looking the other way. In September 1887 he had to go before the City Council to explain why he was not enforcing the anti-gambling ordinances or the Sunday closing law. The issue put Sam crossways with Mayor H. S. Broiles who wanted the police to be a little more proactive cleaning up Hell's Half-acre. The Mayor grew so exasperated with the half-hearted effort of the boys in blue that he began appointing his own "special police" to do the job. When Sam appeared before the Council, he said it was all a matter of miscommunication and said with wounded innocence, "If the Council wishes me to enforce the laws of the city as they are on the statutes, I can and will close every gambling den in the city, and put a stop to Sunday violations." Thereafter, Sam stepped up enforcement of the anti-vice ordinances and mollified the Council, probably saving his job in the process.[14]

This was not the end of Sam's problems with Mayor Broiles, however. Later that same month they butted heads again and again it was over Sam's selective, even arbitrary, approach to law enforcement. Broiles pointed to "certain abuses" by the police force, specifically, how certain saloon owners had the police in their pocket, using them as muscle against their loudest critics, all with the collusion of the Marshal. Broiles "demanded" that Farmer "at once put a stop to" such police harassment. Sam did not like being dictated to, although it was certainly the Mayor's prerogative to issue any orders he wished to his police chief. Unbowed, Sam ignored the criticism and went right on running the Police Department the way he wanted. Mayor and Marshal remained on the outs as long as both of them were in office, two strong-willed men in a power struggle.[15]

On the other hand, Sam had a very good working relationship with Sheriff J. M Henderson (1876–1880). Although the Marshal's jurisdiction stopped at the city limits, Sam joined the Sheriff's posse that was chasing a gang of robbers preying on the Fort Worth-to-Yuma stage in 1879. The posse pursued its quarry all the way to Colorado, finally catching up with them near Leadville; they put the gang out of business permanently.[16] Farmer got his share of the glory and the reward money that came with a job well done, but the weeks on the trail had taken him away from his first responsibility, which was protecting the city of Fort Worth. Chasing outlaws clear to Colorado was not part of the town marshal's job description, and Farmer would soon reveal a disturbing penchant for dropping his normal duties and

Henry S. Broiles served four terms as Fort Worth mayor (1886–1890). He was a strong reformist mayor, not afraid to take on Hell's Half-acre or even his own City Council. He butted heads on several occasions with the obstreperous Marshal Sam Farmer. "Hizzoner" bears more than a passing resemblance to Hollywood character actor Frank Morgan and was about as successful battling the vice lords of Fort Worth as Morgan's Wizard of Oz was battling the Wicked Witch. (Courtesy Fort Worth Public Library, Genealogy, Local History, and Archives Unit.)

skipping town for long stretches. This penchant did not sit well with his "bosses" on the City Council. Sam, for his part, never seemed to have understood that his job security depended on keeping both the City Council and the voters happy.

Still, if not a model peace officer, Sam Farmer did bring a level of professionalism to the FWPD heretofore unseen. Unlike many of his fellows in the lawman's fraternity, he was more than just a gunslinger with a badge. He dedicated himself to running the Marshal's Office like a business, never hiring out his gun or moonlighting as a dealer in the local saloons. Which is not to say he did not pursue other business interests; he just kept them separate from his marshal's duties. Using mostly other people's money as his bankroll, he was extremely active in buying and selling real estate. He wheeled and dealed with some of the biggest players in the Fort Worth real estate market, including the Daggetts (E. M. and E. B.), Robert McCart, and I. M. Terrill. He also closed a few deals with his brother-in-law, Jake Johnson, and his wife, also named Mattie, those transactions being most likely tax dodges. When Howard W. Peak, a member of one of the pioneer families of Fort Worth, lost some land to foreclosure, Sam was there to snap the property up for a song. Then he sealed the deal by putting Peak off the land, using the authority of his badge to intimidate poor Howard into leaving meekly. Ultimately, all this wheeling and dealing brought Sam quite a real estate portfolio. It also brought him more than a few civil lawsuits filed by disgruntled citizens he had snookered. Marshal Farmer spent as much time fending off lawsuits as enforcing the law. In one of his business deals, he attempted to use his Masonic connections to start up an insurance business, calling it the Masonic Mutual Benefit Association of Texas. Sam and his partners were sued by a client who claimed they had been swindled. It was an odd situation for the city's chief defender of law and order also to be one of its biggest defendants![17]

In all, he was elected city marshal eight times (elections were held annually), with a four-year lapse between his first and second tenures. Typically, an election campaign began with a simple announcement in the newspaper, such as this one Sam placed in January 1881 announcing his third run for the Marshal's Office:

> Sam M. Farmer places himself before the people of Fort Worth as a candidate for re-election to the office of city marshal at the coming April election.[18]

While Marshal of Fort Worth, Sam also served two stretches as a deputy U.S. marshal so that his city and federal commissions overlapped, violating a Texas law that said a man "can not hold two offices of honor, trust and emoluments at the same time," but he always faithfully served the good citizens of Fort Worth.[19] Still, his faithful and efficient service did not insulate him against all criticism. Besides his feud with Mayor Beckham, which played out on the pages of the *Fort Worth Democrat*, he was blistered by the editor of the *Democrat* for not being tough enough on crime, and the newspaper never officially endorsed him in any of his runs for office. However, come election time, Paddock could always find something nice to say about the transplanted Missourian, calling him in 1881, "an honest, brave, vigilant, unswerving, trust-worthy and valuable officer." Such a glowing endorsement explains how Sam Farmer was able to get re-elected seven times in ten years even while accumulating a growing list of enemies. Dallas editors also sang his praises. In 1881, the *Dallas Herald* went on about "the efficient, live, wide-awake city marshal of Fort Worth who has made an enviable reputation as [an] officer."[20]

Sam took the public servant side of his job more seriously than any of his predecessors, serving his constituents in countless little ways that were not part of his job description. His good deeds won him fans on both sides of the Trinity. In 1881 he escorted a "consumptive invalid" to Dallas so that the man could catch a train home and even paid the difference out of his own pocket between what the ticket cost and how much the man had on him. The Dallas newspapers applauded the Fort Worth Marshal, which was not something they did very often. A few years later he got up one June morning to discover an old homeless woman (a "bag lady" in modern parlance) had spent the night in his backyard after getting lost while trying to find her way from the city hospital to the poor farm. A severe rainstorm had blown through during the night, and she was lying in the open soaked and shivering when discovered. He brought the poor crone inside and cared for her until she was strong enough to be returned to the hospital. He did not have to do it, but he did anyway. Stories like this were told and retold on both sides of the Trinity. Marshal Farmer owed as much of his re-election success (eight terms!) to his frequent random acts of kindness as to his significant accomplishments as a peace officer. His charitable nature was especially evident around the holiday season every year when he handed out food baskets to the needy in the city's Third Ward. Incidents like the invalid who came to him for help getting home and the old woman who happened to find her way to his house also show that extraordinary things were always happening to Sam Farmer. Nobody ever said he led a normal life![21]

In marriage as in other matters, Sam kept his cards close to his vest. He presented himself as a bachelor for the first ten years he lived in Fort Worth, conveniently forgetting to mention his Missouri marriage. On July 29, 1883, at the age of thirty-six, he tied the knot again. His bride was eighteen-year-old Martha M. "Mattie" Johnson, daughter of a prominent local businessman, John L. Johnson, who had made his money as a self-described "huckster." Born in Gonzales, Texas, Mattie came to Fort Worth sometime before 1876. Her parents, John and Mary Johnson, were enlightened for their day. They saw to it that she received a "liberal education" and "went to the best schools." When she dropped out of college in Waco to marry Sam, her mother was disappointed. Despite her pedigree, Sam's fiancée caused him some grief because Mattie Johnson shared her name with one of the city's most notorious madams, a woman whom Marshal Farmer had crossed paths with on more than one occasion professionally speaking. Sam's fiancée was probably as glad to see her last name changed as Sam was.[22]

They were married in an "impressive" ceremony in the parlor of the Johnson residence on Leuda Street, Fort Worth, distinguished by a "sumptuous repast" and a guest list that included the cream of Fort Worth society. The bride was described in the local newspaper as "a picture of blushing loveliness." Sam was not particularly religious, but a Presbyterian minister conducted the ceremony because that was what the Johnsons wanted. The couple's wedding booty included enough silver to restock the Comstock mines, and for their honeymoon they took a grand, three-week tour by train that included Louisville, Chicago, New York City, and Niagara Falls. Upon their return to Fort Worth, the newlyweds moved into a rented house, which represented another big change in Sam's life since he had been living in boardinghouses or at the city calaboose since coming to Fort Worth.[23]

There is no doubt Mattie was quite a catch for the aging bachelor. Not only was Sam her first love, but she was a girl "whom any man might be proud to win and wear as the choicest jewel in the crown of life." Besides being pretty and charming, she had been educated in "the best schools that the State of Texas afforded." The clincher was that she brought a dowry of $5,000 to the marriage, a wedding gift from her doting parents on top of the honeymoon trip they paid for. The eternal honeymoon that the *Fort Worth Gazette* wished them went stale before the year was out. Although they should have been financially set, she continued to work, teaching music lessons in their home to the children of Fort Worth's best families. And she used her own funds to purchase four rent houses, although under Texas law at that time, all of her property, including what she brought into the marriage, was her husband's to dispose of as he saw fit with or without her permission. And Sam did just that. He took the $5,000 wedding gift from her parents and instead of depositing it in the bank as promised, he spent it constructing and furnishing houses that he rented out to members of the police force.[24]

Their marriage lasted thirteen years, but Sam's commitment to the union was never more than lukewarm. He began mistreating her soon after they were married although she was a "cheerful and loving wife." When he was not treating her cruelly, he ignored her, disappearing for long stretches that included a six-month period in 1886. He seldom told her where he was going or when he would be back. Once, he told her he was going off on "an ant-exterminating trip" like it was some sort of big-game hunting expedition. Whenever he left, he never made any provisions ("not a nickel") for her needs while he was gone, so after a few days she would go stay with her parents until he returned. She did not go hungry, but she could not afford to pay their property taxes or even purchase basic necessities. That humiliating state of affairs was what made her decide to acquire rent property—so she could support herself during his frequent absences.[25]

Sam spent most of his marshal's salary on himself supplementing it with money that Mattie earned and turned over to him. Only rarely did he even buy the groceries with his own money. Yet they were hardly destitute. During their marriage Sam assembled quite a real estate portfolio that included his own subdivision in the Tucker Addition plus other properties in the Daggett Addition. In 1886, their differences were first aired publicly when she sued him for "abandonment" asking the court for "a large slice of her husband's property."[26] She reconsidered and stayed in the unhappy marriage on that occasion, but Sam did not stop being a wandering husband in every sense of the word.

His absences grew more frequent and more prolonged between 1891 and 1895, and he never bothered to write. Even when he was in town he was an infrequent resident at his own home because he preferred renting a room with one of his deputies, Dick Kitts, at Tivoli Hall on Houston Street. In 1893 he took off for Chicago to attend the World's Columbian Exposition although in no official capacity. He did not come home until after the Exposition closed. Only once during the entire time did he even write to her, and then only to send a dollar for stamps so she could write to him! She mailed the money back. During those same years, he was also "consorting with lewd women all the time," according to court papers. He had a fondness for prostitutes, but he was especially enamored with a country girl named Pearl Clements. Pearl lived in Decatur, Texas, and Sam's properties included a stock ranch there, so it would seem many of his "business trips" between 1893 and '94 were to Decatur to stay with her for days at a time. Pearl was not a prostitute, but it was said she had a "low character." And neither one of them was too bright, or perhaps they just did not care, because she wrote her paramour frequently at one of his Fort Worth addresses professing her undying love, and he saved all the letters in an unlocked trunk. Those letters were the smoking gun in the affair.[27]

Sam and Mattie never had any children although it was not because of any physical shortcomings of either one. Sam Farmer may have been a go-getter, but he was all about work and making money, never family. When Mattie got pregnant once, she performed a home abortion using camphor to produce the desired result. Mostly they had a passionless marriage, which was a good thing for her because in 1892 Sam brought home a "loathsome disease" from one of his trips. Mattie only avoided contracting VD because she found out he was infected before they resumed carnal relations.[28]

In September 1895 Sam was part of a manhunt scouring the Indian Territory for the Christian train-robbing gang.[29] He returned home briefly before packing up and leaving for good on October 22, 1895. It was the best way he knew how to get out of a bad marriage and make a fresh start. Their toxic relationship had escalated from constant quarrelling to physical abuse. At the time, they were living on Crawford Street, and Mattie's mother plus one or more boarders were living with them. All later testified that they saw Sam strike Mattie repeatedly. Despite the unrelenting stress and abuse, which had caused her health to deteriorate and her disposition to sour, she continued to hope beyond hope that things would improve. They had bought a lot and hired a builder to construct another house for them, so she had something positive to pin her hopes on. The Crawford Street house was sparsely furnished because Sam had used his money to buy furnishings for several apartments he owned about town. Questioned on his priorities, he told her he had to have "some place to entertain his detectives." Knowing she ranked somewhere behind his girlfriends *and* his men hurt deeply.[30]

When Sam decided to split, characteristically he said nothing, just drew all their money out of the bank and left town. A few months later Mattie filed for divorce on grounds of adultery, cruelty, and abandonment. Her lawyer was R. Y. Prigmore, who had been handling her legal affairs for the past year. Now he became her divorce lawyer, too. The court appointed counsel to represent Sam's interests, but without the plaintiff there to defend his own behavior, the divorce was never in doubt.

When Sam's marriage fell apart it took his reputation down with it. Every sordid thing he had done became a matter of public record. The newspapers primly refused to air the ugly details in print, but they were common knowledge on the street. Sam would have had a hard time getting elected dogcatcher in Fort Worth after 1896, and he knew it.

Meanwhile, life for Mattie was looking up. At some point her relationship with Russell Prigmore turned from strictly professional into something deeper. She fell in love with him, and he had the same feelings for her. Less than two years after terminating her marriage to Sam, Mattie tied the knot with Prigmore on March 4, 1897. They enjoyed twenty-two years together and had two children before he died from natural causes in 1919. She lived another ten years after that and never talked about her first marriage. She made a name for herself teaching and composing music and as the church organist at Broadway Baptist Church. People only knew her as Martha, not Mattie, and that's the way she preferred it. In her obituary her first marriage was not even mentioned.[31]

Mattie had a brother, Jacob, and a sister, Mary. Both Mattie and Mary were musical prodigies who performed on the occasion of the first railroad coming to town in 1876. Brother Jake was a local legend in the late nineteenth century as a "sporting man" and impresario. Jake was a partner in the White Elephant Saloon at one time, a turfman, and proud member of the gambling fraternity. He knew the best people of Fort Worth and he knew the worst. Johnson was able to provide his brother-in-law with a direct connection to Fort Worth's underworld, which proved useful over the years. In fact, Sam had more than a passing acquaintance with some notorious Western outlaw types. Dave Mather, the sometime-lawman, robber, cattle rustler, and gunfighter known as "Mysterious Dave," was briefly employed as a policeman by Marshal Farmer in 1881. Fortunately for all concerned, Mather soon departed for greener pastures, and his criminal activities did not embarrass his boss.[32]

Sam's relationship with John Leer did prove embarrassing, however. Leer was the proprietor of the Red Light Saloon, a low dive and dance hall in Hell's Half-acre, and Sam, while a policeman, shielded him from official harassment. In 1878, Sam was called as a witness in a criminal action against another officer and asked under oath why the police had shut down the Waco Tap but not the Red Light Saloon. He replied glibly that the Red Light did not have dancing, a response which brought a guffaw in the courtroom.[33]

Sam's contacts within the lawmen's fraternity were equally impressive. Up until Sam challenged him in 1879 for the Marshal's Office, Jim Courtright considered him his right-hand man. Although Courtright carried a grudge after losing the election, Sam treated the ex-Marshal with professional courtesy, even hiring him for odd jobs now and then. As Courtright's drinking and fighting grew worse, Farmer gave him more slack than he would have given other men who were not members of the fraternity of the badge. Sam was also considered a friend by Pat Garrett, one of the premier Western lawmen of the era. In December 1881, Marshal Farmer received a surprising gift from New Mexico compliments of Sheriff Garrett: the sombrero and cartridge belt owned by Billy the Kid when Garrett killed him. How Garrett and Farmer were acquainted or why the New Mexico legend saw fit to bestow such a valuable gift on the Fort Worth Marshal is a mystery.[34]

Sam's connections in the lawman's fraternity were more than just personal friendships. He networked widely even before that term existed, exchanging correspondence with fellow law officers as far away as St. Louis and Cincinnati. His long tenure in Fort Worth made him well known to his counterparts in other cities. In 1888 he was contacted by Cincinnati's police chief about the desirability of holding a national convention of police chiefs to share information and improve cooperation. He supported the idea and suggested Kansas City or St. Louis for the convention city.[35]

If such things were the full story, Sam Farmer would go down in history as a model lawman. But good deeds and professional networking are only half the story. Sam Farmer lived two lives: his public life as a hardworking lawman, and his private life as an unfaithful, abusive husband. It is his public life that he is remembered for. He served as city marshal during the boom years of the 1880s when Fort Worth grew from a small town into a full-fledged city. A civilized community needed a professional police force, and Farmer did much to professionalize his department by taking a progressive approach to law enforcement. In 1881 he purchased a pair of bloodhounds for the substantial sum of $100. While Sam Houston and Flora would more than earn their keep in the years that followed, leading manhunts through the nearby Trinity River bottoms, Sam had to pay for them out of his own pocket because the Department had no budget for such things.[36]

He was an innovator in other ways. In 1882 he embraced the latest communications technology by introducing a system for citizens to report burglaries to police by telephone, thereby encouraging reporting and cutting down response time. He also instructed his men to carry a "memorandum book" to keep a daily record of everything that occurred while on duty. Such books are still kept by policemen and even accepted as legal evidence in court trials. His approach to police work emphasized preventing crime, not just making arrests after the fact, and having "probable cause" before making arrests. Many of his precepts were codified in a set of rules and regulations adopted by the Department in 1889.[37]

It was in the middle of his second tenure as marshal that he drew up what became the first comprehensive code of conduct for the FWPD. Those rules and regs would remain the unofficial manual of the Department for the next twenty years. They were not original—Dodge City had adopted a similar code for its police in 1882—but they represented a radical break with past ways of doing things in Fort Worth. The biggest difference was that Dodge City's "rules and regs" were created by Mayor A. B. Webster while Fort Worth's came from within the Department. Marshal Farmer's "Rules and Advice to the Police Force" was published on April 27, 1889, and republished many times thereafter. It never had any legal standing and prescribed no punishments for violating any of the rules, but it marked a major advance in law enforcement locally.

The new rules were a collection of folksy maxims drawn from its author's own on-the-job experience. Farmer set the tone right out of the gate with his opening salutation—"Gentlemen"— then challenged his men to always behave in an exemplary fashion because their acts would "at all times be subjected to the observation and criticisms of the public." "Never forget," he warned them, "your character is your capital." His ten "essential requisites" of a good police officer were: honesty, truthfulness, sobriety, courage, intelligence, good morals, good temper, promptitude, impartiality, and pleasant address. Notably missing from his list were the traditional tools of the Western lawman: quick fists and skill with a six-shooter.

At the same time he wrote "Rules and Advice," Farmer also composed a set of "General Principles of the Laws of Arrests," which contained additional guidelines to educate the beat cop about the legal parameters of his authority. The various rules, advice, and principles were endorsed by the City Council and went into effect on May 25, 1889, about six weeks after municipal elections that saw Sam win an unprecedented seventh term in office.

Sam Farmer was more of a cerebral lawman than a physically intimidating one, and he did not possess a reputation as a fast draw like his immediate predecessor, but he did not back down to any man. Late in his first tenure as marshal, he got into a feud with the Maddox family, which included Sheriff Walter Maddox and future city marshal Jim Maddox. Sam and Jim Maddox exchanged heated words on the street one day, and Maddox was only prevented from killing Sam by the timely intervention of Heck Thomas. In 1884, two Negroes who may have been hired assassins came looking for him, but they were not too clear on what their man looked like because they wound up targeting Jim Courtright. Nobody was hurt, and the two assassins got away, but the episode showed that lawmen had to be careful even after they left office because there were always men who had a grudge to settle.[38]

Sam lived most of his life as a loner. None of his brothers or sisters followed him to Fort Worth, so he never had the strong family safety net of some other Western lawmen, such as Wyatt Earp, or Fort Worth's Walter Maddox. Since he had four sisters and only one brother, he could not have expected much in the way of backup when the going got rough even if the rest of the Farmer clan had followed him to Fort Worth. And while brother-in-law Jake Johnson was a man to contend with, he was no fan of his sister's husband. There was only one recorded visit to Fort Worth by any of Sam's siblings, and that was by Joe Farmer, six years his junior, in 1881. Locals noticed that Joe and Sam looked alike. They also noticed that Joe did not stick around more than a few days.[39]

Still, if Sam could not call on gun-toting brothers to back him in a pinch, he did not seem to need them. There were no showdowns on Main Street on Sam's résumé. On the contrary, he seemed to live a charmed life. He came through the Civil War without a scratch, and he was never shot or otherwise injured during all of his years as a peace officer. As far as is known, he never even pulled his gun in anger. His only known injury came in 1882 when he was thrown from a railway velocipede on a trip to Dallas. Although he sailed over the tops of some trees and was knocked unconscious, he suffered no broken bones and soon recuperated.[40]

Unlike Longhair Jim Courtright, Marshal Farmer did not brawl in the street, bully his constituents, or turn a blind eye to cowboy shenanigans. But he had one habit that put him on a collision course with the City Council: Sam took off from his duties whenever he felt like it, usually to chase after a fat "fee" moonlighting as a deputy U.S. marshal or member of a posse pursuing a fugitive with a reward on his head. At least twice he left town on deputy U.S. marshal errands. Sometimes he just took off to get a little "country breeze."[41] In February 1882, Sam was on his way to Mexico on another fugitive warrant when Mayor John T. Brown telegraphed him to "return to his duties in the city" immediately. In September 1890 he was in New York City for reasons unknown. After he took sick and overstayed his leave of absence "for a week or so," the City Council passed a resolution ordering him home "at once."[42]

Less than a year after being swept into office on Mayor Beckham's coattails, Sam was at odds with the Mayor over the propriety of holding two peace officer commissions simultaneously: city marshal and deputy U.S. marshal. Beckham contended this was a conflict of interest. Sam considered it no big deal and furthermore none of the Mayor's business. When he refused a direct order from the Mayor to surrender his U.S. marshal's commission, Beckham declared Farmer "no longer marshal of the city of Fort Worth" and called a special session of the Council to rubber-stamp the firing. Farmer responded by sending three of the city's best lawyers to argue his case before the Council. They won a reprieve until the next regular meeting at which Farmer showed up with all of his arguments and legal points lined up and the gallery packed with his supporters. He won the test of wills when he won over the Council, and he did that by citing precedent (his predecessors in the Marshal's Office had held multiple commissions) and appealing to public opinion. Nobody could remember a similar case ever arising in the city before, and one Dallas newspaper wondered, "Why all this hue and cry about Farmer holding two offices?"[43] In the end, everybody recognized it for what it was: a personal feud between the Mayor and the Marshal, and the Council overruled the Mayor, allowing Sam to keep both his city job and U.S. marshal's commission. The fight caused a permanent estrangement between Sam and the Beckham faction in the city, but Sam did not mind because he also won the war: R. E. Beckham was no longer mayor after April 1880 while Sam went on to serve six more terms as marshal.[44]

The fight with Beckham was Sam's first clash with city hall, but not his last. Seven years later, during his second extended tour of duty as marshal, he placed himself in the middle of a feud between Mayor H. S. Broiles and City Secretary Henry R. Early over an ethical issue: fees and fines. Those were the principal source of income for city officers who earned the fees by performing various duties and got a cut of the fines assessed violators of municipal ordinances. They provided a lucrative source of income for otherwise underpaid city employees. In the case of Broiles v. Early, the Mayor decreed that the City Secretary was not entitled to a cut of the fees. Early protested, and Farmer backed his protest. The City Council came down on the side of Early, but despite coming out on the winning side again, Sam had acquired new enemies in high places.[45]

Besides enjoying a good fight, Sam sympathized with Henry Early because he himself was not above supplementing his regular pay with income from various schemes and shady deals. For instance, he got cut-rate lumber from his father-in-law, which he used to build small rent houses which he pressured his officers to rent from him. This sort of double-dealing struck some as unethical, but that did not deter him. Some of his other deals got him dragged into civil court, such as the time in 1890 when a Mr. Welbourne obtained a judgment against him in county court for $459.[46]

In 1887, Sam ran for the Marshal's Office again after four years out of office. Perhaps he had gotten tired of being out of the action or his business dealings had turned sour, or maybe he had just grown tired of his marriage and wanted something to keep him away from home. His opponent was Walter Maddox, another well-respected name in local law enforcement. Maddox had served three terms as sheriff from 1880 to 1886, but now he had lowered his sights to the Marshal's Office. Both men were popular, long-serving peace officers, and since Fort Worth did not have any urgent crime problems at the time, the race turned into a popularity contest. The race between the two old-timers went to Farmer. The city would have to wait another four years before a Maddox (brother James Maddox) occupied the office of marshal.[47]

In 1891, twelve years after winning his first Fort Worth election, Sam Farmer retired for good from the Marshal's Office. But retirement did not suit him. The following year he announced his candidacy for Tarrant County sheriff securing the endorsement of the Republican Party. But Tarrant County was a Democratic stronghold, and Elisha Adam Euless, namesake of the tiny community of Euless due east of Fort Worth, won the job. Blocked in that ambition, Sam was back at work as a deputy U.S. marshal for the Northern District of Texas by 1894. He had to range far and wide to earn his fees but did not mind. Since the work was only part-time, he also sold his services to the highest bidder in the private sector. In 1895 that meant riding shotgun on Rock Island passenger trains traversing the dangerous Indian Territory, in which capacity he was referred to in the local newspapers as "Captain Farmer, a well-known United States marshal," which was stretching the truth: he had not been a captain in nearly thirty years, and he was only a deputy marshal.[48]

Sam Farmer's public life ended in the mid-1890s, when he was not yet fifty years old. He left Fort Worth never to return, and the final chapter of his story is the biggest mystery of all: What happened to him after he left Fort Worth? He seems to have dropped off the face of the earth after 1895. In those years the best way for a man to completely drop out of sight, as Butch Cassidy and the Sundance Kid demonstrated, was to relocate to one of the Latin American countries. Family lore says that Sam went to Panama as a bounty hunter where he operated under the name "Carlos Porter," then drifted up to Guatemala where he died and was buried at Guatemala City. To date, no one has been able to verify that story. One intriguing item appeared in the Fort Worth newspaper in 1899, however. Among a number of unclaimed letters advertised by Postmistress Ida Turner that had been sitting in the post office for months, was one to Miss Pearl Clements, correspondent unnamed. There was only one Pearl Clements in the area in recent years, Sam's old girlfriend. Could Sam have been trying to get in touch with Pearl from Central America? We will never know because the unclaimed missive, like others that ended up in the dead-letter office, was destroyed fourteen days after the notice in the newspaper.[49]

In the end, what we can say is that Sam Farmer led a double life bracketed by serious questions on the front end and the back end. Truly, he was a Mystery Man.

CHAPTER 5

Al Hayne: The People's Hero

Today, practically anyone born and raised in Fort Worth knows who Al Hayne was: the celebrated Hero of the Texas Spring Palace. But much of what they think they know is wrong. Hayne is described in various sources as a Welshman, a Canadian, and a fireman, none of which he was. He is sometimes called "Albert" Hayne or "Al Haynes" with an unnecessary "s" on the end of his surname. It has been said that his name was pronounced "Hay-nie" (How would anyone know today?), that he was either thirty years old or forty at the time of his death, and that he died of either internal injuries or severe burns. Will the real Al Hayne please stand up? The only thing that seems certain is that he was a genuine hero, the kind that does not wear a badge or a uniform but steps forward in a time of crisis.

Alfred S. Hayne was born on August 1, 1849, in London to Henry George Hayne and Eliza Rooks Hayne. The family was quite well-to-do in terms of both wealth and social position. He had two sisters, Selina and Georgianna, and a younger brother, Eugene. The family moved to Bromley, Kent, England, where he grew up. His mother died when he was still a boy, and the children were raised by their father. Young "Alf," as the family called him, attended Eton, the most historic and prestigious of all the "public schools" in England. After Eton he attended university where he studied to become a civil engineer—

The only known images of Texas Spring Palace hero Alfred Hayne (left) and his brother Eugene Hayne (right), taken in the Fort Worth studio of John and David Swartz sometime after 1885. (Courtesy Major Tony Gaite, Durrington, England.)

England at that time was producing the finest engineers in the world. In 1875 he emigrated to America where, he believed, "everybody was doing well and making money." He arrived in New York on December 27 aboard the steamer *Germanic*, following his brother over. "Gene" Hayne had arrived three years earlier on August 12, 1872, from Liverpool, and found remunerative work as a machinist. It may have been his influence that was the deciding factor in persuading Alfred to pull up stakes and relocate to America.[1]

After passing through Castle Garden and getting his land legs back, Alfred headed west. He had come with enough money to tide himself over until he could find work worthy of his skills. He made his way west and eventually landed in Texas where the first job he took was with the Texas and Pacific Railway, which was pushing across the state in fits and starts for California. He hooked up with his brother in Marshall, which was headquarters for the T&P. Al spent more time in the field than in town, and his became a familiar face all along the line from Marshall out to El Paso eventually. He worked his way up to "master mechanic" for the entire line. In 1882 he was promoted to "superintendent of waterworks and bridges" for the Rio Grande division. It was in Marshall that he reconnected with his fraternal brothers of the Masonic Order, which he had joined back in England. Now, in 1876, he established his membership with Texas Lodge no. 22 where he continued to pay his dues until 1884. While working for the T&P he somehow acquired the title "Captain," although there is no record that he ever served in the military in either Europe or America.[2]

When the T&P ran into financial difficulties, he left Marshall looking for new opportunities to put his considerable talents to work. Since many of the railroads had interlocking management, functioning like one big, dysfunctional family, he had no trouble finding a new employer. He landed in Fort Worth at a time when the local economy was booming and there was plenty of work to be had for a skilled civil engineer. The newcomer with the odd accent was hardly an object of curiosity to the locals. Fort Worthers were well acquainted with Englishmen and Scotsmen who were flocking to Texas attracted by the business and construction opportunities. Some just passed through, but others, like William F. Somerville who was assistant manager of the Matador Land and Cattle Company, put down roots and prospered. Hayne was somewhere in between the two types. His first job was throwing a bridge across the Trinity River for the city. He drew up the initial plans and specifications for a flat fee of $25, then submitted the winning bid on the project of $3,200. Before that job was completed, he hired on with the Fort Worth and Denver City Railway, but still managed to complete the bridge on schedule and on budget. Even better, he made a $700 profit, which as he pointed out in a letter to his sister, was "not to be sneezed at." Hayne's first big engineering commission in America demonstrated that not only was he a capable engineer but a pretty shrewd businessman! The city fathers of Fort Worth were so impressed they asked him to build another bridge for the booming town. He had to decline because his new job took up most of his time. Still, he found time to do some drafting work in his free time for local businesses.[3]

Miracle on the Trinity! "The Burning of the Texas Spring Palace, on the Night of May 30, 1890." Thousands were caught inside when fire erupted, but only one died. Artist's representation from a photo by J. E. Daniel. (Courtesy Fort Worth Public Library, Genealogy, Local History, and Archives Unit.)

After a slow start, the Fort Worth and Denver City was finally ready to start laying track. Although chartered in 1873, the company did not start construction on the 600-mile line until 1881. It began service between the two cities on April 1, 1888, becoming the first rail line to penetrate the Texas Panhandle and southeastern Colorado. Since the headquarters of the FW&DC was in Fort Worth, Hayne continued to reside there, first in a boardinghouse, then in the Pickwick Hotel, the city's finest.[4]

The driving force behind the project was the team of former Union General Grenville M. Dodge and Colonel Morgan Jones. Both had cut their teeth building the Union Pacific, the eastern half of the nation's first transcontinental rail line. Afterwards, they came to Tex-

St. Joseph's Infirmary in 1890 was Fort Worth's biggest (sixty beds) and best-equipped medical facility. Located on fifteen acres of land adjacent to the railroad reservation, it was the nearest and the best place to bring the burned and injured victims of the Texas Spring Palace fire. But the doctors, aided by the Sisters of Charity of the Incarnate Word, could do nothing for Al Hayne. (Postcard image. Courtesy Fort Worth Public Library, Genealogy, Local History, and Archives Unit.)

as where they collaborated on building the Southern Pacific; Texas & Pacific; Gulf, Colorado and Santa Fe; and Fort Worth and Denver City. Hayne got in, if not on the ground floor, at least in the early stages of the FW&DC before construction began. In September 1880 he did double duty as assistant engineer on the first 100 miles of road and as chief engineer of bridges. He eventually worked his way up to the job of General Dodge's "principal consultant," a responsibility that kept him in the field seven days a week traveling up and down the right of way checking on his crews. Since Dodge and Jones had their hand in several ongoing construction projects, he found himself putting up bridges for both the Fort Worth and Denver City and the Santa Fe with no concerns about conflict of interest. Although he called Fort Worth home, he was away from town for long stretches, sometimes as long as three months. Eventually, when the FW&DC had pushed far into the Texas Panhandle, he moved to Quanah in Hardeman County. It was a tent town that had not even existed before the railroad came. Now it was a terminus town, and even with the influx of workers, provisioners, and vice operators, the population was fewer than a thousand. He lived there for nearly two years (1886–87) making a lasting impression on residents who later remembered him as a "noble, generous-hearted man." Other sources would also agree; he was "well liked by everybody" who knew him—or almost everybody. In 1887 he was sued (along with Morgan Jones) by George D. Clark, a laborer on the Santa Fe, for injuries sustained while building a bridge over the Wichita River. Such suits were part of the business, which is why the railroad kept lawyers on retainer. Hayne let the lawyers handle it while he kept putting up bridges.[5]

Hayne's association with Morgan Jones lasted from 1881 when the GC&SF reached Fort Worth, until the Englishman's death in 1890. In 1886 the GC&SF was absorbed by the Atchison, Topeka and Santa Fe, and Hayne had yet another boss. The Gulf, Colorado had to hurry to lay another 320 miles of track with bridge work to complete its contractual obligations, so Al was still working just as hard if not harder. He had to commute from Fort Worth to Dallas to build the Santa Fe switch on Water Street as part of the Dallas-to-Paris section of the line. Meanwhile, he had not left the employment of the Fort Worth and Denver City, so he continued to apply his skills to pushing that line across the Panhandle toward the Colorado border. By July 1882 it had reached Wichita Falls where construction stalled for the next three years, which is when Hayne did the biggest part of his work for the GC&SF. Before the end of the year the FW&DC's directors had run out of patience with lack of progress and installed Morgan Jones as president with orders to get things moving. He turned to his favorite engineer, and Hayne found himself with all the work he could handle and then some. The Englishman remained on the Fort Worth and Denver City payroll until the line was completed.[6]

Since it is unlikely that Al got time off from his numerous duties with two railroads, it was probably business that took him to Chicago at some point during these years. There was not a direct line to Chicago from north Texas at this time, so he would have had to take a train to Kansas City or St. Louis then connect to Chicago. It was not the sort of trip one took on a lark. In any event we know he was in Chicago because he sat for an undated portrait photograph there, the only known picture of him today. It was taken in the studio of C. D. Mosher, who had been taking photographs of Chicagoans and out-of-town visitors for some thirty-five years. The well-dressed customer who stared into Mosher's camera was a handsome man, with an open face, a high forehead, and level gaze. His dark hair was typically combed straight back, revealing a receding hairline, which only made him look more distinguished. He wore a small, well-trimmed mustache that made his cleft chin and strong jaw even more prominent. He should have been a good catch for any Texas lass looking to "marry up."[7]

Al Hayne was a firm believer in the old Puritan work ethic. He drove himself almost obsessively, taking on jobs whenever and wherever he could get them. Somehow, in 1885 he found time to join with his brother in forming E. A. Hayne & Co., a plumbing and pipefitting firm with an office on Houston Street, Fort Worth. As the name indicated, this was mostly Eugene's project, but Al loaned his talents to the business for two years. The company folded in 1886 after Al moved to Quanah and Eugene got a job with another railroad. It was not a failure as much as a reordering of priorities; their long-term prospects were much better with the railroad than as small-time entrepreneurs.[8]

Al in particular had big ambitions when it came to making his mark on this new land. He had not moved to the United States just to make a big score and then return to England. He considered Texas his home and intended to build a home here, maybe even start a family once he finished the Fort Worth and Denver City project. The railroad paid good wages, starting him out at $75 per month, doubling that after nine months. On top of his salary, he received "expenses when out doors." As he noted in a letter to Georgianna, Americans were building rail lines at a feverish rate, and engineers were in much demand.

He took most of the money he made from his engineering work and built an investment portfolio. He speculated in real estate, purchased stock in the "Denver, Texas, and Fort Worth Railway," and in two banks. At the time of his death he owned 434.4 acres of land in Baylor County outright, plus part interest in another 1,280 acres. He also owned property in Wichita, Callahan, Reeves, Potter, Taylor, Montague, and Martin counties. All of these were north Texas counties that the FW&DC Railroad passed through, and much of the land was town lots in new communities that sprang up along the right of way. Hayne was simply taking advantage of being one of the "boomers" on the leading edge of frontier as it advanced. By beating the waves of homesteaders and townies that followed, he was able to set himself up as a real estate baron. By the time he died, he was considered a "cultured" Brit, "distinguished and rather wealthy." He also joined the Masons.[9]

What he did not do was make a real home or start a family. He never married, perhaps because he was too busy acquiring things, and lived out of hotels and boardinghouses. In the last two years of his life, he boarded at Fort Worth's Pickwick Hotel while maintaining an office over Humphrey's Book Store in the Fordick Building on Main Street. His only personal possessions of any value were a gold watch and chain, his gold Masonic pin, his surveying instruments, and the furniture in his office. His only family in the United States was his brother, Gene. He did correspond frequently with his sister and other family back in England. He seemed to have had no close personal friends in Fort Worth, but was well regarded by the townspeople, counting among his acquaintances, lawyer and future mayor Thomas J. Powell and Major John B. Hawley, a hydraulic engineer with the city.

Perhaps because of the lonely life of being a railroad engineer in the field, he drank immoderately. In the last four months of his life, he took delivery of two and a half gallons of whiskey from Fort Worth's Casey & Swasey distributors. Since this was only his personal stock, it seems likely he imbibed as well in saloons when he was out and about.

Alfred Hayne's date with destiny came on the night of May 30, 1890. He was not living in Fort Worth at the time, and rumor had it that he was "contemplating a return to his native land to enjoy the results of ten years of hard work in America," most of it working for the railroad. In the meantime, he was in town to attend the last night of the Texas Spring Palace, an exhibition of state products housed in an exotic-looking "pleasure dome" on the T&P railroad reservation. Described grandiosely in the local print as "the most beautiful structure ever erected upon the earth," it was actually a firetrap made of wood and completely covered with dried grasses, corn stalks, and wheat sheaves. A larger-than-usual crowd of more than 7,000 was there to celebrate not just the closing of the 1890 season after its three-week run but also national Decoration Day, what we now call Memorial

Day. Al Hayne was there that night "for a pleasant evening" away from work, not as a fireman as some later accounts claimed. He was recuperating from some unspecified illness that had recently befallen him and was not in the best of health. But he felt well enough for a night out on the town. The hardworking engineer had earned it.[10]

It was a brilliant night of music, speeches, and festivities. On the main floor, a grand ball was in progress with couples dancing to the music of the famed Elgin Watch Factory Band. Somehow a fire started on the second floor on the northeast side of the rotunda. The highly flammable materials that went into it and flimsy construction made the building go up like a torch in less than fifteen minutes. Flickering flames quickly ran up the walls and across the ceiling. The air was filled with bits of burning straw and moss, whipped into every corner of the interior by swirling air currents created by the blaze sucking in air through the numerous openings. Nothing could stop the progress of the flames; the fire was out of control as soon as it started. Frantic shouts of "Fire!" echoed throughout the cavernous interior as if anyone needed to be told. The first fire bell was rung at 10:25, nobody knows by whom. Two city firemen were on duty, but they were helpless to do anything. People on the second floor rushed down the four broad staircases to ground level, adding to the panicked throng already there who were pushing and shoving to get out one of the sixteen exits. As the mob stampeded to escape the flames a handful of heroes stepped forward, none bigger than the slight Englishman. He had been on the second floor when the shout of "Fire!" went up, and his first instinct was to run for the nearest exit. He was young and strong and could have muscled his way outside. But instead he chose to stay and help rescue others. He grabbed a rope and lowered several women and children to the ground outside. Then he led others overcome by smoke and heat down the stairs to an exit. As the crowd continued to surge out, he pushed his way back into the building to look for stragglers. Recalled one survivor, "He kept going in and carrying people out. He made one trip too many." Smoke inhalation and his extraordinary exertions on top of his recent illness sapped his strength. He could still have gotten out, but he continued to hunt for victims in the raging inferno. Wisps of burning grass and moss filled the air. He tried to brush them away, but it was no use. The superheated air made it hard to breathe. He could not last much longer. Those outside saw him appear at a second-floor window on the north side of the building with an unconscious woman in his arms. He tossed her to some men on the ground who caught her and carried her away. Then the central dome collapsed with a *whoosh*. With the inferno scorching the clothes off his back and searing his lungs, he jumped, landing hard on the ground eighteen feet below. Already severely burned, he suffered a broken leg and injured his spine in the fall. Four men rushed forward and pulled him to safety. His pain must have been almost unendurable, but his timely and self-sacrificing actions had managed to save more than a dozen people. The hero was still conscious as he was carried away from the fire. He begged his rescuers through horribly burnt lips, "For God's sake, boys, kill me. Please kill me."[11]

His rescuers wrapped him in the first thing that came to hand, a tent fly, and loaded him into a wagon to rush him to St. Joseph's Infirmary, the city's only hospital. St. Joseph's had only twenty-four beds, most of them already occupied by victims of the fire, but Hayne was by far the worst case. Those who saw him that night said he was a "fearful sight." A graphic description of his hideous injuries was printed in a Dallas newspaper three days later:

> He was burned on every part of his body. The flesh had fallen from the fingers of the left hand, and his back was simply cooked. His feet and legs contained spots that were burned to a crisp. Death must have been a relief to him.[12]

The doctors had done what they could, but there was no way in that day and age to treat second- and third-degree burns over 90 percent of his body. His spinal injuries were also untreatable. Until death took him, all they could do was try to make him comfortable by pouring morphine down his throat and placing cool cloths on his fevered body. In the "Day Book" kept by the Sisters of Charity of the Incarnate Word who ran the hospital, the nuns recorded this entry: "Received a patient who was badly burned at the Spring Palace Fire." The last line states that he died in two hours. Later accounts would be as confused on this as on other matters. At the end, no family member was at his side. Gene Hayne was out of the city on business and did not even get back in time for the funeral.[13]

The final resting place of Alfred Hayne in Oakwood Cemetery, where he was reinterred six months after originally being buried in an unmarked grave. Note the Masonic symbols on the marker. (Author's collection.)

The battered, time-worn monument to Al Hayne, Fort Worth's greatest hero until Harold Carswell came along in World War II. Erected in 1893 but never properly maintained. The bust faces west in its latest incarnation; originally it faced south. Note the state historic marker in front of the monument. (Author's collection.)

Doctors at the hospital released no official cause of death. In the absence of such a statement, citizens filled in their own causes. Everyone knew he had died as a result of the fire. Some said he suffocated, others that he died as a result of his terrible burns or perhaps the injuries incurred when he plunged two stories to the ground. Whatever the proximate cause, no one doubted that it had been an excruciating death, all the more reason to sanctify him. When the body was delivered to the undertaker, that gentleman had trouble locating veins to inject the embalming fluid into. The blood in many of the veins was too desiccated from the heat that the body had endured.[14]

The Texas Spring Palace fire was considered the city's "first major tragedy," trumping all earlier fires, epidemics, and flooding.[15] A $100,000 structure had gone up in smoke and forty-three people had been injured, some seriously, but since only one had died, and heroically at that, Al Hayne was all that anyone talked about. Not only the city but the entire state mourned him. The *Fort Worth Gazette* got an early start on the Legend of Al Hayne with its June 1 edition:

> As long as men could stay in and live he stayed, and while great flakes of burning grass and moss were falling on his body, setting fire to his clothes, he stayed there, handing out women and children to those on the outside; and it was not until he was literally burning alive that he abandoned his post, and then all had been saved.[16]

The funeral was at St. Andrews Episcopal Church on Wednesday, June 4, starting at four o'clock in the afternoon. Hayne had not been a particularly religious man, but as an Englishman, it was considered only proper to provide the closest thing possible to a Church of England service, and that meant Episcopalian. The five-day interval between his death and funeral was quite unusual, but it served a definite purpose, allowing time to print up fancy, engraved funeral notices and mail them out to selected friends and dignitaries. This was the first time in Fort Worth history that formal invitations to a funeral had been issued. Afterwards they became collector's items. Since Hayne had no family in the city at the time, city fathers made all the arrangements. The City Secretary appointed the six pallbearers, who included a former mayor and other leading lights. Mayor W. S. Pendleton asked them to serve.[17]

The funeral was unusual in another way. The custom at the time was to hold the service in the home of the deceased, but since Alfred had no home to speak of, it was held in the sanctuary of St. Andrews. No house could have held the crowd that turned out anyway. Hundreds stood outside with bowed heads waiting to join the cortege to Oakwood Cemetery. They formed a procession in carriages and on foot "several blocks" long. Many more stood "in throngs" on the sidewalks along the way paying "silent tribute" to him. At Oakwood they covered the grounds, trampling graves trying to get close enough to see and hear the graveside service. He was interred in a donated plot near the potter's field, with no headstone to mark it.[18]

Hastily buried, Al Hayne would not be allowed to rest in peace for long. Three months later he was dug up and reinterred in a "beautiful lot . . . in the most desirable portion of the cemetery." They had a hard time finding the grave even though it had been such a short time since the original interment. The impetus for the re-interment came from Henry George Hayne, Al's father, who arrived in the city in November, coming over from England as soon as he received the bad news. Mr. Hayne senior purchased the new plot, paid for all the work and also for the very nice granite "monument" atop the grave. Mr. Hayne was shocked at the way Fort Worth had treated his son. Was this any way to treat a genuine hero? More than a few persons agreed with him, which was the genesis behind the grass-roots movement to erect a fitting monument "that will tower to the skies."[19]

In the meantime, Gene Hayne reached the city in the days after the funeral. It was left to him to close out his brother's affairs and dispose of the estate. He dutifully took care of all the financial loose ends, but when it came to honoring his dearly departed sibling, he did it in his own way—by locking up Al's office and leaving it exactly the way it had been on the night of the fire when Al left it for the last time. A shirt lay carelessly tossed across a chair, the daybed was "disarranged," and technical books were piled in stacks on top of the desk. Five years later, the room was still frozen in time covered with dust (fairy dust?) to maintain the spell forever. During all that time, Gene kept the rent paid up but never came back to see the shrine he had created. The curious came, however, to stand on a chair and peer through the transom into the room.[20]

After Gene Hayne departed the city he settled in Houston. He lived in the Houston area the rest of his life, working until retirement as a railroad contractor. He never married, and there is no record that he ever came back to Fort Worth. At the end of his life, he was living alone in the Harris County Home for the Aged.[21]

Testimonials to the fallen hero covered the gamut from maudlin to eloquent with more than a few crossing into hyperbole or worse. A writer for the *Fort Worth Gazette* counted him among the greatest of English heroes, on a par with "Havelock at Lucknow, Garnet Wolseley at Tel El Kebir, Nelson at Trafalgar, and Cardigan at Balaklova," one who was fit to have "graced a seat at the Round Table next to Arthur." Not to be outdone, the *Dallas Morning News* proclaimed, "Centuries will come and go, men's fortunes will wax and wane, but Al Haine's [*sic*] deeds . . . will live on, and his memory will keep green forever." Fort Worth resident Josephine McNamara employed an unfortunate metaphor saying his "world-renowned heroism has forever embalmed him in our affections." Another Fort Worth resident who had witnessed the fire called him "the sacrifice laid upon the altar of the universal heroism of that night." And the newspaper account of his funeral declaimed, "The great heart within him, moved by a universal sympathy for all suffering, impelled him irresistibly to the rescue of the helpless women and children, and so he met his death."[22]

Self-styled poets were also inspired to write memorials. Their verses were printed in the newspapers at the time then quickly forgotten—for good reason. Read today, they evoke more winces than admiration. One such elegy:

> Who scorned the devastating flames
> That raged on ev'ry side,
> To rescue strangers from the fate
> He fearless met—and died.[23]

All the versification and heartfelt testimonials were capped off by the creation of a memorial in stone. It was proposed even before the hero himself had been laid to rest. A Dallas newspaper broke the story two days after the fire: "A movement is on foot to erect a monument to the memory of Al Haines [*sic*]." The *Fort Worth Gazette* confirmed it in announcing, "The people of Fort Worth will build a costly monument to commemorate his virtues." Good intentions are one thing; raising the substantial cost of a stone monument is something else. A. B. Smith, President of the Merchant's National Bank, started a subscription drive that same summer, echoing the drive that had raised the money to build the Texas Spring Palace in the first place. But the drive ran out of steam after the initial outpouring of sentiment dried up. It was not until the ladies of Fort Worth, specifically, the Woman's Humane Association, took over the drive that it shifted into high gear. They secured a sculptor and negotiated his fee ($2,000) to create a marble bust. Then they raised the money via a public appeal, hitting up prominent citizens and organizations. The newspapers also got behind the cause. As word got around, contributions poured in from all over Texas in the form of sizable donations and also nickels and dimes from schoolchildren.[24]

It took three years from the time the project was first proposed, but in 1893 the monument was placed in front of the T&P station on a site where Front Street (later Lancaster), Main, and Houston intersected. It was the first thing visitors saw when they stepped out of the station. In going from dream to reality the marble had been replaced with good old Texas limestone, and those hoping for a larger-than-life-sized statue had to settle for a mere bust of the hero set into an elaborate granite pedestal, the whole surrounded by a pool of water (which doubled as a horse-watering fountain). An inscription carved into the pedestal saluted the hero who, "unselfish as brave, died that others might live." At the dedication ceremony, the Reverend J. Morgan Wells and prominent businessman Thomas J. Powell spoke, the first for his spiritual insights and the second for his lawyerly eloquence. Neither speech was recorded by newspaper reporters at the time or saved in its original form by the man who gave it. All attention was on the impressive stone monument. It was the first the city had erected to anyone since its start twenty years earlier. Al Hayne was no war hero or elected representative of the people, just a simple man who did what he had to do when called upon. The fact that it cost him his life was not his intention, but he laid down his life willingly.[25]

By accident or intent, 1893 proved to be a signal year in the history of the Fort Worth Fire Department. First, the volunteer companies were invited to participate in the "unveiling exercises" of the Al Hayne monument, then later that year the modern full-time Department was created out of the volunteer companies that had protected the community since its incorporation in 1873. It was a move that was long overdue. It had taken the shocking destruction of the Texas Spring Palace to finally persuade city fathers of the need for a regular trained force. With a full-time, professional force on call, it was hoped there would never be any more Al Haynes to spring into action when future fires happened.[26]

While the hero was fondly remembered in the public consciousness, the details of his life and death tended to grow dim as the decades passed. Besides being vague on his nationality and his age at the time of his death, even the date of the fire was misremembered—as either May 30 or May 31 and 1890 or possibly 1893. In 1905 one retrospective on the fifteenth anniversary of the fire stated that "nothing is known of Alfred Hayne except the place of his birth and that he has one brother living."[27]

Legends do not depend on details, or even complete accuracy. On the contrary, they flourish in the absence of hard facts. The legend of Al Hayne as it developed had several facets, including the hero, the engineer, and the businessman. While he was all of those things, one thing he was not was a fireman. Thomas J. Powell, who went on to become Mayor of Fort Worth (1900–1906) and could speak of the Texas Spring Palace fire firsthand, later stated, "So far as I know, he never belonged to the Fort Worth Fire Department." Powell had made one of the two speeches at the time the Al Hayne monument was dedicated in 1893. Neither speech described its subject as a fireman. The story got started later thanks to careless writing by newspaper reporters.[28]

The legend of Al Hayne the Fireman started even before he was laid to rest. By order of the Chief of the Fort Worth Fire Department, the members of the various companies turned out for the funeral in regulation uniform. The Chief's order concluded with the admonition, "All brave firemen should pay honor to him." Thus, the men of the Fire Department claimed him as one of their own from the beginning. When the Texas Firemen's Association met in Houston for its annual convention the following May (1891), its members adopted the following special resolution:

> Whereas, it is a matter of history in Texas that at the burning of the Spring Palace in the city of Fort Worth on May 30, 1890, our beloved comrade, Al Hayne, met a heroic death at the hands of our inveterate enemy, the fiery flames, in attempting to save others from the death which he so bravely met; be it
>
> Resolved, by this association in convention assembled:
> 1. That it grieves our hearts to know that our comrade has been called to report to the great chief of the universe, but it consoles us to know that he has met his fate calmly, bravely and as became a man *and a fireman* [emphasis added].
> 2. That we will ever cherish his memory in our hearts and will hold his acts out to all our comrades as worthy of the emulation and adoption of all the firemen of the state.
> 3. That a copy of these resolutions be printed in our minutes and the secretary be instructed to send a copy of these minutes to his relatives, his father and his brother, Eugene Hayne.[29]

There is no indication that Eugene, still living in Texas, or the family back in England ever received their intended copies of the resolutions.

Within three years of his death, Al had been elevated to mythic status as a combination of Roland, Sir Galahad, and Hector all rolled into one. In 1892 when the Volunteer Firemen of Texas met in Waco for their eighteenth annual convention, a memorial to him was read from the podium and a large bouquet of flowers was presented to the group by the keynote speaker, a retired Waco fire chief. The memorial honored its subject as "the fireman who lost his life at the Spring Palace fire," which definitely gave credence to the misperception that Al had been anything other than a concerned citizen that night. Those attending also used the occasion to launch a drive to build a monument to all their fellows who had lost their lives in the line of duty over the years.[30] Four years later, when the State Firemen's Monument was dedicated on the grounds of the capitol in Austin, the guest of honor for the occasion mentioned just one firefighter by name, Al Haynes [*sic*] saying he represented all those who "live in the hearts and memories of the people as long as time shall last and men are brave and true." At the 1903 convention of the Texas Firemen's Association in Corsicana, Hayne was once again prominently mentioned in the keynote address of Corsicana Mayor E. O. Call, who said, "In every local organization of firemen in the State there is to be found . . . an Al Haynes [*sic*]."[31]

In 1911, when Fort Worth fireman John M. Bennett was killed while racing to a fire, the newspaper noted he was "the first Fort Worth fireman to lose his life while in the discharge of duty." But the story added that he was preceded by Al Hayne, "a volunteer fireman [who] was burned to death in the Spring Palace fire about twenty years ago." Over the years, the newspapers had become the biggest perpetrators of the legend.[32]

It was not just firemen and journalists who kept the legend alive. In 1902 a group of young Fort Worth men organized themselves as the Al Hayne Lodge of the Coming Men of America. Naming themselves after the city's most famous hero seemed like a good way to launch the first local chapter of the organization. Proclaiming itself the "Original Secret Society for Boys," the CMA had thousands of lodges in the United States and other countries.[33]

The Al Hayne monument also perpetuates the legend. On one face of the cupola is a bas-relief of a crossed hook and ladder and fire horn, all traditional symbols of firemen. Below these is a fire helmet, another obvious symbol of the men who make their living fighting fires. Thus, the legend is literally carved in stone. The monument is more a shrine to the legend than to the man. For many years after the fire, its anniversary was the occasion to decorate the monument and hold a memorial service there. The monument was the best spot to meet because the site of the Texas Spring Palace had been taken over by the rail yards and was no longer accessible to the public.[34]

While the man himself and his legend have been highly honored, his monument has not fared so well. The bust was stolen from its pedestal in 1922 and not recovered until 1934, by which time it was so heavily damaged that a new one had to be cast in bronze. Over the years the "Al Hayne Triangle" formed by Main, Houston, and Lancaster became smaller and smaller as streets were widened, encroaching on the small grassy plot. The horse fountain surrounding the monument, no longer needed or affordable in the modern era, is long gone. Meanwhile, pollution and the elements have done their work on the 1934 bust. There is also the matter of its siting: It faces west down Lancaster today instead of south, the direction it originally faced, because it was reinstalled incorrectly. Today the Al Hayne monument is Fort Worth's best-known monument, better known than the statues of Will Rogers, Quanah Parker, or Bill Pickett, but none of them lived and died in Fort Worth. Unfortunately, it is also heavily in need of immediate repairs to keep it from being reduced eventually to a pile of stones and an unrecognizable lump of bronze. Monuments of stone and bronze, theoretically built to last an eternity, in reality require constant attention. Whether the city and citizens of Fort Worth today are willing to commit to saving the People's Hero for future generations remains to be seen.

CHAPTER 6

The Strange Case of Maggie Tewmey

On a blustery winter afternoon in January 1893, Margaret Tewmey set out from her downtown home to give a regularly scheduled music lesson. She wore an old flannel dress over a gray woolen underskirt and pulled a black woolen cloak tight around her to keep out the cold. Atop her head perched a nondescript hat with a silk veil, and she carried her purse and music bag. On the way out the door she said goodbye to her niece, Mrs. M. A. (Frances) Dodd, with whom she lived, but did not say when she would be home; she seldom did. Margaret's destination was 906 West Weatherford, on the western edge of downtown almost to the Clear Fork of the Trinity, where Louis and Anna Reiney and their two daughters, Allie and Lucy, lived. Mr. Reiney had recently been promoted from stock clerk to salesman at Pendery's grocery store, so he could afford private music lessons for twelve-year-old Allie. The distance from where Margaret lived at Main and Sixth to the Reineys' was about twelve blocks going straight up Main to the public square then west on Weatherford beyond the business district. She could take the street car to the square but from there she had to walk the last six blocks. Past Burnett, there were plenty of empty lots on either side of the rutted, unpaved road. She made the trip twice a week. It took no more than thirty minutes, but on this day (January 20, a Friday), she left early because she planned to make a stop along the way, at the establishment of either Mr. Happy or Mr. Wood, both of whom dispensed libations for warding off the winter chill. Both gentlemen knew her as a regular customer.[1]

Margaret would not have attracted much attention on her journey. She was fifty-one years old and wore every year of it on her long, lanky frame. As thin as a pinch of snuff, she had no curves and little meat on her bones. Mr. Reiney described her ungenerously as "an old maid." Later, a Dallas newspaper would be a little kinder, calling her "an elderly maiden lady." Either way, it translated as "lonely spinster." Poor Margaret did not have much to show for her fifty-one years on earth: no husband and no savings. Her prized personal possession was an opal and pearl ring that she always wore. That and her music bag were the only things to distinguish her from the ranks of homeless women who lived unnoticed in the shadows of the city. In addition to her niece, Margaret had a married sister, Mrs. Andrew J. Lawrence (Frances Dodd's mother) who was also a Fort Worth resident. Both women considered Margaret a poor relative and, worse, an embarrassment. They only tolerated her because she was family. Virtually estranged from her two nearest relatives and with no husband or prospects, Margaret Tewmey's only comfort in life was the bottle, which was her constant companion. She drank too much, and not just in the privacy of her own home. She frequently sat and drank in the rear (the "wine room") of Anton Happy's "beer saloon" or H. O. Wood's bar, both on West Weatherford. Her twice-weekly piano lessons at the Reineys' gave her plenty of opportunities to stop in for a little liquid refreshment, sometimes both going and coming.[2]

On this particular day she got an early start tippling. By the time she got to the Reineys', she was visibly tipsy. She even brought along a bottle, stuffed into her music bag, and generously offered a drink to Mr. Reiney when he welcomed her. Shocked by such wantonness, the Reineys cancelled the piano lesson and ordered her to leave. They watched disapprovingly as she "staggered" off on Weatherford disappearing into the dusk about the time she reached the corner of Weatherford and Florence. Margaret Tewmey, *aka* Maggie, was never seen alive again by the Reineys or her own family. Four days later her body was found stuffed into an outhouse. She had been "abused and outraged" before being shot.[3] The mystery of who raped and murdered her, and why, is Fort Worth's greatest unsolved crime of the nineteenth century.

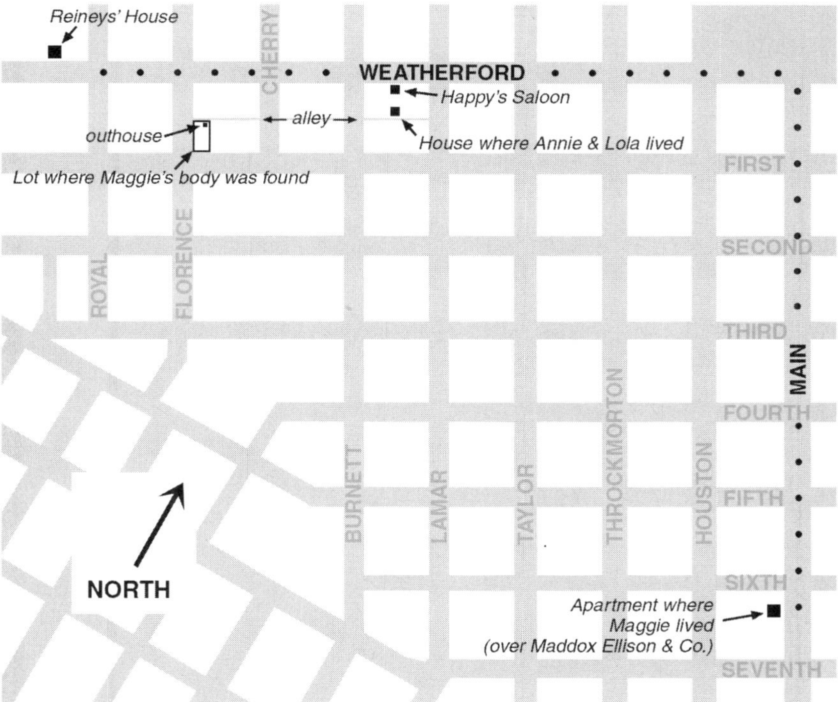

Maggie Tewmey's journey to her last music lesson, January 20, 1893. A composite of Sanborn Fire Insurance Co. maps from February 1893 shows the route she would have traveled to get to her music lesson, and the lot where her body was discovered. Florence Street marks almost the far western edge of downtown. It was unpaved and unlighted, and houses were few and far apart.

The body was discovered by Sam Jones, a "negro rag-picker," about half past three on Tuesday afternoon, January 24. Sam was making his rounds with his little two-wheeled cart, collecting rags and bits of junk wherever he could find them. He had entered the yard behind an empty house on the corner of West First and Florence and noticed a piece of fabric sticking out of the closed door of a "water closet." When he tried to pull it out, it was stuck, and the outhouse door could not be opened because a slat was nailed across it. That seemed strange so Sam peered inside through a crack, and that is when he saw the body. He ran for help, and the first person he found was C. C. McMichael, an officer with the sanitation department (part of the Police Department at that time). McMichael accompanied Sam back to the site, took one look through the door, and then broke it open. Inside was the body of a white woman, sitting doubled over, her head resting in a pool of coagulated blood on the floor. There was a single bullet hole in her head through which blood and brains had oozed out. He also noticed what looked to be chicken feathers and red soil stuck to her clothing and the same kind of soil on her shoes. Deciding it was too big for a lowly sanitation officer, he went to get reinforcements, leaving the crime scene unguarded except for a very nervous Sam Jones. He returned with several regular officers, who started poking around without waiting for the arrival of detectives or the coroner. A little later, Deputy Sheriff Harden D. Gunnells and Justice of the Peace E. B. Randle arrived on the scene, followed shortly thereafter by the undertaker's wagon. As was the custom, JP Randle would serve as coroner of record.[4]

By the time Randle arrived, there was already a crowd of gawkers milling around the yard, drawn to the crime scene like moths to a flame. He got Sam Jones to help him remove the body from the outhouse and lay it out on the ground. This was not easy because rigor mortis had already set in. They found her hat inside, too, and laid it beside the body. In the fading afternoon light, they could also see "corn silks" stuck to her clothing as if she had been lying in a corn crib. No one present could identify the victim so officers shooed the civilians out of the yard so they could go about their business without interference. Since this was a murder investigation, the Sheriff's Office had jurisdiction, but the coroner took the lead. Randle performed a cursory examination of the body and announced that the victim "had been outraged and evidently repeatedly." That hasty conclusion, based on the flimsiest of evidence, would color the investigation henceforward, being repeated regularly to the press and explaining much of the public's fascination with the case. It was Jack the Ripper and "Long Liz Stride" all over again.[5]

Deputy Gunnells was more than happy to let the JP and police do all the work. As far as he was concerned, this was just a random murder of one of the city's homeless nobodies. He casually noted the "corn silks" and red dirt on her clothing and shoes but attached no particular significance to them. After a cursory examination of the area, he went back to headquarters to get out of the cold. As the Sheriff Office's lead officer on the crime, he would not get around to conducting a "thorough examination" until nine months later![6]

All of the other officers on the scene were also working without established procedures to guide them. None had ever received training for this. McMichael, the sanitation officer who now considered himself a "crime scene investigator," hung around trying to be helpful. He was the only one apart from Sam Jones who had the stomach to examine the outhouse searching for clues. That was how he came to notice the silk veil stuck in the pool of blood on the floor. He stuffed it in his pocket. He also retrieved a small liquor bottle that he turned over to Harden Gunnells who took it with him when he left. The bottle contained a remnant of blackberry wine, and the name "H. O. Wood" was visible on the partially torn-off label. The officers knew Wood as the proprietor of a nearby saloon. Two officers went there and brought him back, and it was Wood who first identified the victim as one of his regulars. He was even able to provide the sister's name. Other officers canvassed the neighborhood and found some children who said they had used the outhouse Monday afternoon. This was the first clue in establishing a timeline to the crime.[7]The chicken feathers and red soil seemed to be important clues, too, but matching them up to the place where the deed was done would be the problem.

The body was loaded into the undertaker's wagon for the trip to Gause's mortuary, the official drop-off for unidentified or unclaimed bodies. A couple of officers got the unpleasant duty of notifying Mrs. Lawrence and bringing her to the morgue to make next-of-kin identification. She brought her daughter along for moral support, and, while clutching each other tightly, they made an absolute ID of poor Maggie.[8]

The yard where the outhouse was located furnished no clues. It was an isolated spot with only one other house nearby, across the alley at the rear of the property. The view of the yard from either Florence or West First was blocked by a fence and tall shrubs all around. Yet it was easily accessible via a front gate, a side gate, and breaks in the fence at the rear. The alley beyond the fence at the rear led to Florence Street on the west and Burnett on the east. There was no red soil in the yard or alley and no chickens to be seen either, leading officers to their first theory of the crime, namely that she had been killed elsewhere and dumped in the outhouse. They found no suspicious footprints but noticed a set of wheeled tracks in the alley leading east toward Burnett Street. Two officers set out to follow the tracks and see where they led. They lost the tracks when they got to Burnett, a graveled, heavily traveled street, and gave up. The next day, Police Chief James H. Maddox would follow the same trail but pick up the tracks in the alley across the street and follow them until they disappeared at a point not far from the rear of Anton Happy's saloon. The elderly saloon proprietor lived on the premises with his wife. He was a longtime resident of Fort Worth with no previous criminal record, but his place was known as one of the lowest dives in the city. It was only about a block and half from the crime scene to the yard behind Happy's Saloon, but at least initially there was no reason to suspect him. His name would not be connected to the investigation publicly for months.[9]

The small amount of blood at the scene supported the theory that Maggie had been murdered somewhere else and brought to the outhouse, presumably on a two-wheeled cart, where she was dumped inside like "a sack of corn" and the door nailed shut. Beneath her dress and underskirt, she had on no undergarments and only one stocking, but how and where she had lost them was anybody's guess. There was no jewelry on the body, no purse, nothing that would have identified her if not for H. O. Wood's initial ID. Police believed the crime had been committed nearby because anyone transporting a body through the streets, even at night and in a cart, would have attracted attention, and only someone who knew the house was empty would have picked that particular spot to dump the body. The family formerly living there had moved out just a week prior. Since arriving on the scene, the police had made no progress whatsoever. Who had committed the crime, why, and even where and when were all unknown.[10]

Maggie herself was something of a mystery although she was a familiar sight around town.[11] Fort Worth was still small enough that everybody knew everybody, even if they did not move in the same social circles. She had come to the United States from Canada originally but arrived in Fort Worth from Illinois in May 1892—alone. Family members said she spent her early years in a convent, but if so, she had turned her back on the church as an adult, leading a life of dissipation and debauchery. Whatever her background, it had not prepared her for the world. She was not a sociable person nor even particularly feminine, and aside from her modest musical talents, her only practical skills were as a "wax worker," for which there was not a big demand in Fort Worth. Even her place in the social order was vague. She was not one of the "working girls" who plied their trade out of the cribs and bagnios on the south end of town, nor did she fit in with the society ladies and their tea parties and church socials. She was what polite folks of that day described as "a woman of easy virtue." One newspaper described her ambiguously as being "little acquainted with the ways of the world," supporting the family story that her formative years had been spent in a convent. Her only friend was Mary Shanahan whose family ran a boarding house at 1311 Houston. At twenty-three, Mary was young enough to be Maggie's daughter, but the two seemed to have bonded on some level. Typically, when Maggie failed to come home sometimes for two or three days at a stretch, it was because she was staying with Mary. The Thursday night before she disappeared, she had stayed with Mary. Maggie's alcoholism was part of her dark side: she preferred the city's sleazier bars, places that were off the main drag. There were gaps in her routine when nobody knew where she was or what she was doing. The old-maid music teacher who was also part of the demimonde had shades of *The Strange Case of Dr. Jekyll and Mr. Hyde*, Robert Louis Stevenson's classic novel that had been a sensation since being published in 1886. As more of Maggie's story came out, it too, like Stevenson's fictional character, would contain elements of dual personality, sexual perversion, and personal demons.[12]

At the morgue Dr. H. C. Stevens took over, brought in by the coroner. Stevens was officially described as the "jail physician" on county rolls, making him the acting county medical examiner before such an office existed. He had been a medical doctor for almost forty years, but he was not the brightest bulb. He conducted the postmortem Tuesday evening and as he told it later, the first thing he noticed was "she was dead." Randle did not inform him of the victim's identity so he began his examination with no idea whose body he was working on. What he did was not a full-fledged autopsy but a simple medical examination. As he went through his paces, he made some competent observations, some bad guesses, and one highly dubious conclusion. He examined the single gunshot wound, which had entered the right side of the head over the ear and "ranged downward," coming out the opposite side "about the corner of the eye," and decided it had been the immediate cause of death. He judged her to be forty-to-forty-five years old and to have been dead "a day or two." Examining the body more intimately, he found "evidence of outrage," qualifying that conclusion by stating that she was definitely not a virgin at the time of her most recent outrage. He noted the presence of severe bruising and numerous scratches on the limbs, plus a deep flesh wound on the right leg "as if torn by some rough instrument." He surmised that the scratches had been caused by the fingernails of her attacker or attackers. From the scratches and bruises coupled with the state of her clothing he determined that she had been in a "scuffle." There was no doubt in his mind that she had been "assaulted repeatedly" although "the outrage did not . . . cause her death." How much his medical opinions were influenced by the coroner's aforementioned conclusions is impossible to say, but it was Randle who brought Stevens into the case, so it is not unreasonable to assume that he shared his own conclusions with the physician, particularly since Randle was present during the postmortem. Showing at least some knowledge of forensics, Stevens looked for traces of skin or clothing under her fingernails, but the lack of equipment or training plus the condition of the body dashed that hope.[13]

While stuffed in the outhouse the body had become food for hungry rats that had gnawed off the nose and fingertips. Whatever forensic evidence there might once have been had been destroyed by the rodents. If the body had gone undiscovered for another twenty-four hours, they would have completely obliterated the facial features and marks of violence on the limbs. He noted no chicken feathers, corn silk, or red soil on her clothing, but then his job was to examine the body, leaving the clothing and crime scene to detectives and the coroner. Provoked as much by curiosity as by professional concerns, Stevens nonetheless decided to pay a visit to the crime scene the next morning. He did not have to go out of his way because, as luck would have it, he lived only about 100 feet from where the body had been discovered. As the investigation developed, Stevens would be involved not only as the medical examiner of record, but also as a material witness.[14]

Once Dr. Stevens completed his work, a coroner's inquest delivered the official verdict—homicide committed with a gun of indeterminate caliber—but otherwise added nothing new. To these slim findings law enforcement officers added their own conclusion that two or more men had been involved. As of Wednesday, January 25, that was all they had to go on. Detectives fanned out across the city to begin interviewing anyone who had known her or might have been connected to her. They were immediately struck by the number of saloonkeepers and habitués that she had known.[15]

They tried to reconstruct her movements starting Friday afternoon. She did not return home that evening after leaving the Reineys', but her niece had thought nothing of it, assuming she was at Mrs. Shanahan's. Mrs. Shanahan, however, had not seen her on Friday or over the weekend, nor had her sister. The only other person who had seen Maggie between Friday and Tuesday was H. O. Wood, the barkeep. When questioned, he remembered Maggie showing up at his establishment around mid-day Friday—or maybe it was Thursday; he couldn't remember exactly. He did remember she complained of feeling faint when she came in and made a beeline to the wine room in the back of the saloon. He sold her a bottle of his house brandy "for medicinal purposes," and she left soon after that under her own power. That was all Wood could tell them, and detectives could find no one else who remembered seeing Maggie between Friday and Tuesday when Sam Jones discovered her body.[16]

Trying to fit Wood's recollections into the known facts of the case, detectives theorized that Maggie had been held against her will, probably in a drugged state, but managed somehow to escape whereupon she stumbled into Wood's saloon to brace herself with a brandy before continuing on her way, presumably to file a complaint with the police. However, her captors nabbed her again after she left Wood's place and confined her again until they decided to kill her. As preposterous as that theory sounds, it was the only one they had. Trying to put a timeline on the events, they considered it significant that a number of residents on Florence and West First, including Dr. Stevens, reported being aroused by barking dogs after midnight Monday night.[17]

While the authorities scratched their heads and tried to develop leads, both Fort Worth and Dallas newspapers ran with the story they had, reporting every lurid detail and filling in the gaps with fanciful speculation in the best tradition of the *National Police Gazette*. The *Fort Worth Gazette*, shamelessly taking its cue from its national namesake, set the tone, calling Maggie's murder, "an almost fiend-like atrocity, . . . the worst that has ever disgraced the criminal history of the county of Tarrant." This sort of sensationalist journalism titillated the public and put pressure on the authorities to solve the crime quickly. The authorities tried, but unfortunately, they were sorely lacking in suspects or even clues. Neither the Reineys nor H. O. Wood were ever suspects in the case. Detectives had to look elsewhere, which is what finally brought them back to Anton Happy.[18]

Maggie was laid to rest in the Calvary (Catholic) section of Oakwood Cemetery on Wednesday, January 25, following a service at St. Patrick's Church. The newspapers reported that "a large number of friends were present," which is doubtful because Maggie did not have a large number of friends. She was laid to rest in a Tewmey family plot, neither the first nor the last Tewmey to be interred at Oakwood. Newspapers in both Dallas and Fort Worth gave short shrift to the funeral because that was not what their readers were interested in; the public was far more interested in the on-going investigation. At least neither the *Dallas Morning News* nor the *Fort Worth Gazette* mentioned her drinking or her questionable lifestyle, and they even refrained from calling her "an old maid" on this one day. Still, the haste with which she was buried, without a proper autopsy, called into question the competency of the official investigation.[19]

Though his people were the first on the scene, Police Chief Maddox was a relative latecomer to the investigation. The first time he viewed the body was at the "undertaking establishment." It was the next morn-

Fort Worth Police Chief Jim Maddox devoted more time and effort to solving Maggie Tewmey's murder than almost any other murder during his ten years as police chief. He doggedly pursued every lead, revisited the crime scene, and in general did everything he could to keep the case alive until arrests were finally made. He's pictured here as he appeared in the 1901 Fort Worth Police Department Annual, wearing his custom-made city marshal's badge and "Chief of Police" hat, reflecting his dual roles. (Courtesy Sergeant Kevin Foster.)

ing before he paid a visit to the crime scene. But from that point on, he made solving Maggie's murder his personal mission. For the next week after the body was discovered, he held almost daily press conferences. It seemed he was determined to keep the investigation in the Police Department rather than let the county boys handle it, and that was just fine with the county boys. At every press conference he assured the assembled reporters that his Department was making progress. On Thursday he told them conspiratorially that he was in possession of "new information" that threw "considerable light" on the case, but he could not reveal the "nature" of that information just yet. He added that he was giving the case his "personal attention" and expected to solve it soon. On Friday he said that his men were "picking up [additional] scraps of evidence" but still refused to name any suspects or predict when the case would be solved. His short list of suspects included Sam Jones because of his color and because he owned a handcart, H. O. Wood because one of his private-stock bottles had been found with the body, and Anton Happy because he knew the victim and the cart tracks pointed to his place. But Maddox did not really like any of these suspects, so at every press conference he talked in the most vague terms: there were "new developments"; he was "diligently at work"; there would be an arrest "in the next day or two." About the time of the third or fourth press conference the official view of the case shifted subtly but significantly; now it was "the *two* disappearances" of Maggie Tewmey, which meant that police believed Maggie had been abducted *before* she strolled into H. O. Wood's saloon. That theory would ultimately be discarded but not before police wasted a lot of time trying to make the evidence fit the theory. After the first few press conferences, Maddox's performances ceased to be interesting and reporters began sniffing around for new leads on their own.[20]

A little investigative journalism is how the public learned a couple of days later that detectives had interviewed a possible eyewitness: a man who lived near Main and Tenth who said he had heard a pistol shot on Monday night, January 21. Then, he said, he saw a man place a "heavy roll" in a wagon and drive off north on Main. It sounded promising, but that lead proved another dead-end. Chief Maddox confirmed the newspaper report but never mentioned it again after that, presumably out of embarrassment over the fact that the police seemed to be chasing their own tails.[21]

Four days into the investigation, with no suspects in custody and no solid clues, the Dallas newspaper was saying that "the matter had grown dormant in the public mind," which meant that reporters no longer came running when the Chief whistled. Then the case got new life after police received an anonymous letter on Saturday morning. It was turned over to them by a public-minded citizen who said he had found it in his yard. It was handwritten and addressed to "one of the Fort Worth newspapers." It did not identify the murderer or say exactly what happened, but it did say that the murder had been committed in "an entirely different part of the city from where the body was found." The Chief refused to let reporters see the letter, and he admitted that he did not usually put much stock in such things. He said it was just as likely that "the man" who had written the letter was the murderer, and if such were the case, the murderer either had a "fine sense of humor" or else an "overburdened conscience." The Chief closed this latest press conference by saying cryptically that "the whole crime is clearing somewhat" and that police had "several persons" under surveillance. This was either a brazen lie or a self-delusion.[22]

The truth was, police were completely befuddled. All the talk of "new developments" and imminent arrests was so much blarney. As the days and weeks slipped by, they were no closer to solving the crime than they had been on January 24. And the boys over at the Sheriff's Office were not turning up anything either. Reporters and the general public moved on to other stories.

The case finally broke wide open eight months later thanks to the revelations of a bawd named Annie Edmonds. Twenty-two-year-old Annie had been in Fort Worth about two years after working previously in Houston and San Antonio. For a couple of weeks prior to the murder she had had been living with another bawd, Lola Hindman, in a little house behind Anton Happy's saloon. The house was both their living quarters and their place of work. Only an open yard about fifty feet across and an alley separated the two. They were well acquainted with the saloon proprietor, his wife, and customers, particularly a couple of "sports" named Bob Miller and John Witcher. In fact, they were more than well acquainted; Annie and Lola were implicated in the murder. Immediately after Maggie's body was discovered, both girls had been "searchingly questioned" by the police but revealed nothing because they feared for their lives. Soon after that, her companion left town hurriedly while Annie found another house on Fifteenth Street to conduct her business from. Her conscience finally got the best of her and she went to County Attorney Oscar W. Gillespie to tell her story.[23]

She said four men were involved in the murder, one of whom was the boyfriend of Lola and had threatened them into silence. Several days prior, Maggie had been brought to their house by Happy and the other men and kept there in an inebriated state while they continually "debauched" her. On the fatal night, Maggie had quarreled bitterly with the men and run outside into the yard. One of them pursued her and when he caught her, said, "I told you I'd kill you, God damn you if you did it, and I'll do it now!"

Mary threw up her hands, exclaiming, "May God Almighty save my soul!" She was in the midst of repeating that plea when her assailant shot her and she fell down dead. The shooter and the other three then placed the body in a two-wheel cart and disappeared pushing it down the alley that ran between Weatherford and First streets. When the men returned, they warned Annie and Lola to keep quiet, then went across the yard to Happy's saloon. And that, said Annie, was "the entire, absolute, and unvarnished truth."[24]

Annie and Lola heeded the warnings to keep their mouths shut, and as soon as the initial heat died down, the six scattered to the four winds. Happy sold his saloon, which he had owned for eight or nine years, and moved himself and the missus to Belknap Street. Two of his accomplices decided to skip town for a few months while the fourth chose to lay low in Fort Worth. Lola relocated to Trinidad, Colorado, and Annie moved in with friends on the south end of town. This might have been where the most sensational unsolved crime in Fort Worth history ended but for a prostitute's stricken conscience. Based on Annie's sworn testimony, police made the first arrests in the case in the second week in October. Taken into custody were saloonkeeper Anton Happy, Jack Gunnells, John Witcher, and Bob Miller. Happy was the connection between the four: Jack Gunnells (no relation to Deputy Harden Gunnells) was his son-in-law while the other two were regulars at his saloon. The arrests did not stop there. The County Attorney's Office requested extradition for Hindman, and Colorado authorities complied. Lola was soon locked up in the Tarrant County jail with Annie, and the County Attorney's Office used a little old-fashioned leverage to get them to turn State's evidence. Annie, without whose testimony the case would still be cold, was released and allowed to resume her former life without police harassment. Lola required a little more convincing. She had perjured herself originally when interviewed by police about Maggie's murder and admitted as much when she was back in police custody. As fate would have it, she had an unrelated complaint against her for robbing one of her customers of $35 and a gold watch. In return for the theft and perjury charges being dropped, Lola agreed to testify against the four defendants. If she refused, she was informed, she would find herself behind bars for a long time. The police make similar deals all the time, but in this case it would come back to haunt them.[25]

After so many months of no progress whatsoever, the case took off from this point. The four men had their preliminary hearing before Justice of the Peace John S. Kennedy on Tuesday, October 17. They were represented by a court-appointed lawyer, and through him they denied everything; two of the four even denied knowing the others—or at least until they got acquainted while sharing a jail cell. The preliminary hearing took three days and featured testimony from Dr. Stevens, Officer McMichael, Justice of the Peace Randle, and the niece and sister of the victim. They all had a hard time recalling the events of nine months before, and none used notes to help their memory. They spoke vaguely of this day or that, this time or that, this person or that one. The hearing had more an air of reminiscing than testifying. Still, the State scored points. The most damning testimony against the defendants came from McMichael who stated that he had followed the cart tracks from the murder scene all the way to the rear of Anton Happy's saloon and his stable; furthermore, that the floor of the stable contained red soil such as was found on the clothes and shoes of the victim, and that there was evidence that a chicken had recently been killed in the stable. McMichael did not mention the veil because, as he explained later, "I was not asked about it." With all that evidence, one can only wonder why Happy had not been arrested months before. In the hearing and the trial that followed, the whole police case would appear to have been put together to match Annie Edmonds' confession rather than being built on solid, independent evidence.[26]

At the end of the preliminary hearing, Justice Kennedy remanded the defendants without bail. That same morning, the grand jury, which had just been waiting for the hearing to conclude, handed up indictments charging the four with first-degree murder. Since they had just spent the last three days in court, the County Attorney saw no reason to haul them back into court; he read the indictments to them through the bars of their jail cell. They stood accused of murder in the first degree—and that was all. Despite lurid newspaper accounts, presumably based on Dr. Stevens' report that Maggie had been "debauched" repeatedly, neither rape nor assault was among the charges against any of the four. As the newspaper put it, there was nothing to do now except wait for trial. Lola Hindman was held as a material witness, occupying "comfortable apartments at the [county] jail" until her testimony was needed. Annie Edmonds, the State's star witness, remained free on her promise not to leave the city. [27]

The case was assigned to County Judge William D. Harris' Seventeenth District Court and set for trial on January 29, 1894. Both defense and prosecution were happy with the date and the Judge. They had already done most of their preparation for the preliminary hearing; legal maneuvering and delaying motions were unnecessary. Defense counsel asked for and was granted a writ of habeas corpus for Bob Miller on December 2, which made him a free man until the trial. The other three were not so lucky.[28]

Three developments in the case occurred in the interim between the preliminary hearing and the trial. At the end of October, Maggie's opal and pearl ring turned up in one of the city's pawnshops. Police got the names of the two persons who had pawned it and arrested Sam Smith, a white man, and a Negro woman identified only as "Prickett." Both were charged as "accessories after the fact." But what appeared to be a solid lead turned out to be a dead-end as neither could ultimately be linked to any of the defendants. About this same time, Annie began receiving threats against her life, including one that promised to blow her up with dynamite if she testified. She also told police that she had seen "suspicious characters" lurking around her house at night. Since her house was a well-known bagnio, suspicious-looking characters coming and going should not have been surprising, but police took the threats seriously and offered her protection. She declined the offer to have a policeman posted at her door—for good business reasons—and asked instead for a pistol to defend herself. Police cheerfully obliged. Finally, on January 24, just five days before the trial was scheduled to open, the newspapers reported that Annie had skipped town. The report turned out to be untrue, but police kept a close watch on Annie until her day in court. [29]

The State of Texas v. A. Happy, Jack Gunnells, Bob Miller, and John Witcher finally got underway on the morning of January 29, 1894, and immediately ran aground. The defense team of James Davis and B. D. Shropshire announced itself ready to proceed, but the prosecution team, County Attorney Gillespie and his assistant Wilson Gregg, was embarrassed to admit that all of its witnesses were not present; specifically its star witness, Annie Edmonds, had gone missing. The County Attorney asked for a continuance until the next term in April, which Judge Harris denied, but the Judge did adjourn the proceedings until the afternoon to give the State a chance to round up its witnesses. When court reconvened at one thirty with still no Annie, the Sheriff was ordered to find her. An hour later he stood before the Judge explaining that Annie was "ill in bed and unable to attend." That wrapped up the proceedings for the first day. Judge Harris dismissed the venire pool that had been sitting all day waiting to be examined and ordered the two sides to agree on another date, then adjourned the court *sine die*. There was one final item on the prosecution's agenda before the defendants were returned to jail: Gillespie informed the court that the State was dropping all charges against defendants Miller and Witcher. As Happy and Gunnells were led away, their former co-defendants walked out of court free men. It was just another surprising turn in a case that had more twists and turns than a mountain switchback.[30]

The trial of the two remaining defendants commenced on April 30, 1894, Judge Harris presiding. When Happy and Gunnells were brought into court, spectators, most of whom had never seen either man, gawked at the accused murderers. Belying his name, Anton Happy was an enfeebled graybeard, nearly seventy-eight years old and so crippled with arthritis, he could walk only with difficulty. With his wispy gray hair and shrunken form, Happy looked like many things but murderer was not one of them. He hailed from Germany originally but had lived in Fort Worth for at least thirteen years running his little saloon without attracting any attention. Yet here he was accused of the most heinous of crimes, rape and murder. His son-in-law and co-defendant was much younger, a self-styled sporting man who looked and dressed more like a common day laborer than a sport.[31]

After a jury was seated, the State began calling its witnesses, leading off with Dr. H. C. Stevens then following with Deputy Sheriff Gunnells, City Marshal Maddox, and Justice of the Peace Randle. Their testimony took up the whole day. The following day Officer McMichael, Sam Jones, Louis Reiney, and Frances Dodd testified for the State. None of them offered anything new over and above their testimony at the examining trial except McMichael, who casually pulled out the blood-caked veil that he had pocketed on the day of the crime. The defense took no exception to such blatant disregard of chain-of-evidence procedure, so it was duly entered as evidence. On cross-examination, McMichael stated that he had kept the veil at home since the murder hoping "to find a piece somewhere to match it." McMichael was followed on the stand by Sam Jones and Louis Reiney. Jones was clearly nervous and trying to stay as uninvolved as possible. Reiney attempted gallantly to avoid doing further damage to the victim's reputation, but questioning by both sides brought out Maggie's weakness for the bottle and unsavory lifestyle.[32]

Things picked up in the afternoon when the State put the previously indisposed Annie Edmonds on the stand. Since her previous no-show she had been a guest of the county while she waited for her court appearance. The "entire, absolute, and unvarnished" story that she had told Gillespie back in September had metamorphosed in the intervening eight months into an even better story, which differed in significant details from the original, although both were told under oath. As she explained things now, her house had not been any part of the crime, and everything she had witnessed had been observed through her rear window occurring either in Happy's saloon or in the yard in back of the saloon. As Oscar Gillespie walked her through her testimony, she described how on Sunday night, January 22, she had gone over to Happy's to get some beer and saw Maggie sitting at a table talking nonchalantly to Happy and his wife. After returning home, she heard loud voices coming from the saloon that she identified as belonging to Happy and Maggie. Through her window and the saloon window she could see Happy chasing Maggie around the barroom. Maggie got away and ran outside into the yard followed by Happy. He caught up with her and told her, "You God-damned bitch, if you get away I will get you again!" Then he dragged her back into the saloon. The following night, Monday, at approximately 2:00 a.m., Annie was again looking out her back window when she saw Maggie run out the back door of the saloon with Happy in hot pursuit again. This time, when he caught her, Annie heard a gunshot and then heard Maggie say, "Lord have mercy! Oh, Lord have mercy on me!" That was followed by another shot, then silence. The next thing she saw was four men loading "a woman" into a cart and pushing it down the alley going west. She also added that Bob Miller and John Witcher had visited her and Lola on Sunday and Monday nights but were gone by midnight the night Maggie was murdered.[33]

Annie was obviously the State's star witness, and when it came time for cross-examination, the defense vigorously attacked her testimony, managing to poke an embarrassing number of holes in it. She was forced to admit that she could not identify the body that was loaded into the cart as Maggie's, and that in her previous testimony under oath at the examining trial she had stated that she did not know who Maggie Tewmey was at the time of the murder. The defense also questioned her in detail about her line of work. (Out of consideration for their readers, the newspapers did not print this portion of her testimony.) When counsel asked her why Witcher and Miller were at her house that night she said she didn't have any idea! She admitted that Mrs. Happy had ordered Lola out of her husband's saloon before, but not Annie, and when asked directly if she were "mad" at either of the Happys for making her and Lola feel unwelcome, she replied that she bore them no ill will. The defense led her through her testimony again of how she *and Lola* had stood at her window and watched Happy chase Maggie around the yard *three or four times* Sunday night, then how she had watched a repeat performance the next night climaxed by Maggie's murder without doing a thing, not even ducking when bullets started flying. She explained that she had continued to watch the drama unfolding in the yard even after the first shot was fired because she had no fear of being hit, then backtracked and said that she had not been at the window at all when the shots were fired; she only heard them. She also said that it was "the noise" from the saloon that first attracted her attention, and that she had not been "working" either Sunday or Monday night although she had been home both nights.[34]

When the defense was done, Annie had been thoroughly discredited, but she was not done yet. Her Swiss-cheese testimony forced the State to redirect, which produced more contradictions, loose ends, and non sequiturs from the hopelessly discombobulated witness. Asked about the lighting on the two nights in question, she explained that there were two lights "in my house" (none outside). Asked why she had waited so long to come forward, she said she had been afraid to speak up because Lola (not the defendants!) had threatened to kill her. Given another chance by the prosecution to explain why she had changed her mind, she could only say lamely that her friends had convinced her *over drinks* that she would "never prosper until I told Mr.

Gillespie." These latest revelations led the defense to exercise its right to recross until, when it was finally over, Annie felt like she had been examined by the fiends of the Spanish Inquisition. She did not know whether she was coming or going when she was dismissed.[35]

The jury knew one thing for sure: Annie's story was not sufficient to convict anyone. It was not just that she had glibly admitted on the witness stand to using cocaine and being a prostitute; her testimony sounded suspiciously like it had been fed to her by the prosecution. Obviously, she had not learned her part well enough because the defense had poked it full of holes with the unwitting connivance of Annie herself. Even if the jury accepted her testimony at face value, they could not help but wonder why she had done nothing two nights running to help the poor victim, and why if she posed such a threat to the murderers as an eyewitness, they had not murdered her at the same time as Maggie or at the very least paid her to leave town. The defense did not even need to ask these questions because Annie incriminated herself with her facile, self-serving, and ever-changing testimony.[36]

Before the trial, Oscar Gillespie had cut Lola loose and placed all his chips on Annie, but after Annie's testimony, Lola's "free pass" proved useless. The defense demanded "an attachment" to bring Lola to court so she could testify. Judge Harris issued a bench warrant on the spot, and the Sheriff was dispatched to locate the lady in question and take her into custody.

While that was playing out, the trial continued into the afternoon. The next three witnesses put on the stand by a prosecution trying desperately to salvage its case were Maggie's niece and sister and a man from Houston who had been in the city the night of the murder. At the time he had been residing in the house that backed up to the yard where Maggie's body was found. He testified that he had heard shots around midnight that Monday night coming from the east, which was the direction of Happy's saloon two blocks away.[37]

After Mrs. Dodd and Mrs. Lawrence testified, the State rested. It was the defense's turn now. Spectators expected a parade of rebuttal witnesses, but the lawyers dropped a bombshell by announcing that they did not intend to call any additional witnesses. They rested their case. Clearly, Annie Edmonds had been their best witness, so good in fact that upon reflection, they decided there was no reason to even examine Lola Hindman or any other person on their list. When the

State informed the court that its case was also complete, Judge Harris announced that the argument phase would now commence. He limited each side to two hours but neither prosecution nor defense needed that long to make their closing arguments. During the State's turn, Gillespie dropped another bombshell by asking the jury to acquit Jack Gunnells because the evidence against him was not strong enough to sustain a conviction on the inevitable appeal. Unless the court chose to defy the County Attorney's wishes, Anton Happy now stood alone facing a first-degree murder charge. Unfortunately for Jack Gunnells, he would have to wait for the verdict of the jury at this point in the proceedings. He continued to sit glumly at the defendants' table. When it came the defense's turn, Davis reminded the jury of the complete lack of physical evidence against his client, the unreliability of the State's star witness, and the absence of any *credible* eyewitnesses to the crime. He might have added the shoddy investigation of the Fort Worth Police Department (FWPD) as another reason to acquit, but he didn't. By 6:00 p.m. the Judge was making his charge to the jury. He kept it simple, instructing them that they must either find both defendants guilty of first-degree murder "or nothing." Then he sent them off to their deliberations. Four hours later they still had not reached a verdict, so he ordered them sequestered for the night.[38]

The twelve men resumed their deliberations the next morning, May 2, and wrestled with the case all day. As night was falling on the third day of the trial, they asked the Judge to bring back Officer McMichael and Chief Maddox to repeat portions of their testimony, specifically about the cart tracks leading from the alley behind the outhouse. After hearing the relevant testimony, they retired to the jury room once again. Finally, at 9:00 Wednesday night, they notified the Judge that they were hopelessly deadlocked and asked to be discharged. After consulting with both the prosecution and defense, Judge Harris accepted the following verdict:

> We, the jury, find the defendant Jack Gunnells, not guilty as charged in the indictment. As to the defendant A. Happy, we find it impossible to agree upon a verdict.

Judge Harris then thanked the jurors and discharged them. Jack Gunnells walked out of the court a free man while Anton Happy almost

Maggie was a lifelong Catholic whose dubious lifestyle and sordid death did not prevent her from being buried in the Calvary (Catholic) section of Oakwood Cemetery. (Author's collection.)

broke down when he learned he would have to go back to jail pending the State's decision whether to try him again. Sheriff's deputies half carried him out to a buggy that would take him the short trip back to his cell. His lawyers filed a writ of habeas corpus the next day, which sprang him on bond while he waited for the wheels of justice to turn. He no longer had a business, and not much left of his life either, so he and Mrs. Happy decided to spend their remaining time living in the moment. In September they were arrested and fined in police court for public intoxication. They could barely scrape together the $54 fine.[39]

Eventually, all charges against Anton Happy were dropped. The County Attorney's Office had no desire to go through the expense and trouble of another trial with a case based almost solely on the testimony of Annie and Lola. And it was a good thing, too, because nine months later, the Texas Court of Criminal Appeals threw out Lola's deal with the County Attorney's Office because the theft charge and the murder case, with its related perjury charge, were "unconnected" and therefore could not be linked in a plea bargain.[40]

Like the rest of the city, the FWPD moved on, but Jim Maddox always had his own theory about the case. As he saw it, Maggie knew the four men well; they were all longtime drinking buddies. One aspect of that "friendship" included surrendering herself to their sexual pleasure when she was in her cups. The fact that her sister was quite well-off may have led the defendants to believe that she would bankroll their gambling and drinking indefinitely. But either she didn't, or else they tired of her. Or perhaps she finally resisted their advances. Whatever provoked the act, they did away with her as coldly as one might put down an old dog. Maddox could never prove any of this, however, and after the County Attorney decided to drop the case, he quit trying. But he never gave up his pet theory.[41]

Maggie Tewmey's murder went in the books as an unsolved case, which is not surprising. The investigation had been botched from the beginning by an appalling lack of attention to detail and even rudimentary professionalism. The crime scene was compromised, evidence was improperly handled, investigating officers did not take notes, and jurisdiction was never clearly established. On top of all that, the County Attorney's Office seems to have coached Annie and Lola to get their testimony against the four defendants. The fact that two of the defendants were set free even before the case came to trial, that the case against the third was dismissed by the prosecution during the trial, and that the last remaining defendant got a hung verdict is the final proof for the incompetence of the State. The simple fact is, the local authorities did not have either the training or the expertise to investigate a crime where so much of the case depended on forensics evidence and shrewd police work. The case was too complicated for the city or the county boys in 1893. Only Chief Maddox's dogged determination kept it alive for nine months.

Yet if Maggie's case was unsolved, it was far from forgotten. Thirteen years later it was back in the news as part of a retrospective of "Some of Fort Worth's Many Unsolved Murder Mysteries." The writer, *Star-Telegram* crime reporter J. B. Roberts, vaguely recalled some of the basics of the case but got all the details wrong, including the date of the crime, 1885; the victim's name, "Molly Tewmey"; and the name of the accused, "John Hoppy." Other inaccuracies he perpetrated included saying she was strangled by two men using strips torn from her skirt and that other portions of her skirt were stuffed in her mouth. The irony was that Jim Maddox, who had been police chief at the time of the murder, was back in the chief's office when the article was written in 1907, and the reporter claimed to have interviewed him for the story.[42]

J. B. Roberts' fanciful telling was not the last or even the worst misrepresentation of Maggie's story. In 1953, Fort Worth historian Oliver Knight spun the story off into another whole universe, or more accurately, a historical twilight zone, telling the story of "Sally," a "dance-hall girl" who was murdered in the Acre in a particularly grisly fashion. The context of the story suggests that it was 1887. Sally would be nothing more than a footnote in Fort Worth history except for the shocking manner of her death: She was found "nailed to an outhouse behind the dance hall where she worked."[43] Knight footnoted most of his stories, but strangely he provided no documentation for this one, which would lead one to believe that it was local lore he picked up in the course of researching *Fort Worth: Outpost on the Trinity*. In the years since *Outpost* was published, it has become the standard, one-volume history of Fort Worth, and thanks to Knight, Sally has achieved the status of historical celebrity. Local historians have always wondered about Sally; some of us have even combed through microfilmed rolls of old newspapers trying to find her, wondering why such a sensational story was not headline news in the Fort Worth or Dallas newspapers or both.

Now we know, and Sally can be put to rest once and for all. Her story is too similar to Maggie's to be coincidence: a poor, benighted woman, brutally murdered, Ripper-fashion, and nailed into an outhouse; a shocked city; an unsolved crime. All the basic elements are there. Sally is Maggie, filtered through journalistic imagination and years of careless retelling. What J. R. Roberts started, Oliver Knight put the stamp of historical fact on. But whereas Sally appears now to be nothing but a local legend, Maggie was a real, flesh-and-blood victim.

CHAPTER 7

Black Sheep Jeff Daggett

Jeff Daggett was bad news his whole life, from his unwelcome birth in 1863 to his unfortunate end fifty-four years later in a hail of bullets in the Tarrant County Courthouse. He was born in 1863 on the plantation of Captain Ephraim M. Daggett, remembered as the Father of Fort Worth. His mother was Matilda Smith, a slave on the plantation. It was a small plantation by the standards of the Old South, no more than ten or fifteen acres with the slave quarters right behind the big house. Slaves and their master's family lived and worked close together. Jeff's father was Ephraim "Bud" Daggett, the only son of Ephraim Merrell Daggett. Bud Daggett had been born in Kentucky in 1838 to E. M. and Pheniba Strauss Daggett. The mother died while Bud was still a child. The father fought in the Mexican War where he acquired the rank of captain while serving with the Texas Rangers. He came to Fort Worth in 1854 with his family, livestock, and slaves, settling on a survey about three-quarters of a mile south of the bluff. Daggett had remarried in the meantime, but Bud Daggett was mostly raised by a black mammy who was like a second mother. Growing up in a slave-owning family, race was a fact of life and living in such close proximity the lines between the races were sometimes blurred. With his father often away on business and being the oldest male in the household, Bud was the man of the place.[1]

A rare image of Captain E. M. Daggett (1810–1883), unacknowledged grandfather of Jeff Daggett. Seen here in a studio photograph, subsequently colorized, the youthful-appearing Daggett is probably in his fifties, which would date the picture sometime in the 1860s. No indication where it was taken or by whom. (Courtesy Fort Worth Public Library, Genealogy, Local History, and Archives Unit.)

He may have been the only son and even the man of the house in his father's absence, but E. B. Daggett was hardly the "good son." Just the opposite, he was the black sheep of the family, estranged from his father for most of his adult life. The son was such an embarrassment that in 1876 Daggett senior wrote out a will leaving all of his property to a nephew upon the old man's death. When E. B. subsequently married a white woman and started a respectable family, Daggett senior tore up the old will and wrote out a second one leaving everything to his daughter-in-law and whatever children she had by E. B. As for her husband, he remained the family outcast the rest of his life, and when Daggett senior died in 1883, his only son received nothing.[2]

What could E. B. have done to bring his father's undying opprobrium down on him? He was not a badman in a criminal sense. On the contrary, he held his head up high in the community, even serving a term on the City Council. His sin was not breaking one of the usual laws but violating racial taboos by committing miscegenation, which was also against the law but was never enforced against the slave-owning class. The crime that could not be named was having intimate relations with a family slave that produced an offspring, Jeff Daggett.

The boy who came into this world on July 3, 1864, was just one day shy of being "a real live nephew of his Uncle Sam."[3] More importantly, if he had been born a year later, he would have been born a free man. As it was, there was no birth certificate since Matilda was a slave, and for the rest of Jeff's life, public documents such as census records and death certificate listed his father as "unknown." His father was not unknown, just unnamed. The only clues that Jeff's parentage was unconventional were that he was routinely described as "mulatto" for the rest of his life and when he struck out on his own he proudly retained the last name of his former master. The facts that Bud Daggett was the only other adult male in the Daggett household besides the old man, and that Captain Daggett, who was widely known as a kindly and solicitous master, never made any post-Emancipation provision for Jeff, are corroborating evidence. If Jeff had been just another freed slave, rather than the awkward reminder of his son's illicit relationship, old man Daggett would have surely helped the young man get started in his new life as a free man. Silence does not mean guilt, but the complete absence of any contemporary reference to Jeff Daggett's connection to the white Daggett clan is, to say the least, suspicious. The clincher is the surname, which was not acquired naturally at birth (since slave mothers did not have last names to give to their children) but adopted willfully by the adult Jeff, thus establishing beyond a doubt his family roots. (See also the case of Hagar Tucker in chapter 3.) Jeff's genealogy was the Daggett family's dirty little secret, and although it was common knowledge in the little community on the Trinity, it was something that was never publicly acknowledged.[4]

In 1865, when news of the Emancipation Proclamation reached Texas, Ephraim Daggett freed his slaves, including Matilda, but he continued to take a paternal interest in their welfare. All "or nearly all of them" settled down nearby, "living within his call." Those who were old or unable to find work, he provided a home for life on his lands, while even those who moved away continued to come to him "for advice and assistance." The former master's relationship with his former slaves was a marvel to his friends and neighbors. It was said that the freedmen "worshipped him" and "were ever ready to go to him . . . at his bidding."[5]

After emancipation, Matilda stayed on as a servant in the Daggett household. Jeff grew up knowing whom his father was, living under the same roof with him, but since the official family line was that his father was unknown, he was forever after labeled a bastard. Being unacknowledged by his father yet still wearing the Daggett name made for a very confused and angry lad. Even his ethnic heritage was problematic since neither parent's race really claimed him, and in the Deep South, a man without strong roots in one race or the other could never be certain whether he was fish or fowl. Jeff's own conflicted feelings can be seen in the fact that he could never settle on a single surname: in city directories, court proceedings, and newspaper interviews, he used "Daggett"; when he married, however, and when the census taker came around, he called himself "Jeff Smith." If he ever forgot where he came from, he had only to roll up his sleeve and see the letters "J. D. S." (for Jefferson Daggett Smith) tattooed on one burly forearm.[6]

Jeff made things hard for himself by defying the laws and conventions of his father's world. He resented any and all authority and acted out his resentments at the slightest provocation. He carried a perpetual chip on his shoulder, ready to fight anybody at any time. In fact, he was an equal-opportunity brawler, picking fights without regard for race, creed, or color, making life hard for everyone who had the misfortune to cross his path. He had the attitude and physical tools to win most of his fights and under different circumstances might have had a successful career in the ring. But the discipline of training and even the simple rules of boxing were not for him. Instead of channeling his aggression he became a notorious hell-raiser and wastrel—an embarrassment to his white family and a source of heartbreak to his elderly mother. Following in his own father's footsteps, he sired an illegitimate son, but his parenting was limited to teaching the boy how to gamble and fight like his old man.[7]

As a physical specimen he inherited his grandfather's powerful physique only without the Captain's gracefulness and height. Jeff was a fireplug of a man, standing just five foot three and weighing 174 pounds. He had the classic short man's pugnacity, which may also have been a cover for his lack of formal education. He never learned the three Rs growing up in the servants' quarters. He reached adulthood still unable to read or write, but this did not prove an insurmountable obstacle when it came to making his way in the world. What did cause him no end of grief was what his prison record called "intemperate habits," meaning he drank and swore and fought too much. Like his grandfather he had a prickly pride and resented the frequent slurs that came his way. In 1885 he bashed a white man over the head with a club for some unknown insult, inflicting a "large gash" that brought a doctor and the police running. He was arrested but the charges were dropped, one suspects, because of his name. He was just twenty-one.[8]

Jeff's long rap sheet began before 1885 and included illegal gambling, disturbing the peace, petty theft, and aggravated assault. By the late 1880s the Fort Worth and Dallas newspapers practically ran a regular "Jeff Daggett" column to keep readers updated on his latest brushes with the law. In August 1888 he beat a white man so severely that he was indicted by a grand jury for assault with intent to kill. Four months later he got into another brouhaha with another white man but this time got the worst of it, being so "badly cut up" he was lucky to escape with his life. But the experience did not humble him or make him less belligerent. A month later he was arrested with stolen property in his possession. He beat that rap, but his gambling activities combined with his short fuse got him into trouble regularly.[9]

Jeff did not confine himself to fists, knives, and clubs when it came to conflict resolution. He was equally adept at using invective when his sense of honor was offended. Twice he was hauled into court for using "abusive language" against whites who he claimed had insulted him. Since the law in such cases was always going to be on the side of the whites, he lost. On the second occasion, he backed up the invective by waving a pistol at his defamer. Jeff's endless dust-ups eventually won him a certain kind of fame when the *Dallas Morning News* anointed him a "Third Ward celebrity." Whether he was a celebrity or just a hard case, he definitely got the attention of the white establishment that he hated so virulently, which may have been what he had in mind all along.[10]

Jeff's life did not have to be a war against the world. Growing up he had two advantages over his mother's people: he was lighter skinned than most blacks, and he always had enough money. Ironically, that combination also made him an object of envy and resentment among blacks. White society was not any more accepting, treating him as a second-class citizen or worse. He was described in the newspapers as a "Negro," a "colored" man, or a "Son of Sam," but in private conversations whites used more offensive terms that could not be printed in family newspapers. Sometimes he was also called "a maroon," which in the vernacular of the day referred to the distinctive eye pigmentation of many mulattos as well as to the mulatto individual himself. A Dallas newspaper characterized him as a "Third Ward Negro sporting man." Jeff Daggett was the "Zip Coon" stereotype at its worst.[11]

Jeff lived with his grandfather until Ephraim M. Daggett died in 1883, then at the age of nineteen he was forced to move out of the only home he had known and start taking some responsibility for himself. He met and married a mulatto woman named Hester that same year, and they set up house in Irish Town, a black neighborhood on the eastern edge of the Acre. It is not known what happened to Matilda, whether she had already died or left town, but either way she dropped out of the picture. Jeff's life might have gone in a different direction after marrying Hester. She was four years older than her husband and not inclined to rock the boat. Nothing is known of her life before she married him. They had three children, none of whom were living in 1910. If Jeff raised them to be like himself, it is no wonder. During the thirty-four years they were married, Hester remained far in the background while her husband carved an angry path through Fort Worth. Only once did she get into the newspapers, and that was when Jeff severely beat a white man for insulting her. While he might have been justified, he was still found guilty of assault in police court and fined five dollars plus costs.[12]

Jeff's decision to follow the career path of the "sporting man" (an actual career choice in the nineteenth century) is understandable. The gentleman gambler could enjoy a life of leisure, even respect. Luke Short and Bat Masterson were members of the white sporting fraternity. In Jeff's case, the decision was not hard; he had no desire to work as either a tenant farmer or a day laborer, the two occupations open to black men after Emancipation, so he chose the life of the sporting man. He opened a gambling joint in the Acre and did well. He was also smart enough to make himself useful to the authorities by "aiding them in finding thieves and other petty criminals in the Acre." He was so good at it, some unnamed officers praised him in the press in 1889 for being a big help to the police. In criminal circles that would have made him a snitch, but no man would dare call Jeff Daggett that to his face. Cooperating with the police was not something he did because he was public spirited but working another angle to get ahead, just like he used his race and family name. Besides enjoying the favor of the authorities provided a valuable entrée into white society. Gambling was still his first calling. His favorite haunts were the low dives in the Acre, and his principal associates were gamblers, thugs, and con men.[13]

Thanks at least in part to his friends uptown, he was able to build a successful gambling operation serving the black community. With his ever-present .45 and blackjack, he policed his own joint. When one of his monte dealers gambled away a "sack of silver" that belonged to the house playing poker, Jeff made an example of him by beating the man senseless. He was charged with assault, but since it was a "black thing" and Jeff was a friend of the police, the charges were dismissed. Jeff had a sweet deal, but like he did with everything else, he pushed it too far, crossing the line into new criminal territory when he murdered a man on the morning of June 18, 1889. The victim was Dick Vann, a gambler and sometime barber, who was also a regular at Jeff's gambling joint. The newspaper described Vann as "a half-breed Comanche Indian and Negro," not the sort of man who would have been found in the company of either "Gooseneck Bill" McDonald or Quanah Parker. Daggett put two bullets into Vann after the gambler had scammed some money off him and taken additional money by force from another one of Jeff's customers. That was two strikes against Vann, and Jeff did not need a third. The victim died about noontime. Two police officers went to Jeff's place and placed him under arrest.[14]

Jeff would not beat this latest rap, despite all his courthouse connections. He was denied bail and held in the county jail until indicted by the grand jury on September 10. To the credit of the Daggett family, they did not turn their back on him. Late that same afternoon, E. B. Daggett quietly sold a piece of property in the Daggett Addition to R. L. Carlock. News of the reason behind the quick sale got out, but that did not prevent the money from being put to good use helping pay for Jeff's defense.[15]

The charge was second-degree murder. He pleaded not guilty, and the trial was first put on the docket for September 27. That date came

JEFF DAGGETT, Saloon Man

In 1907 Jeff Daggett, "Saloon Man," was a respected businessman in the black community, a fact which was recognized in the Fort Worth Colored City Directory. Although it is a poor image, we can still see that Jeff knew how to "dress for success." (Courtesy Fort Worth Public Library, Genealogy, Local History, and Archives Unit.)

and passed and on October 6 Jeff's lawyers got a continuance. Pre-trial motions and legal maneuvering delayed it until March 1892. When his day of reckoning finally came, the all-white jury was less than sympathetic. They found him guilty and sentenced him to ten years in the state penitentiary. His lawyers filed an appeal, but quietly dropped it after an off-the-record deal with the county attorney's office promised Jeff time off for good behavior in return for dropping the appeal. He took the deal and was booked into Huntsville on April 5, 1892. The Daggett family connections back in Fort Worth quickly went to work, and a little over two years after being sent away, the governor issued a full pardon for Jeff on August 5, 1894. The prodigal son was back home in Fort Worth after serving just one-fifth of his sentence. At the time he was processed into Huntsville, as inmate number 7888, Jeff described himself as a "waiter." After being released he seemed determined to turn over a new leaf.[16]

He went from small-time gambler to community activist, joining the Republican Party, which was struggling to live up to the legacy of Abraham Lincoln, and got himself elected as a Third Ward delegate to the Republican's county-level convention in March 1904. He was one of four delegates from the local African American community at the convention, reflecting the national party's drive to create a "black and tan" alliance as a power base in the South. Unfortunately, none of the local black delegates were selected to represent Tarrant County at the state convention, and Jeff's political career died aborning.[17]

His new, reformed image was definitely less remunerative than his former life. He could only find employment as a janitor ("porter") or as a private security guard ("special officer"). He worked mostly as a porter, first at city hall, then later at the Moore Building.[18] Married life may also have worked a calming influence on him, or at least Hester did. She is barely mentioned in the historical record, but before Jeff's stretch in the penitentiary, they resided as a happy couple at 1408 Morgan Street. After he returned from Huntsville, they moved to 1503 Chambers Avenue, also in the Third Ward.[19]

After Huntsville, city fathers were glad to see Jeff turn his life around and give up the gambler's life in favor of honest employment. They were particularly pleased that he was no longer an embarrassment to the esteemed Daggett family. The Fort Worth Police Department even threw him a bone in 1909 when they made him a special officer on the city rolls. This was a rare sign of respect for a black man; Jeff was just the third to be so honored. His beat was (Frederick) Douglass Park, the city's only recreation area for African Americans, located just north of the Trinity River on undeveloped land.[20] As a commissioned special officer he was not on the city payroll, but drew a modest salary from the park's owner, Tom Mason. There were other perks, however, that came with being a special officer: the right to wear a badge, carry a gun, and call himself a "policeman." His grandfather would have been proud of him.

His commission would be revoked after just two months because once again he had overstepped the bounds. On the night of July 5, he attempted to question two suspicious-acting white men in the park, and despite the fact that Douglass Park had been designated a black park, whites were still inviolable there. The two took exception to being accosted by a Negro, even one with a badge and a gun, and administered a beating. When white officers arrived, they administered a second beating to emphasize the point. The two white men walked, Jeff spent the night in jail, and after he recovered, his special officer's commission was revoked.[21]

Convicted murderer "Jim Toots" (center) facing a very uncertain future in this 1895 photograph of the Tarrant County Jail gallows chamber. Special officer Jeff Daggett stands to his immediate left. (Courtesy Fort Worth Star-Telegram Collection, Special Collections, University of Texas at Arlington Library, Arlington, TX.)

By 1917 Daggett's earlier lapse of judgment had been forgiven, and he had his commission back. He was working as an "out-guard" or "doorkeeper," i.e., bouncer, at a Negro nightclub on the corner of Eleventh and Harding streets, which was in the middle of Irish Town. It was an area avoided by whites unless they were looking for trouble.[22]

On Saturday night, October 20, Tarrant County Detective Ben LeGett showed up at the door of the club and demanded entrance. Just the year before, LeGett had been a defense lawyer representing minority clients, but he had switched sides and gone to work for the county attorney's office. Now he was squaring off with one of the most dangerous men in Fort Worth. Ben LeGett was also as tough as they come. His boss, the county attorney, characterized Ben as "unusually vigilant in hunting negro lawbreakers," which was old boy codespeak for saying LeGett took a Klan-type approach to dealing with minorities. In the early twentieth century that was not a hindrance to working in law enforcement in Fort Worth.[23]

The man known as Ben LeGett (or Legett) was born James Benjamin LeGett in South Carolina in January 1866. The years after the Civil War were a bad time in South Carolina so the family came west, eventually settling in Texas. At eighteen he was a guard at the Rusk Penitentiary, the state's second oldest prison, in Cherokee County. From that he moved up to deputy sheriff for Cherokee County. Rusk's sizable African American population and Ben's Deep South roots made for a volatile tenure enforcing the law in the community. LeGett left Rusk and settled in West Texas where among other attractions there was hardly a black person to be seen. He was high sheriff of Lubbock County for one term (1896–1898) at a time when the county covered hundreds of square miles of the Texas Panhandle. When he left Lubbock he continued his westward migration, settling in Chaves County,

The "old" Tarrant County Jail at the time of this Labor Day parade, ca. 1898. The building was equipped with a gallows to accommodate executions that had been moved indoors in the 1880s. This is a rare photograph of the building. Jeff Daggett was standing on the jail's gallows beside Jim Toots in the 1895 photograph. (Courtesy Fort Worth Public Library, Genealogy, Local History, and Archives Unit.)

New Mexico, and trading in the badge for a herd of cattle and his own spread. He mixed easily with New Mexico Territory's large Hispanic population, which he apparently did not find as distasteful to his Southern sensibilities as African Americans. In 1907 he relocated to Fort Worth and hung out a shingle as a lawyer. How he learned the law is unclear because he never attended law school, and if he read law with an established lawyer, there is no record of it. At this time there was no state bar association in Texas so he did not have to demonstrate his familiarity with the law before hanging out his shingle. He practiced law in Fort Worth for nine years, representing defendant Louis Flores in one of the most famous murder cases in the city's history, the murder of Officer Peter Howard in 1915. (His client lost.) After the Flores trial in 1916, he gave up his law practice and returned to law enforcement, joining the County Attorney's Office as a Tarrant County detective in April 1917. Five months later, he was administering a dose of old-fashioned Southern justice to Jeff Daggett.[24]

In 1889 while living in Rusk, Ben had married Anna, and they had six children in the next eleven years, all of them except the last born in Texas; the youngest was born in New Mexico. When Ben left New Mexico he not only turned his back on stock raising, he also left behind his family. He arrived in Fort Worth alone and declared himself a "widower." In 1910 or 1911 he married Lottie, fourteen years his junior, and started a new family. By 1917, James B. LeGett was firmly established in Fort Worth as a husband, father, and solid member of the community.[25]

On the evening of October 20, 1917, LeGett showed up at the black nightclub where Jeff Daggett worked security and demanded entrance, claiming to have "official business" inside. The Detective's business there was never specified, but he was there without a warrant or even backup, which was a no-no even in those days. He later issued a statement to the press that such clubs were "the central places of meeting for all the criminal Negroes and [also] where the biggest part of crimes committed by Negroes are fermented [*sic*]," which still did not address the question of what he was doing there on that particular night. There is no uncertainty about what happened next. Daggett was not about to step aside for any man, but especially a white man far off his turf. He was shorter than LeGett but outweighed the Detective and was confident he could take him if it got physical. But LeGett had no intention of getting into an argument or a street brawl. When Daggett refused to step aside, LeGett pulled out his gun and administered a pistol-whipping, then stepped over Daggett's body and entered the club. It all happened so fast, Jeff never knew what hit him. By the time he came to, LeGett had finished his business, whatever it was, and left. Nursing a sore head, Daggett vowed "to get" his assailant the next time he saw him.[26]

It did not take long for that threat to get back to LeGett nor for the two men to meet up again. On Tuesday afternoon, October 23, at about four o'clock, Daggett came to the courthouse to lodge a formal complaint against the Detective who had assaulted him. This was the new, responsible Jeff. In the old days, he would have simply hunted LeGett down and killed him. This time he had witnesses and intended to take legal action. But this was still the Jim Crow era, and there were very different standards of justice for whites and blacks. At the courthouse, he was not allowed to use the front doors but had to enter through the basement doors like all members of his race, and make no mistake about it; as far as white Fort Worth was concerned, Jeff Daggett was a Negro, regardless of who his daddy was. He entered on the north side of the building and took the elevator up to the second floor where the county attorney's office was located. When he did not find Marshall Spoonts in, he went back down to the first floor looking for anyone in authority to hear his complaint. He found Commissioners Rufe Snow and O. W. Gibbons, but got no sympathy from either of them. Before walking away, however, he made the mistake of uttering threats against LeGett. He was on his way back upstairs when Ben LeGett showed up.[27]

Snow and Gibbons had located County Attorney Spoonts and informed him that Daggett was in the building looking for trouble, and he hurried off to find LeGett. He found the Detective at the County Tax Assessor's Office and alerted him to the threat. LeGett was standing in the hallway when he saw Daggett inside the elevator cage on the other side of the rotunda and stalked over to confront him. Jim Shivers, the Negro elevator operator, saw him coming and held the door, thinking he merely wanted to ride to another floor. LeGett stopped at the door and pulled out a pistol, firing three shots at point-blank range. All three found their target, striking Daggett in the neck, shoulder, and right breast. Jeff died where he stood. Neither man had said a word before the shooting started. Daggett did not even have time to react, although unarmed and trapped in the elevator cage, there is little he could have done. In the tradition of Luke Short, Wyatt Earp, and countless other Western shootists who lived to a ripe old age, LeGett was not about to give his opponent a fair chance to defend himself. It was kill or be killed; shoot first and ask questions later, such as, "Have you been threatening me?" "Are you looking for trouble?" Shall we take this outside?" But this was not an invitation to a duel or a gentlemanly dispute and had their situations been reversed, Jeff Daggett would have done the same thing. For the second time, LeGett had effortlessly gotten the drop on Jeff, who had long enjoyed the reputation of being a tough guy and a terror to his enemies. There would be no third act in this drama.

A stunned crowd in the rotunda, including various county officials, law officers, and ordinary citizens, stood frozen as the last echoes of the gunshots faded. When they did finally react, they did one of two things: either ran to get as far away as possible in case there was more shooting; or raced over to the elevator to stare down at Jeff Daggett. One of the officials present who would play a key role in what followed was Justice of the Peace Hugh Small.

The aftermath was anticlimactic and more than a little bizarre. While LeGett calmly surrendered himself to his friends, several men got the unwelcome job of seeing to the victim. He was beyond medical help, so they used the elevator to take the body downstairs and dump it in a corner of Justice Small's courtroom. It would remain there until Jeffrey & Company, the Negro mortuary, could come and take it away. They searched the dead man's clothes and found no weapon, only four shotgun shells, and a pocketknife. Meanwhile, an impromptu inquest was convened in the courtroom, Hugh Small presiding. The JP charged Ben LeGett with murder and released him on $1,000 bond. It only took a matter of minutes.[28]

Two days later (Thursday), Jeff Daggett was quietly laid to rest in Old Trinity Cemetery, the segregated section of Oakwood. Besides Hester, the funeral was attended by business acquaintances from the black sporting fraternity and former political allies from the old "black and tan" alliance days. It would be comforting to think that white members of the Daggett clan were also present to pay their final respects, but there is no indication in the scanty newspaper reports that they were there.

The city's white community did, however, close ranks behind one of their own. Public officials were unanimous in defending Ben LeGett and denouncing Jeff Daggett. The latter's reputation made it easy to cast him as the villain, not the victim. Rumor and innuendo did the rest, compounded by irresponsible reporting. The day after the shooting, the *Fort Worth Star-Telegram* led off its account with a report that Daggett had already tried to kill LeGett once by taking potshots at someone in an auto near the Stop Six neighborhood whom he believed to be the Detective. It was not, and nobody knew why Daggett was shooting in the first place. Since Daggett had more than a few enemies and had never been shy about confronting them, it could have been anybody in the car. The rest of the story explained how Daggett had come to the courthouse looking for LeGett, even declaring to witnesses, "They might barbecue my hide but I'll get him first!" Those words were reportedly overheard by Marshall Spoonts while he was standing across the street from the courthouse. Regarding the killing of Jeff Daggett, which resembled nothing so much as an execution-style slaying, the newspaper explained, "Though he carried no weapon, Daggett had four shotgun shells in his pocket." The *Star-Telegram* completed its character assassination by noting that Daggett "is said to have killed two or three Negroes" previously, and the *Star-Telegram* was not even the most racist of Fort Worth's two daily newspapers; that would have been the *Fort Worth Record*. With the race card in play and virtually all public officials on board, there was little doubt how the criminal justice system would deal with Ben LeGett.[29]

The case did not come to trial for more than a year, during which time Ben LeGett not only walked around a free man, but continued to work as a county detective. After twelve months of the case being in limbo, county officials were pressured to bring closure to the affair. Better to go through the motions of a trial than to try to sweep things under the rug. LeGett was formally indicted by the grand jury on November 8, 1918. The indictment said the defendant did "unlawfully with malice aforethought, kill and murder one Jeff Daggett by shooting him with a pistol, from the effects of which said shooting, the said Jeff Daggett did then and there die." The defendant pleaded not guilty, of course, but what made the case more interesting than most was the list of subpoenaed witnesses. It represented a Who's Who of county government: County Attorney Spoonts and Assistant County

Attorney Frederick Garland “Fritz” Lanham; and County Commissioners Rufe Snow, H. R. Wall, and James Childress. Spoonts was at the trial not only as a witness for the defense but as the prosecutor for the State, a conflict of interest that did not seem to trouble anyone unduly.[30]

On November 13, 1918, Ben LeGett’s trial opened in Criminal District Court.[31] The prosecution could generously be described as halfhearted while the defense team had more lawyers than a state bar convention. The defendant pleaded simple self-defense. The State asked for a second-degree murder conviction, and the deck was stacked against it. The testimony of two county commissioners and the county attorney was sufficient to establish that the deceased had threatened LeGett’s life and, equally important, that LeGett had been informed of the threat, giving him the right to arm himself and preemptively shoot his would-be assailant. County Attorney Spoonts testified that he had been at the courthouse that day when Commissioners Gibbons and Snow “told me of the threats and I informed LeGett without loss of time.” No one seems to have asked the obvious questions, such as how did Gibbons and Snow come to inform Spoonts of the threat? Did they seek him out or was it a chance encounter? How did Spoonts find LeGett to give him the warning? If Daggett was uttering threats, why didn’t someone arrest him instead of letting him walk around the courthouse? What was LeGett doing standing around the hallway if he had just been warned his life was in danger? And was he already armed when informed that Daggett was looking for him or did he arm himself and then go looking for the other man? These were all valid questions, but none of them were raised at the trial. The jury also seemed to have disregarded the fact that Daggett was unarmed and trapped inside an elevator at the time he was shot, which called into question the whole premise that he was looking to kill LeGett. By all appearances, the prosecution merely went through the motions, and the jury already had its mind made up before retiring for its deliberations. This was an open-and-shut case for all the wrong reasons. Everyone in the courthouse rotunda that afternoon had been a friend or colleague of Ben LeGett. He was a member of the old boys’ network. On the other side was a black man with a beef, uttering empty threats and challenging the cozy power structure at the courthouse. The trial lasted just one day, and the jurors’ seats in the jury box barely had time to cool before those gentlemen brought back a verdict of not guilty. To no one's surprise, Ben LeGett walked out of the Tarrant County Courthouse a free man.

Jeff Daggett's story resonates for reasons beyond the simple facts of his life. There was more to his death than just a personal feud between two men. As a mulatto, Daggett had for too long been an affront to white society, a violation of "natural law" and an uppity black man trying to act white. On top of all that, the incident occurred just four years after the 1913 Third Ward race riot provoked by the murder of policeman John Ogletree. It was a time when Fort Worth's white population was growing increasingly uncomfortable with its burgeoning black minority, and white authorities were even more uncomfortable with black men having guns and badges. The lines were clearly drawn. No black officer, regardless of his rank or status, was permitted to arrest any white person. That was an immutable law of Southern-style justice, and Jeff Daggett in particular because of his race and being only a "special policeman" would not have been considered a member of the exclusive lawman's fraternity. He made a serious error in judgment when he tried to stop Detective LeGett at the entrance to the Negro nightclub, just as he had made a serious error in judgment eight years earlier when he tried to stop the two white men in Douglass Park. LeGett, on the other hand, obviously felt no need to explain himself, not even to a fellow officer, and had no qualms about assaulting that selfsame officer when pressed. Later, at the courthouse, circumstances continued to build toward a fatal climax. Daggett would never have been granted the run of the place if he had not been well known to those working there. But he was pushing his luck strolling around the building because he was perceived as a black man, there to cause trouble. Finally, Ben LeGett was not just any law officer; he was a respected veteran with a reputation for being hard on lawbreakers and not just African Americans.[32] This combination of circumstances and bigotry coupled with his own belligerence proved fatal for Jeff Daggett and provided yet another argument for those who believed that the last thing law enforcement needed was black officers. Better to keep things the way they had always been. Jeff Daggett was no innocent victim, but he did not deserve to die the way he did. If the law enforcement community had not cut him so much slack on previous occasions when he crossed the line, perhaps he would not have been in the courthouse on that Tuesday afternoon. It seems clear he was not looking to kill Ben LeGett at that time. What would have happened if he had caught up with LeGett before the Detective found him is uncertain, but knowing the two men, we can assume it would not have been pretty. Daggett had a permanent chip on his shoulder and was not above killing an opponent, but LeGett was a racist and a loose cannon, who saw nothing wrong in assaulting anyone who got in his way or even shooting down an unarmed man. There were no heroes and no winners in this affair.

Ben LeGett's career in law enforcement lost steam after this. He left the County Attorney's Office and became a deputy for Sheriff Sterling P. Clark, a demotion. A few years later he left law enforcement altogether and moved to Clackamas County, Oregon, with his wife, Lottie, and their child. There he took up chicken farming as Jim Legett, dying on July 1, 1936. It is doubtful if his fellow farmers knew the full story of his checkered past as a Texas lawman.[33]

Unlike the two families of Thomas Jefferson, his white descendants and the offspring of his relationship with slave Sally Heming, the Daggett family of Fort Worth never reconciled the black and the white sides of the family. As far as can be determined, they never even acknowledged each other. Considering the generations of hard feelings in the extended Jefferson-Heming family before they finally reconciled, perhaps that was for the best, since, as the Scriptures say, "He that troubleth his own house shall inherit the wind."

CHAPTER 8

Quanah Parker: Fort Worth's Adopted Native Son

In the heart of the Fort Worth Stockyards National Historic District stands a statue of legendary Comanche Chief Quanah Parker. It is fitting that the statue stands in front of a hotel because Quanah himself was never more than a visitor to Fort Worth. He never resided here, did not have family roots here, and visited the city only rarely. Yet this son of a Comanche father and an Anglo mother became Fort Worth's "native son" in the truest sense of that term. The city virtually adopted him. City fathers such as W. T. "Tom" Waggoner and Samuel Burk Burnett called him friend and he always had a special place in his heart for the town even while making a home among his people in Oklahoma. How Quanah Parker came to be Fort Worth's Native Son is one of our city's great stories.

It is the remarkable story of a man straddling two cultures, alternately embraced and rejected by both, who in the end helped heal the wounds of war and hatred. He was born and grew up in the world of the fearsome Comanches but died in the white man's world after making peace with his people's longtime enemies. His given name, Quanah, was Native American and the only name he needed among his father's people. Years later he added the surname Parker as acknowledgment of the white half of his ancestry. The two names symbolized the two worlds that Quanah Parker lived in.

The A. F. Corning daguerreotype of Cynthia Ann Parker and daughter, taken in Fort Worth in December 1860, is one of only two known images of Cynthia Ann. The miserable woman staring into the camera with her hair chopped off—a traditional Comanche sign of mourning—believed her husband and sons were dead and her bleak future was as a "captive" of the whites. (Author's collection.)

Quanah is an elusive historical figure. Take his birth date, for instance. He once wrote a friend offhandedly that he thought he had been born "about 1850," yet the subsequent chronology of his life does not fit someone born in 1850. The authoritative *New Handbook of Texas* states that he was born "about 1845." Various biographers have placed the date as early as 1845 and as late as 1852. There is no way of telling for certain since the Plains Indians relied on oral history to preserve their history, not written records, so there is no documentation for any of the suggested dates. However, 1845 seems most likely based on the chronology of his subsequent life.[1]

By Quanah's own account, as related years later to Charles Goodnight, he was born in a Comanche tepee in the shadow of Oklahoma's Wichita Mountains. His mother was Cynthia Ann Parker, who had been captured in May 1836 by a large Comanche-Kiowa-Caddo war party in a raid on the Parker family compound at the headwaters of the Navasota River in central Texas. She was nine years old at the time and would not see her family again for twenty-four years. The raiders escaped with five white captives, including Cynthia Ann and her brother John. The Comanche might have ransomed her back to her people, which is what happened to the other four captives, but they admired her toughness and her striking blue eyes. So they adopted her into the Quahade ("Antelope-eaters") band, giving her the name Naduah ("Someone Found").[2] A few years later, Chief Peta Nocona (or Noconi) took her as his wife. According to Comanche lore, Naduah was the only wife Peta Nocona ever had, an extremely rare departure from tribal custom. Although not a "Boston marriage," the term then current for a proper church or civil ceremony, theirs proved a long and happy union on both sides. Cynthia Ann grew into womanhood thoroughly assimilated into the culture of those who called themselves Numunuh ("the People"), and the three children she had by him were all raised in the Comanche way. Quanah's given name translates as "the Eagle," and indeed he would soar higher than any other of his people in Native American history. By 1860, he had two siblings, a ten-year-old brother, Pee-nah, usually translated as "Pecos," and an infant sister, Toh-Tsee-Ah, *aka* "Topsannah" or "Prairie Flower."[3]

Quanah Parker's formative years coincided with the height of Comanche power in Texas. Originally, the tribe was a branch of the Shoshones who rode out of the Wind River region of Wyoming a century earlier and settled on the southwestern plains where they perfected a remarkable talent for buffalo hunting and raiding. Comanches lived up to the name given to them by the Utes, "the people who fight all the time," ranging from Kansas and Colorado all the way down into Mexico. International boundaries and state borders meant nothing to them. They made war indiscriminately on other Indian tribes and white settlers. Texans retaliated just as bloodily against the Comanches whenever they could catch them. At the time Quanah was born, the Comanches were at the height of their power, battling rival tribes and encroaching Anglo settlements for possession of a sprawling territory known as "Comancheria." After the Civil War, the Comanches went into rapid decline as an independent power on the Great Plains.[4]

On December 18, 1860, Cynthia Ann was recaptured by a white raiding party on the Comanches' winter camp on the Pease River near the Oklahoma border. The raiders were led by future Texas governor Lawrence Sullivan "Sul" Ross. The Quahades, mostly women and children, were caught off guard and massacred, including the woman who had been a companion to Cynthia Ann and a second mother to Quanah. Cynthia Ann, who was nursing Toh-Tsee-Ah at the time, was recognized as white and returned to her white family. Quanah, Pee-nah, and their father were away from the camp on a hunting expedition at the time, so they, too, survived.[5]

After entering politics Sul Ross would tell the self-serving story that he personally had killed Peta Nocona that day, an assertion that Quanah vigorously refuted all his life, telling a Texas audience in 1909, "This . . . damn lie. Sul Ross no kill my father. My father no there on Tongue River [*sic*]. Gone to Plains for hunting." The following year, at a public event held in Dallas to honor him, he told the audience he wanted to set the record straight. "Texas history says General Ross killed my father. The old Indians tell me that not so. He no kill my father. I want to get that in Texas history straight up."[6]

Cynthia Ann began her long, unhappy return to civilization at Camp Cooper. Ross and the others thought they were liberating her, but they could not have been more wrong. Her uncle, Colonel Isaac Parker, identified her, and escorted her on the return trip. They came back through "Fort Town" (Fort Worth) on the way to his homestead near Birdville in northeast Tarrant County. Mother and child were objects of curiosity and pity, which only reinforced her belief that whites were no longer her people. Local lore says that school was closed the day Cynthia Ann arrived in Fort Worth so that all the town's children could come and stare at the strange pair on display in the general store, the mother clutching her tiny child to her breast. The town photographer, A. F. Corning, was summoned to record the event for posterity.[7]

Although returned to her birth family, at heart Cynthia Ann remained a Comanche. The Parkers had to forcibly prevent her from leaving. The Texas legislature appointed Isaac and Benjamin Parker her legal guardians, but she was bounced around among members of the family. She only remained at Birdville three months and never returned to the Fort Worth area. The sense of isolation and cultural shock she had overcome twenty-five years earlier proved too much to endure this time. She learned that Pee-nah, or Pecos, had survived the Pease River raid, but then came the news that he had died of smallpox in 1863. That same year, five-year-old Toh-Tsee-Ah died of the fever.

In 1870, at the age of forty-three, Cynthia Ann herself died. The official cause was influenza but most people who knew her believed she had grieved herself to death. She never saw her sons or husband again after December 1860. She was buried in Fosterville Cemetery, Anderson County, in the same grave as Toh-Tsee-Ah.[8]

Quanah was not present when his mother died, nor at her funeral. If he had shown up for either event, he would have been promptly seized, perhaps even killed. Despite being separated from her for most of his life, the bond between them was undeniable. In Native American culture, children growing up spent their childhood years in the company of the womenfolk while the men were mostly away hunting and making war. It is no surprise that Quanah so cherished the memory of his mother. He never outgrew her influence and moreover, always believed they would be reunited in the next life. He told a sympathetic Anglo audience many years later,

> My mother was a good woman whom I always cherished. She has gone to her resting place. I, myself, may die at any time. When I do I want to meet my mother in the great beyond.[9]

He held her memory so dear that his only request when he first came in to the reservation was for help to find where she was buried, and after he traded in his tepee for a house, he commissioned an oil painting of her (from the famous photograph) to hang in his bedroom.[10] When one of his daughters married A. C. Birdsong, who worked for the Indian Service in Oklahoma, Quanah enlisted his son-in-law's help in locating Cynthia Ann's grave. Birdsong and others unearthed the remains of mother and child and transported them to Oklahoma. Upon first seeing the pitiful remains, Quanah asked Birdsong if he was sure it was Cynthia Ann. Birdsong assured him it was, but Quanah asked a second time. Upon being reassured again, he commented simply, "Then I am satisfied. I have looked for a long time." Quanah had his mother and sister reinterred together in the same casket in Post Oak Cemetery near Cache, Oklahoma, and bought an adjacent plot so he could be buried next to them eventually.[11]

Quanah's father died two or three years after the Pease River fight, still grieving the loss of his wife and daughter. When Quanah lost Pee-nah it was the fourth personal loss in young Quanah's life.

In March 1909, Quanah (center, on white horse) and some friends dressed up in full native regalia to put on a show in the North Side Coliseum. The audience consisted of manufacturers attending the thirteenth annual National Feeders and Breeders Show (Fat Stock Show). This particular show was one of the first put on in the recently completed Coliseum. The picture is taken from the west side bleachers. (Courtesy North Fort Worth Historical Society.)

Compounding the multiple tragedies was that, reportedly, it was only on Peta Nocona's deathbed that the old chief informed Quanah that his mother had not been Naduah, full-blooded Comanche, but Cynthia Ann, white captive. Whether this is true or not, he must have already realized that his mother was not of Indian blood.[12]

The next decade saw Quanah's star rise among the Comanches as he grew into manhood. He easily assumed the mantle of war chief because all his boyhood had been spent training to be a warrior fighting for plunder, honor, revenge. It was how Comanche boys were raised. By the time he turned fifteen he had already been on his first raid and killed his first enemy, thereby performing the traditional blood rite of passage for a Comanche male. He was now a member of a warrior caste as ferocious as the Don Cossacks of Russia or the Mongols of China.

In December 1885, the beaux-arts-style Pickwick Hotel, just recently opened, was Fort Worth's finest, with gas lighting, first-class restaurant and bar, and private bathrooms with some rooms. Its location at Main and Fourth was Fort Worth's "hotel corner" for ninety years (1870s–1960s). Quanah and Yellow Bear only rated the hotel's "annex," but the fact that they were even accepted as guests is a mark of what esteem Quanah was held in—as well as the high-powered friends he had. (Drawing prepared by Bob Smith, Fort Worth architect.)

He was a magnificent specimen of manhood, possessing the best qualities of his two peoples. Typically, the Comanches were short with stubby legs, but having all the physical tools to survive in the harsh environment of the Great Plains. They also possessed a natural dignity. One contemporary observer described them as "uncommonly fine-looking men and women . . . muscular and athletic." Anglos tended to be taller, leaner. Quanah combined the compact, powerful muscles of his father's people, with the longer build of his mother's people. By the time he reached adulthood, he stood more than six feet tall, a fact emphasized by his erect carriage. He had the light gray eyes characteristic of his mother's people, but otherwise his face was all Comanche, with high cheekbones, a jutting brow and prominent, Roman nose. He learned the ways of his father's people. According to whites who regularly dealt with them, Comanches were "cunning" but also "generous to a fault," and "mostly honest." These things were drilled into them from birth. Unfortunately for whites, they were also merciless in war.[13]

Quanah led his share of raids on the Comanches' enemies, yet he never displayed the cruelty or taste for blood that his father's people were notorious for. His name was never associated with the torture of captives or the massacre of innocents, although this may have been less a matter of historical fact than of rewriting history by later white apologists.[14]

Quanah took a Comanche wife, To-nar-cy, stealing her from the tepee of her father, before he was twenty. They never had any children, but he was loyal to her in the Indian way the rest of his life.[15] By 1867 he was sitting in the Quahade councils of war, and joined the older chiefs in rejecting the Medicine Lodge Treaty whereby all the Southern Plains Indians agreed to settle down in the Oklahoma Territory and submit to assimilation.[16]

Quanah was always a mixture of his two heritages, white and Indian, as these two studio photos show. The one on the left was taken in the 1870s, the one on the right, in the 1880s. In both photos he wears his hair braided and ears pierced in the Indian fashion, yet is dressed in a white man's suit and tie. (Young Quanah courtesy University of Oklahoma Library, Western History Collections; Older Quanah courtesy Fort Worth Public Library, Genealogy, Local History, and Archives Unit.)

This photograph of a still-young Quanah, ca. 1880s, shows him sitting in full Comanche regalia in his bedroom at Star House. Note the painting of Cynthia Ann and Toh-Tsee-Ah (from the photograph) in the chair beside him, suggesting that he had just gotten it but had not made space for it on the wall yet. (Courtesy Research Center of the Oklahoma Historical Society.)

The Quahade held out for another seven years. During that time they launched the last Indian raid into Tarrant County in June 1871, chasing homesteaders John P. Daggett and John B. York through the scrub oak north of town, but there were no deaths and no kidnappings on this occasion. Subsequently, Indian depredations continued to plague Parker County, due west of Tarrant, but Fort Worth's days as a frontier settlement were over.[17]

The Quahade took one more shot at defending their ancestral lands against white encroachment in June 1874 when Quanah led a war party of some 250–300 warriors against twenty-eight buffalo hunters who were forted up in a trading post known as Adobe Walls on the Canadian River. The attack was repulsed with heavy Indian losses, and Quanah himself was wounded. Afterwards, even the most diehard Comanches had to admit the truth: the white man owned the Great Plains, and their life of freedom was over. There was no longer any place to hide and no way to survive on the run. In May 1875 Quanah led the pitiful remnants of the Quahade band—fewer than 100 men, women, and children—to Fort Sill, Oklahoma, and surrendered to Colonel Ranald Mackenzie.[18] Quanah identified himself to Mackenzie simply as war chief of the Comanches and son of Cynthia Ann Parker, although at the time he did not know if she was alive or dead.[19] Quanah promised the colonel that he would diligently apply himself to adopting the white man's ways.

The Comanches reluctantly settled down to reservation life, living on handouts and staying within the boundaries set by the U.S. government. Quanah's native intelligence and flexibility allowed him to make the transition to reservation life with the same ease that he had shown going from being a boy to being a warrior. Government agents, the new overlords of the Plains Indians, recognized his leadership qualities and designated him a "tribal chief" over all the Comanches, to serve as a liaison between his people and the Bureau of Indian Affairs. In effect, it represented a promotion from being merely a war chief of the Quahade. He proved a shrewd and pragmatic leader, encouraging the Comanches to take up stock raising and farming, educate their young in government schools, and sign contracts with whites. In return, he was embraced by the overlords as an "assimilationist," who could be a role model to his fellow Comanches.

Led by Quanah, many Comanche males rode the capitalist trail and became relatively prosperous by leasing their grazing lands to white cattle barons such as Samuel Burk Burnett and W. T. Waggoner, both of whom eventually called Fort Worth home. The first leases were signed in 1883, a proud day for Quanah. He himself proved to be a shrewd stockman who proved as successful at managing his herds and lands and he had been at raiding and making war. The money he made from leasing his grazing lands, he invested in railroad stocks and real estate, becoming a businessman of some means, perhaps even the wealthiest Native American in the United States at the time.[20] His friends, Burk Burnett and Tom Waggoner, built him a spacious ranch-style house at the foot of the Wichita Mountains, which he named "Star House" for the distinctive white stars painted on the roof, but he spent as much time on the road as he did at home.[21] He traveled widely on business and tribal affairs. He participated in Wild West shows, posed for photographs, and gave speeches, which were eloquent in their construction if not in their English vocabulary.

Along with his personal wealth, his influence also grew. Washington consulted him on Indian affairs, whites feted him as a "noble savage." Quanah, Texas, dubbed a "Panhandle metropolis" after it was founded in 1886, was named for him, and the Quanah, Acme and Pacific Railway was dubbed the "Quanah Line" by those it served.[22] Although the title "tribal chief" came from whites who needed to know they were dealing with the head man, his own people treated him with deference, too, first, because he had proved himself as a warrior, and, second, because white authorities listened to him. He served as a judge on Comanche tribal courts, which were a combination of white man's process and Indian judges, and encouraged the establishment of a tribal police force to assist white authorities in maintaining law and order on the reservation.[23]

Chief Quanah became the leader of the so-called "progressives" (*aka* "blanket Indians") among the Comanches, advocating, among other actions, leasing Indian land to white cattlemen like Texan Burk Burnett. Burnett came to see Parker, and they not only hammered out a business deal, they forged a friendship that began in 1882 and lasted the rest of their lives. The crusty cattleman admired the shrewd, scrupulously honest Indian chief. Burnett got the use of 300,000 prime acres of pasturage and the Comanche got six and a half cents per acre. After Burnett built a home in Fort Worth in 1900, Parker was welcome at the Ninth and Lamar residence whenever he was in town. Many years later, Quanah said of Burnett, "I got one good friend, Burk Burnett. He big-hearted, rich man, cowman. Help my people good deal."[24]

Not impressed by Parker's business dealings and friendships with the white man were the more traditional members of the tribe. They denounced him as a half-breed lackey of the whites, an "Uncle Tomtom," as it were, criticizing his ostentatious lifestyle, his affectation for white man's clothes, and his publicity seeking. What they failed to recognize was that the same pragmatic, openhanded qualities that made him a leader of his own people also allowed him to move easily in white society. He learned to drive an automobile and, when traveling, wore a business suit complete with patent leather shoes and bowler hat. Yet he never completely turned his back on tribal ways. Rather, he walked a thin line between the two races. He preferred moccasins instead of boots and under his very bowler wore his hair in long braids down his back.[25] He also remained faithful to the old religious ways. Historically, the Comanches had never practiced organized religion, but they did believe in spirits and mystical visions. Quanah encouraged them to keep praying to the ancient spirits and even led the movement to use peyote in their religious ceremonies, which helped them cope with the humiliations of being "blanket Indians." Here again, he mixed white and Indian heritage in his religion, practicing a highly personal brand of Christianity along with peyote worship, seeing no apparent contradiction in his beliefs. His personal use of peyote coupled with his open advocacy of it among his people would eventually result in his being recognized as a founding father of the Native American Church.[26]

He made it his life's mission to keep peace between the two races. Under his leadership, the Comanches did not join the popular uprising known as the Ghost Dance movement when it swept through the Plains Indians around 1890, thereby avoiding the excesses committed by the Sioux up north. Quanah himself seems to have received a free pass from whites for his years of leading war parties. Ranald Mackenzie declared that he "certainly should not be held responsible for the sins of former generations of Comanches," ignoring Quanah's own past aggressions.[27]

In preserving the old Comanche family structure, however, he was on shakier ground. Comanche men had always been polygamists, and Quanah stubbornly retained that part of his heritage. Estimates of the number of wives he took during his lifetime vary from six to nine, and at the time of his death in 1911 two were still living under his roof.[28] Ironically, this defiance of Victorian morals got him into more trouble with the authorities than his years of raiding white settlements ever did! Government agents sniffed at his "much married condition," and even thought they had convinced him to get rid of all but one. In 1897 he promised the Secretary of the Interior that he would take no more wives over and above his current four, but there is no indication that he kept this promise.[29] The BIA tried to be helpful by referring in their reports to all but one of the women as "mothers" rather than wives. But he kept the harem, including To-nar-cy, wife number one, or the "show wife," who often traveled with him.[30]

Quanah's two best Fort Worth friends were Martin B. Loyd (above left) and Burk Burnett (below). Quanah leased grazing lands to Burnett and hosted the cattleman and his friends on their hunting trips to Indian Territory. Burnett's son, Tom, was the defendant in a paternity suit brought by a woman claiming to be Quanah's daughter. Loyd was Quanah's banker, pictured above in his office at the First National Bank with Quanah and an unidentified wife (Dunas?). The triangle is completed with Burk Burnett being Loyd's son-in-law. (Loyd picture courtesy Fort Worth Public Library, Genealogy, Local History, and Archives Unit. Burnett picture courtesy Private Collection, Amon Carter Museum Archives, Fort Worth, TX.)

Quanah's intransigence on this matter finally got him dismissed from the tribal court in 1898, at which time he publicly acknowledged five wives. By his various mates, he eventually sired twenty-four children, of whom nineteen grew to adulthood and sixteen survived him. This remarkable patriarchy was a monument to both his virility and his love of family.[31]

Despite Quanah's best efforts, the Comanches continued to lose ground to advancing white civilization even after accepting resettlement in Oklahoma. In 1885 they numbered about 1,600 people living on some 8,000 square miles of reservation alongside the Kiowas and Wichitas. Yet, though pacified and living under watchful eye of the federal government, they were still part of what was officially known as "the Indian Problem." Until 1901, government policy was to keep the Comanches confined to the reservation and deal with them as a tribe. In that year, however, the policy changed to one of breaking up the reservation and redistributing the land in parcels of 160 acres to the men of the tribe willing to take up farming. Many Comanches moved away rather than become tillers of the soil, but Quanah continued to find success in a third way, using his land grant as ranchland and acquiring surrounding parcels until he owned a spread of truly baronial proportions. He still acted as tribal spokesman even after the Comanche diaspora.[32]

Personal tragedy continued to dog Quanah's life, however. In 1906 his eighteen-month-old son died of whooping cough, and he took the death "very hard." Later that same year, his eight-year-old son was dismissed from the public school in Lawton, Oklahoma, because the parents of his white classmates considered the boy a "half-breed." Quanah had enrolled the boy in public school to begin with because "I want my children to become educated men and women." Now he was forced to re-enroll the boy in the local Indian school, but the old chief was "nearly heart-broken" by the blatant discrimination.[33]

Another slap in the face was the fact that in the eyes of the U.S. government he was not even an American citizen despite being born on American soil and having an American citizen as a mother. As Quanah Parker, non-citizen, he could sign treaties, serve as sheriff of Lawton, Oklahoma, negotiate contracts with whites, even own land, but he could not vote nor enjoy the basic civil rights protections of the Constitution. That situation did not change during his lifetime. Not until 1924 did Quanah Parker's children receive U.S. citizenship along with all Native Americans after President Calvin Coolidge signed the Indian Citizenship Act into law.

Quanah never escaped the discrimination, but late in life he derived some satisfaction from being a national celebrity whose fame crossed cultural and racial boundaries, much like Geronimo for the Apaches but with more dignity and influence than the last war chief of the Apaches. He was feted by business leaders and civic representatives. Practically everyone who met him in person came away an admirer. A Congressional investigator in 1904 stated, "If ever Nature stamped a man with the seal of headship she did it in his case. Quanah would have been a leader and a governor in any circle where fate may have cast him—it is in his blood."[34] It should never be forgotten that that blood came from both his mother *and* his father.

Besides Burnett and Waggoner, other notable men of the day who called him friend were legendary cattleman Charles Goodnight, banker and businessman M. B. Loyd, and President Theodore Roosevelt. Loyd was the longtime president of Fort Worth's First National Bank. Starting in the 1880s, Parker always paid a call on Loyd whenever he came to Fort Worth and probably kept at least some of his money in Loyd's bank. (Unfortunately, as a capitalist, Parker was much better at making money than saving it.) An undated photograph taken by a bank employee sometime in the late 1880s shows Quanah and one of his wives sitting with Loyd in the latter's office. Quanah's relationship with Theodore Roosevelt was even closer. He corresponded with the President and even traveled to Washington, D.C., to take part in the President's 1905 inaugural parade. When Roosevelt subsequently came to Texas to hunt and keep his political fences mended, he invited Quanah to join his hunting party and spoke warmly of his Comanche friend from the platform. But it was Dallas and Fort Worth where Quanah always got the warmest welcome whenever he left the Indian Territory. It was the only place south of the Red River where he could be assured of being treated like a chief rather than "a poor half-breed Indian." The locals considered him very much "a superior class of red man."[35]

He was regularly invited to be the guest of honor at public events in both cities, including the Texas State Fair, the annual convention of the Texas Cattle Raisers' Association, and the annual Fort Worth

Fat Stock Show. He was popular with white audiences because he was a celebrity and because he told them what they wanted to hear. "Some my Indians no good," he told a Dallas audience. "Some white people same. I tell you reason why some no good. You see man buy bottle [of] whiskey and play cards. That reason some [Indian] men no good. Some white people do that, too." He also admitted that he once made war on whites, stole their horses, and battled the U.S. Army. He related his past without bragging but also without shame.[36]

The hosts of these events typically invited him to bring his family, which usually included one or more wives and sons plus fellow chiefs and assorted traveling companions. Befitting his exalted position, Quanah never traveled anywhere alone. His entourage at the 1904 cattlemen's convention and fat stock show in Fort Worth—two wives and one son—was unusually small for him. At the Fat Stock Show in 1909, he brought thirty-eight members of the tribe down with him from Oklahoma, and they set up their tepees near the imposing North Side Coliseum, not far from where the current statue of Quanah stands. In these public appearances, he played his war-chief image to the hilt. Although he spoke better than adequate English, his grammar and syntax were always awkward, which is why he preferred to use an interpreter when making set speeches at public events. His fractured English was notorious and sounds to modern ears like something out of a bad Hollywood movie, but it did not seem to matter during his lifetime because white audiences expected him to speak like a stage Indian. Public expectation is also what caused him to participate in countless Wild West shows dressed up like a cigar-store Indian leading his "braves" in suicidal attacks on wagon trains. It could be argued in retrospect that he was demeaning himself, but those well-attended performances won him a loyal following among whites, which helped the causes he fought for. The shows were not just about his own image either. The stylized Indian attacks that were the centerpiece of every show helped shape a neo-heroic image of the Comanches who had historically been regarded by whites as cowardly savages.[37]

Quanah's remarkable personal popularity crossed racial and social lines alike. One adoring newspaper reporter said his life was "tinged with romance" and recalled "many important historical facts in the march of civilization in the Southwest." Even his mother's descendants, the Parker family, could not bring themselves to hate him. They joined the chorus that proclaimed Quanah "the greatest of Comanche chiefs," a questionable historical claim, but undeniable if "great" means celebrity status. Quanah himself always believed his mixed heritage was a positive thing. Shortly before he died, he mused that white men and Indians were "all same people, anyway".[38]

In time Quanah became part and parcel of Fort Worth lore. The town adopted him as an unofficial citizen at a time when Geronimo's Apaches were still terrorizing neighboring Arizona. It is not known when exactly he first visited Fort Worth, but his was already a familiar face here when he stopped over in November 1885 with four of his followers on the way home from New Mexico. Around this same time, the *Fort Worth Gazette* called him "the most influential man in the Comanche nation." The following month he came down from the Indian Territory on a dual mission to consult with Captain Lee Hall, the U.S. government agent for the Comanche-Kiowa-Wichita reservation, and to purchase "a large amount of wire and fencing material" that would be used to enclose Indian pasturage being leased to Texas cattlemen. Lee Hall, a legendary Texas Ranger before going to work for Uncle Sam, would play an important if forgotten role in what followed.[39]

The purpose of the meeting with Captain Hall was to discuss rents paid by Texas cattlemen on their leases, but the mystery is why the two of them chose to meet in Fort Worth. Hall's headquarters was at Anadarko, Oklahoma, the "capital" of the Indian Territory and a short ride from Quanah's ranch, so they could easily have met there to conduct their business. But Fort Worth it was. Accompanying Quanah was Yellow Bear, also a Comanche chief and one of Quanah's three living fathers-in-law. The two came in on a Fort Worth and Denver City train on Saturday evening, December 19. They checked into the Pickwick Hotel but were put up in an apartment on the second floor of an adjacent building occupied by Taylor & Barr on the ground floor. Whether the hotel was full or simply did not cater to Indians is unknown, but the apartment they were given was quite nice, with indoor plumbing and gas lighting. However, the fact that it was not part of the regular hotel and therefore there were no other guests nearby helps explain what followed. Quanah left his money with Yellow Bear and went out with a "cowboy friend" to enjoy Fort Worth's night life.

(One newspaper account suggests uncharitably that Quanah was on the prowl for female companionship.)[40]

After Quanah left, Yellow Bear retired for the night, blowing out the light but apparently not turning off the gas jet. When Quanah came in a few hours later, he went to bed without checking the gas valve. Sometime during the night he awoke feeling "awful sick" and disoriented ("crazy"). He tried to get up and open a window but collapsed on the floor unconscious. It was thirteen hours before the two were discovered. The room had been closed up tight the whole time. Fortunately, the valve on the gas jet was not all the way open or they would have both died long before they were found—or else blown up the building with even more loss of life. A housekeeper finally discovered them on Sunday afternoon when she came to clean the room. Yellow Bear was lying on the bed and Quanah was stretched out on the floor, both men overcome by gas. She brought the desk clerk on the run, and he quickly ventilated the room and summoned doctors. It was too late for Yellow Bear, but they administered stimulants via "hypodermic injections" to Quanah and he rallied. A coroner's jury attributed Yellow Bear's death to asphyxiation ("the inhalation of gas") caused by the carelessness of one or the other guest; the six jury members did not hazard a guess as to which one. Quanah probably survived because he was lying on the floor, and gas tends to rise. While convalescing for the next two days, Quanah was moved to room 78 in the Pickwick, and doctors attended him closely. It was Tuesday before Quanah was able to explain what had happened. There was no doubt it had been an accident, but everyone wanted to know how such a thing could have happened. A *Fort Worth Gazette* reporter came to the hotel to interview him with the help of an interpreter. Quanah's explanation was vague and slightly garbled in translation.[41]

Three days after his near-death experience, Quanah returned home. The body of Yellow Bear had been prepared by Fakes & Co. undertakers, and it went home on the same train. Lee Hall, who had hovered nearby for the last three days, made all the arrangements including transporting the body. He also went along to escort the still-woozy Chief and help explain to Yellow Bear's family how he had died. Quanah worried that his in-laws would blame him personally and asked Hall to bring along a copy of the inquest proceedings to show them. He understood the power of such legal documents in the white man's world and hoped this one would have the same power among his own people.[42]

The story was carried in newspapers all across the country, but they did not all have the same take on the tragedy. The Dallas and Fort Worth papers expressed relief that Quanah had survived for the very practical reason that if he, too, had died, "it would have been difficult to explain to his people that he and Yellow Bear had not met with foul play here, and some trouble might have resulted in the Territory." Other newspapers surmised that one or both chiefs had indulged in too much "firewater" and were too drunk to know what they were doing or, being ignorant savages, simply did not understand modern technology. Despite his brush with death as a guest of the white man, Quanah never held any hard feelings against either the hotel or the town. In fact, he retold the story on later visits to Fort Worth, and it was always a crowd-pleaser[43]

In the next quarter-century, Quanah returned to Fort Worth on more than a few occasions, often just passing through on the train but sometimes as a guest of the city's cattlemen. He was not personal friends with all of them like he was Burk Burnett, but they all considered him the key to getting grazing rights for their herds in Indian Territory. Quanah's official visits were irregular, almost always in late winter around Fat Stock Show time. Three years passed after his 1901 attendance at the cattlemen's annual get-together. Five years passed after his 1904 visit. But his visits were always newsworthy. After the 1909 Fat Stock show, he told one reporter, "Had big time; big show; lots fine cattle, lots people; cattleman, Fort Worth people, old-home folks, all treat me as brother—think big man."[44]

The city received alarming reports in the summer of 1897 that their favorite Native American had been foully murdered. There were conflicting details, and the murderer was never named in any of the reports, but the story was carried in every north Texas newspaper. Tellingly, none of the reports was credited to any member of Quanah's family; they were all just vague rumors. After several days of "sensational" reports, the truth finally emerged at the end of August: Quanah was alive and well. He was sighted with his usual entourage at a cowboy reunion at Seymour, Texas, in fine fettle. When queried about the premature reports of his death, he was not as quick on the reply as Mark Twain under similar circumstances, but he did offer the following self-evident comment: "Tell them Quanah is alive and having a good time here with his people."[45]

Quanah Parker died on February 23, 1911, at 12:05 p.m., which may explain some of the confusion surrounding the exact date of his death. The end came at his beloved Star House. What white men had not been able to do when he was a feared war chief, pneumonia did in his seventh decade on earth. His entire life had been a riposte to convention, and his death was no different, defying the old Comanche proverb, "A brave man dies young." Nobody ever questioned Quanah's bravery. The tombstone over his grave says he was sixty-four years old when he died, but that was just a guess since nobody knew for sure, not even his family. Medical doctors at the time believed his death resulted from a combination of rheumatism and asthma. Some of his own people believed he had been poisoned by his enemies since he had taken ill suddenly while visiting the Cheyenne tribe in Arizona, and they vowed to launch an investigation. Another version of his death told and retold in the white community in later years was that he had died coming home drunk, fell off his horse into a creek and drowned, defying common sense since his advanced age and physical infirmities made him barely able to mount a horse, much less ride any distance. Sadly, variations on this particular tall tale were told about many old Indians at the end of their lives. At the time, however, the murder conspiracy failed to stir up much interest, and he was quietly buried in a combination Indian-white service near his beloved home.[46]

At his own request he was buried not beside any of his five or six wives, but beside his mother and sister in the Post Oak Mission Cemetery. In 1957, the remains of Quanah, Cynthia Ann, and Topsannah were dug up and moved to the military cemetery at Fort Sill. This time an impressive monument was placed over the two graves. If the size of the tombstone indicates the importance of the deceased, then Quanah Parker had finally achieved the recognition he deserved nearly half a century after his death.

Quanah's death marked the passing of an era in more ways than one. After his death, no Comanche was ever again called "chief." The Comanches themselves had never favored the title, and since even the concept of war chief was passé, they adopted the white man's title, "chairman" for their elected leaders henceforward.[47] Quanah's death cut the last ties to the old days when Comanches roamed the southern plains at will, making war on anyone who dared to trespass on their domain, terrorizing white settlements and other Indian tribes alike. For more than four decades Quanah Parker had been the public face of those Comanches. He was also their first and last media star, filling the same role that Geronimo filled for the Apaches, Sitting Bull for the Sioux, and Chief Joseph for the Nez Percé. Unlike those others, however, Quanah made the transition smoothly, almost effortlessly, from savage warrior to successful entrepreneur and public figure. In the tradition of Pocahontas, Massasoit, Ely Parker, and Cochise, he became a "good Indian" who helped forge the bonds of peace between the two races.

Despite the fame and honors that came his way, Quanah Parker was also a tragic figure in some ways. Beginning with the separation from his mother and the deaths of both parents and siblings when he was very young, then the deaths of a beloved son, he seemed to always be losing those closest to him. He also endured the loss of a certain amount of pride when he was forced to lead his people into captivity. Then, after he led them to the reservation, even that was taken away from them by the double-dealing government in Washington. All the wealth and honors in the world could never replace all that he lost during his lifetime. Yet he never allowed himself to sink into bitterness or depression. On the contrary, he was never anything less than honorable and dignified, even heroic in filling the role of "last Comanche chief."

His memory looms large in Fort Worth history, logic be damned. In the same way the city appropriated Butch Cassidy and the Sundance Kid to represent its outlaw heritage, it appropriated Quanah Parker to represent some sort of mythical Indian heritage. Fort Worth's image as "the city where the West begins" requires not just the cowboy and the outlaw but also the Indian to be authentic. Quanah Parker represents Fort Worth's tie to a time when Native Americans "owned" north Texas and defied whites to take it from them, and his connection to the city continued even after his death. Recently, a historic marker for Cynthia Ann Parker has been placed in downtown Fort Worth on Main Street, between Seventh and Eighth, as part of the city's Heritage Trail. Two descendants, Lance Tahmahkera and Lance's nephew, Monroe Tahmahkera, put down roots in Fort Worth and raised their families here, although they could easily have chosen to live among their own people in Oklahoma. Monroe was a direct descendant of one of Quanah's twenty-five children, making Quanah his great-grandfather. Both Tahmahkeras performed traditional Comanche ceremonial dances, continuing a performance tradition begun by the Great Chief himself so many years before.[48]

Quanah Parker is an enigma, inside a riddle, wrapped up in an Indian blanket. What we know of his life today comes from his own occasionally faulty memories shared late in life and from the recollections of whites who claimed to have known him more or less well. Quanah grew up in the oral traditions of the Comanches and never went to school, so he knew little if anything about the basic tenets of historical reporting. Unwittingly, he contributed to the confusion about the chronology and events of his life, not surprising for one who grew up in a culture that counted time by the seasons and passed down their stories around campfires.

His parents' deaths also became part of the mythology. For many years Texas Governor Sul Ross made political hay out of claiming that he killed Peta Nocona in hand-to-hand combat. It was a great story, but a boldfaced lie. As for Cynthia Ann, for years, historians repeated the tale that she had died of a broken heart in 1864, four years after being reunited with her white family. Somebody finally checked the 1870 U.S. census, which reported her as alive and well and living in Tarrant County. She died later that same year, and no one ever interviewed her about the last ten years of her life when she was a stranger in her own family.

Quanah's years as a war chief of the Quahade are shadowy because we cannot trace his movements and because, according to his Comanche descendants, he never called himself a "war chief." Yet for whites, "war chief" was a handy description and besides, he was the only Comanche leader most whites knew, so he was blamed for every Comanche raid be it on an isolated farm or wagon train anywhere in Texas. Even if he had wanted to, he could not have led every Comanche raid personally. The only attack on whites that he led personally that we know anything about was the Second Battle of Adobe Walls in 1874. He lost that one badly, and his command leadership on that occasion suggests that he was a much better peacemaker than war chief.

The two sides of Quanah Parker: in full Comanche regalia and in the business suit and bowler that he typically wore when traveling. Both photographs were taken on the front porch of Star House, sometime before the turn of the century. (Author's collection.)

Still, his place in history is secure. He was the last chief of one of the great warrior nations of history, *aka* the Lords of the Plains. For 150 years the Comanches ruled the southern plains, alternately fighting and negotiating with the Spanish, Mexicans, Apaches, and Americans until they went down in complete defeat in the canyon lands of the Texas Panhandle in 1875. They stand side by side with the Iroquois and Lakota Sioux in successfully resisting white civilization for any extended period of time. It was Quanah's unfortunate fate to preside over the end of what one historian calls "the Comanche Empire." He went from being a war chief whose territory covered thousands of square miles to being a "white man's Indian" who tried to usher the remnants of his people into the modern era. But in his frequent public appearances, his eloquent speeches in the Comanche language, and his insistence on wearing traditional native dress, he also kept alive a unique culture.[49]

The shame is that we know so little about him and much of what we "know" is wrong. Even the name "Quanah" is actually a mangling of his Comanche name, "Kwihnai." And the meaning of his given name has been misunderstood for years by biographers who translated it as some variation of "fragrance." The origins of that mistranslation are unknown, but it was already in wide circulation in 1910 when a Dallas newspaper reported that when Quanah was born, the tribal elders went to Cynthia Ann and asked her what she wanted to name him. She reportedly "lisped 'Quanah,' signifying 'sweet odor' or 'in the bed of flowers,'" and thus he was dubbed. That is so much nonsense, but what is not nonsense is that Quanah was always equally proud of the Parker side of his family. When he finally settled down on the reservation, he added his mother's surname, which was never used by his fellow Comanches. Even by white custom and law, a child takes his father's last name, not his mother's, so neither as a Comanche nor as a white man should he be known as a "Parker." But he is.[50]

Quanah outlived all the great Indian chiefs of American history—Geronimo, Sitting Bull, Crazy Horse. He even lived long enough to play himself as a Hollywood Indian before there was a Hollywood, making him unique among the great chiefs. His brush with the movies came in a small role in *A Bank Robbery*, a 1908 production of the easily forgotten Oklahoma Natural Mutoscene Company. The entire film was just nineteen minutes long, and Quanah's cameo lasted only a few seconds. Since at the time he was the second-most-famous Native American in Oklahoma after Geronimo, who was too old and in poor health for such shenanigans, Quanah was the natural choice to play the token "red man" in this all-Oklahoma production, which really had nothing to do with Indians.[51]

One of his wives, Topay, lived another five decades, giving her last public interview in 1960 when she was at least ninety years old. She was the mother of five of his children, three of whom died in infancy, and filled the role of "foster mother" to most of the rest of his children. Although she lived near Cache in southern Oklahoma and refused to speak much about her husband, she remained an object of curiosity for Fort Worthers who had kept her husband alive in their collective memory.[52]

Although there was not a single Comanche raid on Fort Worth during its years as either a military post or a frontier settlement—Fort Worth was too far east of the area known as "Comancheria"—Quanah's statue stands, bigger than life, in the middle of the Fort Worth Stockyards National Historic District. The famous picture of Cynthia nursing her infant daughter, taken by local photographer A. F. Corning in 1861, is one of just two historic pictures identified with Cowtown, the other being the picture of Butch Cassidy and the Wild Bunch. Quanah and his mother have become Exhibits A and B for Fort Worth's Indian heritage during American Indian Heritage Month every year since 2006. All of this makes the Quanah Parker we know today about equal parts self-made legend and icon to Victorian romanticism, white mythmaking, and civic boosterism! In any event, Fort Worth proudly claims Quanah Parker as one of our own.

CHAPTER 9

Wayward Policeman Thomas Finch

There is a big difference between dying while a police officer and dying in the line of duty. Ever since 9/11 there has been a wave of popular sentiment nationally to honor fallen peace officers, including those who died decades ago and have been forgotten. Thomas Finch was a commissioned, badge-wearing Niles City policeman when he died, but he did not fall in the line of duty. He was a victim of the unwritten law that has governed marriage since ancient times. The only question is whether he violated that commandment or was set up.

Thomas E. Finch was born in Wise County, Texas, in July 1877 to Amos and Emma Boyd Finch. The Finches came to Texas from Mississippi during Reconstruction, and Thomas was the first of four children born to them in Texas. His brother Jessie came along in 1879, sister, Stella, two years after that, and brother Drew on January 7, 1885. That was a date Thomas never forgot because Emma Finch died giving birth to Drew. Papa, who was a Wise County justice of the peace, was left to raise three young children and an infant on his own.[1]

All of Wise County in 1880 had only 579 people. The small hamlet of Decatur was the county seat. The last Indian raid had occurred three years before Thomas was born. Before 1882, regular stage service linked Decatur to Fort Worth, forty miles away. In that year, the Fort

Worth and Denver City Railway reached Decatur on its way north, making travel between the two towns much easier and faster. Because of Amos Finch's work the family lived in town. He carried out his JP duties in what was generously called "the courthouse," a forty-by-forty foot, two-story frame building with weatherboard siding erected in 1861. The little town's population jumped to 1,746 by 1890, and it built a beautiful granite courthouse that rivaled Fort Worth's, but it still lagged behind Fort Worth in all important measures.[2]

What is known of Thomas' upbringing is that the apple did not fall far from the tree. Like his father, he was drawn to law enforcement although in a different capacity; he preferred to put his faith in a Colt and a Winchester rather than a set of law books. Also, he did not answer the calling until relatively late in life. His personal life, what little is known about it, was quite conventional. He married a Wise County girl, May, and they had two children. The youngest, born in 1898, was named for his brother Drew. Something unfortunate happened because soon after the turn of the century Thomas was single again, and his children were living with their maternal grandfather. While still living in Decatur he met Leona Helm, older by one year, and they married in December 1904. Thereafter, he did not speak of May nor acknowledge their children, leaving the impression that Leona was the only wife he had ever had. He started a new family with her that eventually grew to four children: William (b. 1908), Mary Emma (b. 1910), Ruth (b. 1912), and Lundy (b. 1914).[3]

Looking to make a better life for himself and his family, Thomas brought them to Fort Worth in 1911 where there were more opportunities for an ambitious young man with a growing family to support. He was not interested in either farming or ranching, which were still the principal occupations back in Wise County. He had struggled trying to sell life and casualty insurance to his friends and neighbors; now he hoped to parlay that experience into a better position in the same field in Fort Worth. He went to work as an agent with Southland Life Insurance Company and did well enough to buy a small house in the Diamond Hill Addition of North Fort Worth, three-quarters of a mile from the stockyards. He and Leona got used to the unpleasant smells emanating from the stockyards and packing plants, which were not so very different from the smells of the farming community where they grew up. The following year, after Ruth was born, he moved the fam-

Officer Thomas E. Finch, looking natty in this group photo of the Niles City Police Department in about 1916. The NC police uniform consisted of the traditional brass-buttoned jacket, an English-bobby-style helmet, and the badge on the left breast. (Reproduced from *In Old Fort Worth*, Mack H. Williams, ed., 1986.)

ily into a larger house on North Main, still within smelling distance of the stockyards, however. His brother Drew came down from Decatur and found work as a barber in North Fort Worth, moving in with Thomas and Leona until he could find a place of his own. Brother Jessie, after losing his wife, also opted for the bright lights of Fort Worth over Decatur; he married a girl named Jennie and went to work for Stripling's dry goods store.[4]

In 1916 Thomas Finch made a life-changing career move; he left the insurance business and took a job with the Niles City Police Department as a "deputy marshal." Compared with Fort Worth's Police Department, the Niles City force paid less but was easier for a rookie to break into. Niles City was only five years old in 1916, having been created as a tax dodge by the giant meatpackers Swift and Armour. Dallas newspapers dismissed it as "the packing-house town," which was only slightly more disparaging than what they typically said about Fort Worth.[5] The tiny municipality may have lacked big-city services and amenities, but it would thumb its nose at its overbearing big sister until 1922 when it was finally annexed by Fort Worth. In the meantime, the most important qualification for a Niles City police officer was to get along with the bosses at Swift and Armour because the two meatpacking giants were the sole support of the little township.

One of the many North Side residents who worked at the plants was William A. Jobe, born the same year as Finch and a resident of

North Fort Worth since 1916. Prior to that he had lived in Smithfield, where he met and married Minnie, seven years his junior, in 1903. The first of their two children, Laura Viola, was born the following year, and Jennie Irene came three years later. The Jobes lived in Fostepco Heights, a working-class neighborhood wedged in between North Main, Fortieth, Decatur Avenue, and Twenty-ninth. Jobe worked as a millwright at one of the packing plants and kept a jealous eye on his young, flirtatious wife.[6]

Although North Fort Worth was a small community, there is no indication that the Finches and Jobes knew each other. For Thomas and Leona, life was good. They had no complaints living in a company town, even if many of their neighbors were recent immigrants from Eastern Europe and Mexico who worked as common laborers at the packing plants. In 1917 their home was at 505 Armour, within the boundaries of Niles City as opposed to Fort Worth. When they wanted to shop or put a little more distance between them and the stockyards they could hop a streetcar and be in downtown Fort Worth in less than thirty minutes. Sometimes they did not go together. On Tuesday afternoon, November 27, Tom was strolling down Main Street on the south end of Fort Worth's business district, not in uniform so, it can be presumed, not on duty.

Also present on south Main that same afternoon were William A. and Minnie Jobe. They lived in Riverside, a new residential addition just across the river to the east of downtown. Whether they came into town together or simply happened to wind up at the same place at the same time is not clear. If sheer coincidence, it was the granddaddy of all coincidences. Just prior to Tom, William, and Minnie coming together, Will was inside Monnig Dry Goods Company, the city's largest and most popular department store, taking up most of the block on Main between Twelfth and Thirteenth. He was there ostensibly to pay a bill while Minnie waited outside for him. She did not mind. Fort Worth was a vibrant city of nearly 100,000 people in 1917, and it was a pleasant day to be out, so the downtown streets were filled with people going about their business. Still, it stretches the bounds of credulity to believe that Will Jobe was inside while his wife just happened to be standing outside on the sidewalk when who should stroll up but Tom Finch. To paraphrase Humphrey Bogart in *Casablanca*, "Of all the sidewalks in front of all the stores in all of Fort Worth . . . ." No possible alignment of the planets or conspiracy of fate seems possible to have put the three of them at that place at that precise moment. Yet that is the story that would be told under oath later.

Ordinarily, a chance encounter on a public street would not have had any meaning, but Tom Finch and Minnie Jobe were quite well acquainted. In fact, later testimony would suggest that their meeting was no accident but part of a pattern because Tom and Minnie were having an affair. She had first met him when they were passengers on the same North Side streetcar, perhaps the first affair ever to start on a streetcar. They continued to meet secretly thanks to the convenience of public transportation, and he invited her to a movie. The affair blossomed from there. At least twice, they skipped the streetcar and the movies and met at hotels. But hotel rendezvous could not continue indefinitely, so his rented room at Mrs. D. F. Finley's boarding house on Florence Street became their love nest.[7]

By that Tuesday afternoon, Will Jobe was onto them. It was never explained how he found out since they had tried to be very discreet, but he eventually figured out they had been carrying on their affair right under his nose. Apparently, Leona Finch did not keep close tabs on her husband, or perhaps she was just a more trusting soul. If Will Jobe still had any doubts, however, those were swept away as soon as he walked out of Monnig's and found the two of them deep in conversation. They had been talking for about five or ten minutes, and Finch was pressuring Minnie to make some excuse to get away from her husband so that she could meet him in "a [hotel] room" nearby. The sight of the two lovebirds together sent Jobe into a rage, and without saying a word, he pulled out a pistol and put a single bullet into Finch. Since he was standing no more than ten or twelve feet away at the time, he could hardly miss. The question that was never answered was whether Will Jobe was expecting trouble that day or was just "packing" like so many men in Fort Worth in the old days. Because of Fort Worth's recent frontier roots, carrying a gun was still part of the town's culture.[8]

Ironically, Tom Finch, the policeman, was not armed that day, perhaps because he was expecting to find a little romance downtown, not trouble. He and Minnie typically met whenever he could get a day off from work. But this time things went horribly wrong. He barely had time to wheel and face his assailant, just in time to take a bullet in the face. It entered his left cheek just below the eye and although it did not kill him instantly, it would have been fatal even if he had been standing in the entrance to the City-County Hospital; he was a dead man.[9] He collapsed to the sidewalk and lay there in a spreading pool of blood. Jobe tried to put a second bullet into his victim, but his cheap revolver misfired. He did not stick around to gauge the effect of the first shot or argue justification based on the unwritten law. He did not even say a word to his shocked wife. Instead, he sprinted away trying to put as much distance between himself and the scene of the crime as possible. Nobody tried to stop him. He reached the corner of Twelfth and Main and turned east toward Commerce. Halfway down the block his luck ran out when he ran into Officer George W. Cummins, an MP patrolling the Acre as part of the U.S. Army's war on vice to protect the soldiers at Camp Bowie that first summer of World War I. As soon as Cummins heard the gunshot, he knew what it was and came running. When he saw a man running toward him with a pistol in hand, he arrested him on the spot. Jobe offered no resistance. Except for that chance encounter with an MP, Jobe might have gotten away scot-free.

Back at the crime scene, the echo of the shot had brought other people running. Monnig's clerk Aline Tindle ran outside just in time to hear Minnie Jobe scream out, "Oh, my God! He's killed a man. I wish it had been me instead of him." Things were too chaotic right then to wonder exactly what Minnie meant by the last part of her exclamation, but later it would cause tongues to wag. A crowd quickly gathered to stare at the victim and at the sobbing woman standing over him. Somebody dashed inside and used the store's telephone to summon an ambulance. The ambulance arrived in short order and took Finch to the nearby City-County Hospital where doctors pronounced him dead on arrival.[10]

Meanwhile, Cummins had frog-marched Jobe to the jail at City Hall and turned him over to Fort Worth police. Technically, the MP had only made a citizen's arrest since Jobe was not a soldier and had not assaulted military personnel. The Fort Worth police in turn passed the prisoner on to county authorities to be formally charged with murder. At the courthouse, Jobe gave his statement to County Attorney Marshall Spoonts saying that he was being cuckolded by Finch and had only done what any husband would do under the circumstances.

He was locked up until an examining trial could be held in Justice of the Peace Court to decide the matter of bond. That proceeding was originally scheduled for Wednesday afternoon, but Jobe did not go before a judge of any kind until the afternoon of Friday, November 30. In the meantime, his father and brother came to visit him in jail. Afterwards, his brother issued a statement that Tom Finch had been warned previously to stay away from Mrs. Jobe and ignored the warning, a bit of brotherly dissembling that was patently untrue. Will Jobe had suspected his wife of being unfaithful but only had his suspicions confirmed the night before. Minnie Jobe did not visit her husband in jail in the first few days and was conspicuous by her absence. She did make a statement to reporters on Friday, however, that Will had been consumed by jealousy for no reason because her relationship with Finch had been "perfectly innocent." Leona Finch issued no public statements, instead retreating into seclusion with her children. In the circus that followed, she managed to keep her name and her opinions out of the papers.[11]

The service for Tom Finch was held on the morning of Thursday, November 29, at the family residence on North Commerce. The turnout was smaller than usual for such occasions in part because he was not personally known to most members of the Fort Worth Police Department or other law enforcement agencies, but even more because of the questionable circumstances surrounding his death. Fort Worth newspapers had to scramble to find something nice to say about him. The best the *Record* could come up with was to call him "one of the best *known* policemen in the vicinity of Fort Worth [emphasis added]." It was damning by faint praise and fooled no one.[12]

At Will Jobe's examining trial before Justice of the Peace Hugh L. Small he was represented by Charlie Mays of the firm of Mays and Mays. Reporters jammed the courtroom anticipating that a lot of dirty laundry would be aired. They were disappointed. Not only did Jobe put up a stoic front, but he waived his right to an examining trial, thereby abruptly terminating the proceedings. Judge Small remanded him to county lockup to await the actions of the grand jury. Charlie Mays announced he would be filing a writ of habeas corpus to get his client out on bail. Before being escorted out of court by sheriff's deputies, Jobe uttered a cryptic farewell to no one in particular: "Well, good-bye, good luck to you all."[13]

Exterior of Monnig Dry Goods Company at Twelfth and Main in 1912, looking from the east side of Main Street. Thomas Finch died on the sidewalk just outside the front door, to the far left in the picture, on November 27, 1917. (Courtesy Fort Worth Star-Telegram Collection, Special Collections, University of Texas at Arlington Library, Arlington, TX.)

Interior of Monnig's, already one of the main emporiums for Fort Worth shoppers by the time this photo was taken in 1910. It had opened in 1889, and expanded steadily in the years thereafter. For years, the staff was all male. (Courtesy Dalton Hoffman of Fort Worth.)

Mrs. Jobe and the two girls were present in the courtroom, sitting at the defense table beside Will. Observers noted that she appeared "wan and nervous" and spoke not a word to anyone, even her husband. Whatever she was there for, it was not moral support for Will. At one point, he leaned over and tried to say something to her, but she turned her face away. He did better with the children who did not understand that their daddy was on trial for murder or that their mommy was shamed. Minnie allowed him to embrace and kiss the girls, the older of whom cried quietly. Minnie's demeanor at her first court appearance was consistent with her reaction at the crime scene and afterwards in her first statement to reporters: She and poor Thomas Finch were the victims. She continued to play the role of the aggrieved wife right through the examining trial, but shortly thereafter, she underwent a change of heart, telling reporters on Friday afternoon that she supported her husband completely. The turnabout came after her first private conversation with her husband since the shooting. On the way out of the courthouse, the Sheriff's deputies kindly allowed the couple to go into an empty room alone where they could talk away from all the lawyers and reporters. Minnie subsequently compromised the privacy of that conversation when she shared the substance of it with reporters later that day. As she told it, neither one of them had brought up the painful reason they were there, preferring to stick to mundane matters. She had asked Will if there was anything he needed. He requested a few modest personal items, and she promised to bring them. When it was over, the Jobes, to all appearances, were a family again, which was good news for the defense.[14]

As promised, the defense filed a writ of habeas corpus, and a hearing was scheduled in Judge George E. Hosey's Criminal District Court for Saturday, December 15. This was Tarrant County's newest court, created specifically by the legislature to handle the overload cases on the dockets of the Forty-eighth and Sixty-seventh district courts. It had opened for business in July with Judge Hosey moving over from County Civil Court to be its first sitting judge. This was one of the Court's first cases of note, and Judge Hosey would oversee the *State of Texas v. W. A. Jobe* from start to finish.[15]

On December 6, the grand jury had indicted Jobe for second-degree murder (manslaughter), so the defendant's first appearance before Judge Hosey was merely to decide where he would spend his time until trial—in jail or at home in his own bed. The court met in brand-new, "commodious" quarters in the newly opened county jail. If spectators had come expecting a show, they got their wishes. The habeas corpus proceedings proved to be a dress rehearsal for the upcoming trial. Much testimony was taken, and both sides revealed the strategy they would follow in the trial. Plus, it was all squeezed into one day so the details made it into the late Saturday edition of the newspaper. And there were plenty of juicy details to titillate readers. The biggest news was that Minnie had changed her story under oath, admitting that she and Tom Finch had indulged in what she delicately called "improper relations." The remainder of her testimony was enough to indict herself either for gross stupidity or for secretly desiring to get her lover killed. As she now told it, she had confessed to her husband the night before the shooting that she knew Tom Finch, had rendezvoused with him on the q.t. at least twice, and was determined to "be with him again." That confession had "made him mad" and a "fuss" followed. Further questioning by the district attorney brought out the fact that she had met up with Officer Finch at hotels on the two previous occasions, and that he had not been in uniform either time. Yes, she had lied to her husband about the affair, she admitted, but she did level with him that "she had met Finch and been with him" and would probably do so again![16]

That conversation occurred Monday night. Against all common sense, she had still planned to meet Finch on Tuesday morning, she testified. The brazenness of her confession astounded observers in the courtroom. She seemed unconcerned that she was admitting to the crime of adultery as well as infidelity and shirking her maternal responsibilities. Will Jobe then took the stand to testify that he had gone to work as usual Tuesday morning but was alerted to the situation when a neighbor called to inform him that someone had telephoned for Mrs. Jobe but "she was in town." (This was in the day when several neighbors might rely on one telephone in the neighborhood.) That information was all it took to send him storming off to town where he caught up with the careless couple in front of Monnig's and shot down the dirty dog who had violated his marriage. It was sympathy-inducing testimony that would appeal to an all-male jury, except that it did not explain the timing of his presence inside

Monnig's, reportedly paying his bill, just before he shot down Tom Finch. Seemingly, this would be a point for the defense to explore at the trial. [17]

Minnie Jobe's testimony put her in a legal bind, because on the day of the killing she had made a statement to Assistant District Attorney P. W. Seward and Chief of Detectives John A. Connelley that she had "never had improper relations with Finch." As she now explained it, she only lied to them out of a desire not to humiliate poor Mrs. Finch. She also added that her meeting with Finch on the morning of the twenty-seventh had been purely "an accident," contradicting what she had just testified to only minutes before![18]

When it was all over, Judge Hosey granted defense counsel's habeas corpus petition. There were enough extenuating circumstances to the crime, and Will Jobe was, after all, a solid citizen—never in trouble with the law, owned a home and had a steady job—to justify it. The Judge set bond at a modest $7,500, which the defendant posted on the spot. Jobe was a free man until his trial whenever that might be.

Setting a trial date proved maddeningly elusive. It was first put on the docket for January 28, 1918, then bumped back on the court calendar repeatedly. It almost happened on February 7, with voir dire even scheduled for that morning. An unusually large jury pool of 250 men had been summoned in anticipation that a large number of potential jurors would be challenged by one side or the other. What the prosecution did not consider was that the defense would file a motion to quash the entire venire on the grounds that it had been improperly summoned because Sheriff Nace Mann had contacted most of the men by telephone, thereby violating state law that required that all veniremen be served in person.[19] Modern communication technology may have simplified the Sheriff's job, but it did not change state law.

The trial was rescheduled two more times in February, first on the fifteenth then on the eighteenth. On the second date, another large venire, this time of 200 men, was summoned, and all strictly according to state law. But once again the proceedings did not get out of the gate. The defense asked for a continuance because Mrs. Finley, the boardinghouse proprietor, was out of town, and her testimony was crucial to prove the State's argument that Finch and Mrs. Jobe were having an affair. Judge Hosey granted the defense motion, and the case was rolled over to the April term. But the legal maneuvering was not all on the defense side. The prosecutor had his own ace to play. That same day he filed a perjury charge against Mrs. Jobe for lying under oath about her relationship to Tom Finch. She had opened herself up for it with her flatly contradictory statements on November 27 and December 15: No, she was not having an affair; yes, she was having an affair. Both sides were playing high-stakes poker with Will Jobe's life. The prosecution hoped to use the indictment to intimidate her into recanting her bond-hearing testimony and standing by her original testimony that she and Officer Finch were *not* having improper relations. That testimony at the trial would remove the unwritten-law argument that the defense was depending on and make Will Jobe nothing but a coldblooded cop killer. The perjury indictment would hang over Mrs. Jobe until shortly before her husband's trial some six months later, when the district attorney abruptly dropped it without explanation.[20]

On the other hand, Minnie Jobe's capricious testimony also smacked of collusion with her husband's defense counsel. In her first public statement on the day of the shooting, she had proclaimed her own and Tom Finch's innocence, then in her first court appearance she had pointedly snubbed her husband. But after a private meeting with Jobe that same day, she changed her story 180 degrees stating, yes, she had been seeing Finch and had admitted as much to her husband less than twenty-four hours before he gunned down Officer Finch. That story, if it stood up in court, would earn Will Jobe a free pass from any jury of red-blooded males. Clearly, she was the key to her husband's fate. So Minnie was being pressured by both sides: the defense to get Will off scot-free and the prosecution to help nail him to the wall. The holes in her testimony reveal the difficulty she was having getting her story straight.

After the second false start in February, the defense managed to delay things for the next six months, getting one continuance after another. Their hope was that public opinion would swing in Will's favor and that the marital bond would prove stronger than the State's threats against the wife. It was a brilliant strategy. Charlie Mays began his stalling tactics at the February 18 proceeding by pleading successfully that one of his key witnesses was not available. He continued to stall through the summer, and since Will Jobe was out on bond living a normal life, he had no objections. In fact, he had left everything in the hands of his lawyers and taken a job in a munitions plant in Tennessee. While he was serving his country in the Great War, the lawyers continued their legal sparring back in Fort Worth. But just as the tide of war in Europe had turned in the Allies' favor, the tide of public opinion in Fort Worth had turned in the defendant's favor. The initial shock over the brutal murder of a policeman on a public street had given way to open sympathy for a cuckolded husband. Mrs. Jobe and the children had stayed in Fort Worth while her husband worked in Tennessee, but reports that the couple were back in love and facing Will's impending court date together did not hurt his cause.

The case was finally set for trial on September 4, 1918, a Wednesday, but circumstances once again outran the legal system. Jobe had recently been overcome by gas fumes at work, and while he was back in Fort Worth recuperating, there was some question whether he would be well enough to start trial. The public had been reading about soldiers being gassed in Europe, and having one of their own victimized in the same way struck a responsive chord. Some people were saying poor Will Jobe had been punished enough.[21]

Despite concerns for the defendant's health, the *State of Texas v. W. A. Jobe* opened as scheduled on the morning of September 4, Judge Hosey presiding. The dynamics of the case had shifted dramatically in the ten months since the indictment had been handed up. The State, represented by Assistant District Attorneys William R. Parker and Fritz G. Lanham, had not lost its determination to prosecute Will Jobe to the full letter of the law, despite the rising tide of sympathy for him in the community. On the contrary, the State had refiled its case, raising the charge to first-degree murder—"unlawfully and with malice aforethought killing one Tom Finch." For its part, the defense, now led by Frank Graves, was chomping at the bit to put the case in the hands of a jury that they knew would consist by law of men only and probably family men, at that. Jury selection and preliminary motions took up the entire first day. The lawyers had to sift through the entire jury pool to find twelve men acceptable to both sides. The defense used all fifteen of its challenges; the State, fourteen. Thirty men were sent home for one reason or another. The real show did not start until the second day, so what went into the books as a two-day trial really lasted less than one day. Knowing it held a bad hand; the prosecution was not seeking the death penalty, but had reasonable hopes for a manslaughter conviction even from a jury packed with husbands and fathers.[22]

The testimony phase of the trial commenced on Thursday morning. The prosecution's strategy was to keep the jury focused on the act of murder itself not the provocation behind it. The defense's strategy was to invoke the unwritten law, portraying the murder as a justifiable crime of passion. During the defense phase, Frank Graves called ten witnesses, among them four described as "housewives," to testify to what a good husband and father Will Jobe was. Then he called Mrs. Jobe, whose testimony, as anticipated, checkmated the State's case. On the witness stand, she meekly repeated her previous confession to having "improper relations" with the deceased. When Assistant District Attorney Parker on cross-examination asked her why she had lied, she burst into tears. Between sobs, she finally explained, "I did not want to say anything that would reflect on him [Tom Finch]."[23]

She also added further damning details to the testimony she had given at the habeas corpus hearing. She related how on Tuesday morning she had gotten word to Tom Finch that "he looked good to me," and she wanted to meet him. When she started getting ready to go into town, her husband asked her what she was doing, and she retorted that she "didn't know as it was anybody's business." So Will Jobe went to work, and Minnie went to town with every intention of meeting her lover at the agreed-upon spot in front of Monnig's. Yes, she also admitted, she knew Finch had a wife and children.[24]

With that testimony, the defense had succeeded in making Mrs. Jobe the villain in the piece, not her husband. Frank Graves also put on the stand some of Tom Finch's fellow policemen, who testified that Finch had a "bad reputation" in general and "was bad on women" in particular. The longer the trial went on, the worse Tom Finch was looking.[25]

The defense played its trump card by putting Will Jobe on the stand to look the jury in the eye and plead the unwritten law: He had been defending the sanctity of his marriage. Still showing the effects of his job injury, the defendant cut a pitiable figure. After testimony wrapped up and the two sides delivered their summations, there was one more thing to be done before the case was turned over to the jury. Judge Hosey delivered a nine-page charge of the court to guide the jurors in their deliberations. After reviewing the finer points of first-degree murder, he contrasted premeditation versus a sudden act of passion, then defined the finer points of second-degree murder as opposed to first-degree. Tellingly, he included adultery as one of the mitigating circumstances for a finding of second-degree murder. The Judge spent much more time explaining the legal definition of manslaughter than first-degree murder.

The jury took its cue from Judge Hosey, but was still not willing to let Will Jobe off the hook completely for what he had done. After nearly four hours of deliberation, interrupted by dinner at the county's expense, they reached a verdict of guilty of first-degree murder. Following the Judge's guidelines, they could have sentenced the defendant to a date with the gallows or, alternately, to confinement in the penitentiary for a term of five years to life. But having decided that the convicted was a cold-blooded murderer, they threw away the guidelines by making a gratuitous recommendation to the court. The verdict, as read by foreman Max Kaminsky from his own notes, said:

> We the jury find the defendant guilty and assess his punishment at confinement in the state penitentiary for 5 years. We further find that the Defendant has never heretofore been convicted of a felony in this or any other state and recommend to the court that said sentence be suspended.[26]

Judge Hosey bowed to the jury's wishes and without batting an eye suspended the entire sentence. Will Jobe had spent a total of seventeen nights in jail, and not a single night after December 15. Now he walked out of the courtroom not just a free man but a vindicated one as well. If one was inclined to read messages into verdicts, then every cuckold in Fort Worth had license in the future to take the law into his own hands.

As for Thomas Finch, he was dead and beyond caring, but whatever honor had ever attached to his name was gone forever. He had forfeited the traditional goodwill enjoyed by policemen going about their duties; the good citizens of Fort Worth now wrote him off. Having shamed both himself and his family, his memory was erased from Fort Worth law enforcement history. His death had been neither heroic nor in the line of duty. Leona Finch, the only innocent victim in the entire affair, continued to live in Fort Worth, raising her children and residing at the same house where she had lived with Tom. County authorities took pity on her and hired her to be a deputy district clerk the following year, continuing a long and commendable tradition of taking care of their own without actually guaranteeing any benefits or long-term relief. She became a working mother at the age of forty-one, and continued to work for the county well into her fifties.[27] Official pity did not extend, however, to the county providing any pension or death benefits. After Niles City folded in 1922, that put an end to any financial support she might have applied for even if she had been so inclined.

The conclusion seems inescapable: Tom Finch and Minnie Jobe had an illicit relationship. They were having an affair right under her husband's nose. What is less certain is whether Minnie set Tom up on the last day of his life. Confessing the affair to her husband the night before, then going right ahead and meeting Finch the next day, the fact that Will Jobe showed up at their rendezvous carrying a pistol, and finally, Will and Minnie's reconciliation during the run-up to the trial: it all seems very suspicious. We will never know for certain, of course. What we do know is that the story of Tom, Minnie, and Will is a classic love triangle, not a romantic fairy tale. It is a sad tale of ruined reputations, innocent victims, male chauvinism, and perverted justice. When it was over, a marriage had been sundered and a promising law-enforcement career snuffed out along with a life.

CHAPTER 10

Crazy Mary Rea: A Real "Corker"

Every family has a black sheep, and the Rea family of Fort Worth was no exception. The Reas were known as a family of lawmen, marshals, and sheriffs. Then there was Mary Rea, who was only related by marriage, but still, she wore the family name and that was all that mattered. She was an embarrassment to the family and a dilemma to the city. No one knew what to do with her. She could have been the poster child for all that was wrong with the justice system when it came to dealing with the mentally ill.

When mentally troubled individuals came through the criminal justice system, a myriad of factors determined how they were treated. First and foremost was their place in the community. Status and family connections were all-important in determining sanity and placing those who were judged "insane" or "incompetent." For many defendants, a trip through the justice system began when family members dropped them off at the county jail, in effect turning them over to the Sheriff. This occurred when the family members could no longer control the person or were just tired of shouldering the burden.[1]

In Mary's case, she was tolerated as an eccentric and allowed to go about her business because of the prominence of the Rea family. They were part of the second generation of Fort Worth pioneers who arrived after the railroad in 1876 and helped turn Cowtown into a thriving city. The Reas produced a bumper crop of lawmen that included William, Edward, Henry, James, and John T. The most famous of the brood, William M. Rea, served twelve terms as Fort Worth marshal, *aka* chief of police, five terms as deputy sheriff, and two terms as sheriff in a thirty-five year career in law enforcement. Around 1879, Mary, a Fort Worth resident, married Confederate veteran John Rea who was sixteen years older, widowed, and raising a son at the time. He had followed his older brother to Fort Worth and also into law enforcement. He eventually served fifteen years on the police force, twelve of those years under William Rea before retiring in 1905 as the second-oldest member of the force.[2]

Subscribing to the theory that children were cheaper by the half-dozen, John and Mary had five children of their own, three sons and two daughters. The family lived comfortably enough in a house on Arizona Avenue. Mary had a fragile psyche and raising six children while fulfilling all the obligations that came with being a member of Fort Worth's version of the famous Earp family was more than she

J. T. REA,
Patrolman.

Fort Worth Police Officer John T. Rea, Mary Rea's husband, whose years as a policeman could not have prepared him for dealing with "Crazy Mary." (Reproduced from 1901 FWPD Annual, courtesy Fort Worth Police Historical Association.)

could handle. At the very least those were contributing causes to her very public mental breakdown. Over several years her behavior became more and more eccentric, eventually crossing the line into the bizarre. The beginning of her "long day's journey into night" came in 1909 when she got into a bitter dispute with the Magnolia Rebekah Lodge, the women's auxiliary of the Odd Fellows, of which John was a longtime member. The lodge expelled her, and she filed suit. When that went nowhere, she filed another suit against the Grand Lodge of Texas. Both suits came before Judge James Swayne in the Seventeenth District Court, and he summarily dismissed them. That was not the end of it, however. John had refused to be a party to her suit; in fact, he had spoken out publicly against the action. Convinced that her husband was in cahoots with her enemies, she gave him no peace.

After nearly a year of this, the sixty-seven-year-old husband filed for divorce, citing as grounds, that he had "experienced no peace of mind" since the lawsuit and that "married happiness had ceased to exist" for him. The case landed in the Seventeenth District Court, so Mary once again found herself standing before Judge Swayne, this time as a defendant. It did not make any difference; she lost again as John's divorce petition was granted. It was an ugly breakup. Everyone knew John was not trying to trade in his wife of more than twenty years on a younger model; he simply wanted to be free of her. The children became pawns in the bitter quarrel, especially the three youngest, who included fifteen-year-old Roy. John was free, but he had to split $40,000 of community property. Mary got the house on Arizona Avenue, the bank account, and "a good deal of [additional] property." She also got custody of the two daughters. Roy went to live with his father.[3]

Mary must have been humiliated by the whole messy affair playing out in the newspapers. It certainly embarrassed the Rea family. On top of that, the divorce really settled nothing. John and Mary continued to quarrel, landing in court at least twice in the next eighteen months. The first time was about Roy, who had a minor deformity (six toes on one foot). John wanted to have the sixth toe surgically removed and engaged a couple of local doctors, J. B. Kelly and E. P. Hall, to do it. Mary opposed the surgery and got a temporary injunction against her ex and the two doctors to stop it. Mary Rea was the sort of person who practically kept a lawyer on permanent retainer because she saw enemies everywhere and was always doing battle with someone. This latest brush with the legal system brought her back before Judge Swayne in May 1910, and again he ruled against her; the surgery would go forward. The second case arose because she seemed a little fuzzy over who got which property in the divorce settlement. In the spring of 1911 she hired workmen to do major plumbing and carpentry work on some of John's rental property. Not only was the work unauthorized, but she was charging it to him!

Furthermore, purely out of spite, she hired men to "pile rubbish and waste" on the property. John Rea had to go to court to get yet another injunction to make her "cease and desist" from running up bills in his name and from "molesting" his property." The court order to that effect came from Judge Swayne, representing one more strike against him in her book. As for poor John Rea, he was at a definite disadvantage battling his ex after suffering a stroke in 1910 that left him partially paralyzed. After 1911 he was a homebound invalid who only lived two more years. He finally escaped the troubles of this world in 1913 at the age of seventy. There is no record that Mary attended the funeral, and it is unlikely that the family desired her presence.[4]

With her nemesis removed from the picture, Mary might have faded into obscurity, but fading away was not in her nature. She remained active, managing her property, and running a small boardinghouse on East Front Street. She also continued to be an active member of the Fort Worth Woman's Club, although the members must have wondered if one day she would sue them as she had the Magnolia Rebekah Lodge. Her club work and business affairs still left her plenty of time to pick fights. Authority figures were her favorite targets. In 1911 she threatened to sue the city for damages caused by a public water project on East Twelfth. The claimed damages were only $100, but she pressed her suit as if thousands of dollars had been at stake. In example after example, if there were any way to avoid a fight, Mary would provoke one. Her behavior could be unpredictable, even violent, making her not just the family's problem but a community problem as well. Among themselves, family members called her "a corker," but they did not cast her adrift. Even if they had wanted to, she was still the mother of five Rea children. The community at large called her "eccentric," stopping just short of "crazy," more out of consideration for the family than any inclination to give her the benefit of the doubt.[5]

In modern parlance, Mary Rea had serious anger-management issues. Even while occasionally sparring with her invalid ex-husband, she sought out new dragons to battle. Her battles always seemed to bring her back to James Swayne's court. As the *Star-Telegram* put it in 1912 on the occasion of her latest trouble, she had "a long-standing grievance against the Seventeenth District Court judge." She was attending the trial of John Beal Sneed for murder and did not like the way the proceedings were going. There was more than a sneaking suspicion that she was just at the trial to pursue her vendetta against Judge Swayne. In any event, she attended every session of the trial until February 19. On that day when she arrived a sheriff's deputy posted at the door would not let her enter. Swayne had ordered her barred from the courtroom after receiving information that she was carrying a gun and out to get him. He did not, however, order her searched. She sat outside in the corridor and steamed until court was adjourned. When Swayne ordered court officers to bring her in, she resisted mightily all the way down the aisle forcing the deputies to manhandle her rudely. She broke free and began berating the Judge, starting with "That man wrecked my home. He tore my child away from my arms. Where is he [Roy] now? That man and his band of agents ruined my home!"

Swayne interrupted her tirade, telling her to hush and warning her, "I will fine you . . . and put you in jail two days." He continued, "I understand that you have brought a six-shooter into this building."

"Produce it! Produce it!" she taunted.

"Not only that," he said calmly, "but you told a lady that you were coming here to kill the judge today. . . . I understand that you have said that when I get outside you are going to fix me."

"Prove it! Prove it!" she sneered.

Swayne cited her for contempt of court and ordered the deputies, "Take her to jail."

"I will accept it," Mary crowed, triumphant over getting the last word.

Once at the county lockup, the jail matron searched her and found a pistol "of large dimensions" wrapped in a newspaper in her purse. The gun was unloaded, but it was proof that at least half of what Judge Swayne had heard was true; she had indeed come to court that day armed. She served her time but never did pay the $100 fine, and

Swayne tried to give her a break by not making an issue of it. He could only hope that his compassion coupled with the shock of two nights in jail would bring her to her senses. Nothing changed, however.[6]

It was following this incident that local officials finally began to take Mary seriously. The County Attorney filed "lunacy charges" against her. This was the first step in getting her committed, but it placed Sheriff Bill Rea in an awkward position since his deputies would have to take her into custody until a court could determine her fate. However, there was no urgency to schedule a hearing since no one at this point thought Mary was actually dangerous, just unbalanced, or maybe just a little crazy where Judge Swayne was concerned. Even after the courtroom confrontation and contempt citation, she refused to call off her vendetta against him. If anything, it escalated. When she encountered him on the street one day in June while out strolling with Roy, she commenced berating him loudly. Roy joined in, demanding his mother's pistol back and making other insulting remarks. Mary stood to one side during most of it, but the Judge had good reason to believe that she was armed and only waiting for an opportunity to use the weapon against him. Then there was the afternoon she stood on the courthouse lawn for three hours shouting vile things against the man she considered to be the Antichrist. Swayne issued orders from the bench that she was to stay away from the courthouse unless she had official business. Naturally, she ignored this latest order as she had all the others. A few days later when she tried to enter the building, officers were on the lookout and stopped her at the door. Upon searching her they found a gun in her purse and placed her under arrest. The next day she was taken before Judge Tom Simmons in the Sixty-seventh District Court. Although it was Swayne's order that she had violated, he could no longer adjudicate her run-ins with the law because he had become part of the melodrama. It was now Judge Simmons' turn to try to tame her. He fined her $100 for contempt and offered to release her to her brother-in-law, William Rea. When she refused that offer he sentenced her to two days as a guest of the county. Neither the fine nor the jail sentence, however, got to the root of the matter; she hated James Swayne and was not going to stop going after him as long as she drew breath. The next day she and her lawyer, Charles Rowland, were back in front of Simmons for a habeas corpus hearing. It should have been a routine proceeding, but it was

Fort Worth Marshal/Police Chief William Rea in group photo on the steps of City Hall, 1901. The marshal's badge on his vest was custom-made. Compassion for his brother did not extend to his sister-in-law. (Courtesy Sergeant Kevin Foster.)

far from it. Swayne was there, having excused himself from his own court in order to attend as a material witness, and Mary was visibly angry and agitated in his presence. Simmons practically pleaded with her to promise that she would not "injure or abuse" Judge Swayne, but she was having none of it. Then Charles Rowland tried wearily to get his client to "let matters drop," but she rebuffed him, saying, "I told you last night that I wanted you to do nothing but get me out of jail on habeas corpus."

After a pregnant pause, Judge Simmons announced, "I guess we'll overrule the application [for a habeas corpus writ]."

Swayne was up next. When asked to tell his side of things, he explained, "Mrs. Rea's feeling against me dates back to decisions in my court in which she was interested." He went on to explain why he had issued the contempt citation during the Sneed trial and how he had been accosted on the street more recently by the woman and her son. When Simmons asked him if he anticipated "personal violence" against his person from either Mrs. Rea or her son, Swayne said he did, but added hopefully, "If she were to tell me she had no intention of bothering me, I would believe her."

Given yet another chance to avoid jail, Mary refused still to make nice with Swayne. When Simmons queried her about her intentions, she replied cryptically, "Perhaps I ought not to talk." At that, the Judge ordered her back to jail. Unexpectedly, she broke down sobbing. In between sobs she said would rather do her time in jail than apologize to the man she hated more than all others. Simmons warned her that such behavior might get her declared "insane," but that only drew another defiant answer.[7]

By this time Mary's troubles and her war with Judge Swayne were general knowledge to the public thanks to the newspapers, which were now carrying frequent reports as if they were baseball scores. What every judge who came up against her failed to realize was that jail time did not cow her; it only got her Irish up. Quite simply, no one knew what to do with her. They could keep locking her up but sooner or later they had to let her out and she was as unrepentant as ever. Even her lawyer, Charles Rowland, dumped her as a client.

Things only got worse for Mary. In 1914 Roy joined the ranks of her enemies—real and imagined. He had moved back in with her briefly after the death of his father but had recently married, and now, he claimed, his mother bore "ill will toward him and his wife and has threatened bodily harm to [her]." Complicating the issue was the fact that he was nineteen, still a minor in the eyes of the law, and therefore blocked from inheriting his father's substantial estate. He wanted his inheritance, but he would have to pry it loose from his mother's clutches. Naturally, it turned into another legal imbroglio and just as naturally it landed back in Judge Swayne's court. In September, Roy filed application in the Seventeenth District Court to have his "disability of minority" set aside so that he might claim his inheritance or at the very least, to have W. R. Hurley, an old friend of his father's, appointed his legal guardian. As long as he was a minor, his mother would administer the estate. Without the court's intervention, he would continue to be Mary's ward until he reached the age of twenty-one. Mary opposed the petition and girded herself for another courtroom battle. Whether she was really that greedy that she was unwilling to give up control of the estate or was just displaying her usual hardheadedness and persecution complex is impossible to say.[8]

The lawyers for Mary and Roy almost accomplished the impossible. They reached an agreement that represented a win for both sides. Roy would get his petition granted while Mary would receive a nice financial settlement. On September 22, a Tuesday, the lawyers presented the deal they had worked out to the court, and Judge Swayne signed off on it. As the court was preparing to move on to other business, Mary barged into the courtroom and demanded that Swayne read the terms of the settlement aloud. She was convinced that the Judge was part of an unholy conspiracy "to break up her home, drive her children and friends from her, and get her property."[9] Since it was a slow day and the courtroom was almost empty, Swayne obliged her demand hoping against hope that it would satisfy her and she would leave. To keep the proceedings informal and therefore non-threatening, he stepped down from the bench and took a seat in the empty jury box. If he thought this ploy would soothe the agitated woman he was badly mistaken.

Declaring that she did not intend to "be robbed of her property" as she had been of her family, Mary pulled out a revolver and opened fire. Thinking her purse might be searched when she entered the courtroom, she had hidden it in what the newspaper delicately called "her bosom," which was a place no officer would ever search. Mary's attorney, Durward McDonald, had half-expected trouble so he was not caught completely by surprise. After the first shot he knocked her wrist up and grappled with her. She proved surprisingly strong, keeping her grip on the pistol and squeezing off round after round until it was empty. Fortunately, the quick-thinking lawyer had managed to deflect her aim. The first shot hit the wall just above Swayne's head; the next five all went into the ceiling. McDonald wrestled his client down the aisle and out of the courtroom, keeping a tight grip on the wrist of her gun hand. Out in the rotunda, he finally got some help. Two sheriff's deputies appeared, and the three men finally subdued her. While the deputies hustled her off to jail, a shaken McDonald returned to the courtroom. Miraculously, no one had been injured.[10]

That same afternoon a grand jury happened to be in session in the courthouse, one floor above Swayne's courtroom. The gentlemen of the grand jury took time out from their deliberations to hand up the quickest indictment in Tarrant County history. They charged Mary with one count of "aggravated assault with intent to murder" (a felony) and one count of "carrying a pistol" unlawfully (a misdemeanor). The quick indictment could not cover up several potential problems in the case. To begin with, Durward McDonald, one of the very few members of the legal establishment that Mary trusted, had to recuse himself because he was now a witness in an attempted murder case. He turned her defense over to the firm of Baskin, Dodge, and Eastus. That was only the beginning of the legal conflicts of interest. Because of her past history with both Simmons *and* Swayne, the case had to be placed in the Forty-eighth District Court, Judge R. H. Buck presiding. Neither the State nor the defense sought a change of venue; they were confident that a local judge and jury could administer justice and expected an easy verdict. The trial was put on the docket just three days later, and with its case to prepare and so little time, Mary's legal team did not even bother to ask for bond. They knew there was no way they would get it anyway because of Mary's history.[11]

Meanwhile, the Rea family closed ranks. No one made any public statements about the case. Among friends, when Sheriff Bill Rea was asked about Mary's latest troubles, he could only shrug and say, "She's my sister-in-law; what can I do? You can pick your friends but not your relatives."[12]

When Friday, the twenty-fifth rolled around, the defense and the State were ready to go to trial. The defense had subpoenaed a remarkable sixty-seven witnesses, turning in its list just the day before. The Sheriff's Office had to work overtime delivering all the subpoenas. On Friday other business took up the court's day, so Mary's case had to be continued. By the middle of October, the case had still not been reset on the calendar, so defense counsel filed a habeas corpus motion on Friday, the eighteenth. Judge Buck set bond at $1,200, which was an amount Mary could not immediately post. Nor did the Rea family step forward. Finally, on Monday she produced the money and was released on bond.[13]

Mary's case did not finally come up for trial until March 18, 1915, before Judge Marvin H. Brown in the Sixty-seventh District Court. It had first been placed on the docket of the Forty-eighth District Court, Judge Bruce Young presiding, but a murder trial had taken precedence, so it was moved to the Sixty-seventh. Defense counsel, now with Durward McDonald back on the team to keep the defendant happy, adopted the most obvious strategy: a plea of insanity. The case should have been cut and dried. Any judge would have been glad to institutionalize Mary, and since no one had been injured, the public would have accepted it. But two problems arose: First, defense counsel could not get Mary herself on board; she expressed "strenuous objections" to the strategy. Secondly, although her behavior for years had demonstrated serious mental problems, the strategy did not come without some risk attached. Both sides were no doubt aware of the history of insanity pleas. Only about 15 percent typically succeed; when a crime is committed juries like to have someone to pin the blame on. With a shaky legal case and an unsympathetic client, Baskin and McDonald, the lead attorneys for Mary, did not want to risk serious prison time. They decided to roll the dice with an insanity plea.[14]

The defense initially subpoenaed sixty-six of their original list of sixty-seven witnesses, including three doctors, a college professor, four judges, several policemen, one deputy sheriff, a dozen lawyers, and Sheriff Bill Rea's wife. They subsequently supplemented that list with additional names. By the time the trial opened, however, they pared the list down to a handful of witnesses. To prove a defense of insanity, they only had to show a "preponderance of evidence" supported their case, not prove it "beyond a reasonable doubt." The prosecution initially prepared a full-court press, too, subpoenaing nine witnesses, but by the day of the trial they too decided to go with a stripped-down case. A reasonable assumption can be drawn that both sides wanted to cut things short and were hoping for a settlement before the trial started. Mary was left out of the negotiations, a decision everybody thought was for the best.[15]

When they could not reach an agreement out of court, the trial opened as scheduled on March 18, a Thursday. The first day was taken up with the usual preliminaries: seating a jury and hearing defense motions. Finding a jury of twelve men was easy as neither side challenged any of those who were examined, and Judge Brown entertained just one defense motion—an unusual request that in the event of a guilty verdict, the sentence be suspended. He granted the motion based on the defendant's "standing in the community," code words for the power of her married name in Fort Worth. Tension in the courtroom was still thick, however. With two previous incidents on her record, the prosecution asked that Mary's person be searched to see if she was carrying a pistol, and defense counsel did not object. Judge Brown, however, demurred, refusing to inflict such an indignity on the lady sitting meekly before him, instead accepting her "word of honor" that she was unarmed.[16]

On Friday, Durward McDonald took the stand to be examined by his co-counsel, A. J. Baskin. He testified matter-of-factly about what Mary had told him on various occasions, waiving client privilege without consulting Mary herself to ask how she felt about it. No one raised any objection, and the proceedings moved along quickly. When McDonald stepped down he resumed his place at the defense table and took the lead examining James Swayne. All this time, Mary and daughter Camilla sat "at some little distance" from her lawyers because she had disdained being associated with them. Her only friend in the whole courtroom it seemed was her daughter. As a further courtesy from Judge Buck, she was neither physically restrained nor closely guarded despite her history of outrageous behavior in courtrooms. The last witness examined on Friday was Dr. J. B. Kelley, Mary's family physician for twelve years. Although not trained as a psychiatrist, Dr. Kelley testified that he considered his patient "a paranoiac on court matters." He did not offer his professional opinion on her mental state in matters unrelated to court proceedings or, specifically, on Judge Swayne. Kelley was just the first in a parade of "medical experts" called by the defense to explain to the jury the finer points of paranoia. Two more defense experts, Drs. Wilmer Allison and Ross Trigg, took the stand the next day, Saturday, to offer supporting opinions that poor Mary's mind was completely unhinged. They were followed by George Harris, a clerk in county court records who testified about another insanity case filed against the defendant in February 1912, which had never gone to trial. Throughout all the testimony, Mary seemed to follow the proceedings closely. On the third day of the trial, she was in what observers described as "a particularly good humor," laughing and chatting with counsel for both sides, apparently oblivious to her legal predicament.[17]

The prosecution finally got its turn Saturday afternoon. They argued that her assault had been calculated "with malice aforethought" and therefore was not the evidence of "a disordered mind." Mary followed their presentation intently, frequently nodding her head in agreement, which observers thought was odd in itself. The truth, however, was that she did not want to be judged insane, not even as a legal ploy to stay out of prison.[18]

The State's presentation was short, and the case went to the jury at 6:00 p.m. Saturday. Those twelve gentlemen took only an hour and twenty minutes to return a verdict of guilty, assessing punishment at five years in the penitentiary but with a recommendation that judgment be suspended "during good behavior." It was an extremely lenient sentence by any standard. Judge Brown pronounced the verdict from the bench saying that he was in agreement with it, but if he thought that wrapped things up, he was mistaken. Mary, stubborn as always, refused to accept the court's proffered mercy. She argued that she had never asked for it and that her lawyers were not following her wishes when they filed the application for leniency. Therefore, she declared indignantly, "I refuse to accept it!" On the contrary, she went on, she intended to appeal and if she lost, to go to the penitentiary with head held high.

She was just getting warmed up when Judge Brown cut her off in mid-rant, ordering her "released on her own recognizance." He then added, barely hanging onto his judicial dignity, "I don't give a hang where you go! You are now released." Before she could say anything else, he brought the gavel down adjourning court *sine die*.[19]

Mary Rea never did serve any time in the penitentiary. She continued to wage her one-woman war against the judicial system until she died on August 26, 1925, at the age of sixty-one. She was an occasional observer at trials involving her friends or matters in which she had a personal interest. In 1916 she attended every session of the trial of Robert Moore for auto theft in Sixty-seventh District Court because she and the defendant's mother were close friends. She assured Mrs. Moore at the outset that she would see to it that Robert got a "square deal." There is no record of what Judge Brown thought of having Mary in court every day, but everyone probably breathed a sigh of relief that it was not Judge Swayne's court. [20]

She lived out her final years in Fort Worth, but not in the home she had occupied for so many years. That now belonged to Roy Rea, who shunned his mother until the day he died at the premature age of twenty-four. Roy left behind two children who never got the full story about their crazy aunt from family members. Mary and Roy were buried side by side in Greenwood Cemetery, although neither had expressed any desire at the end to be interred in the same ground. Mary outlived her son by six years, long enough for public memory to fade and for skeletons to be locked up tight in the family closet. Fort Worth newspapers at the time of her death showed admirable compassion for both the deceased and for surviving members of the Rea family, not mentioning her long, losing fight with mental illness or her history of legal problems.[21]

In all its quirks, Mary Rea's case reveals the complete inability of the old judicial system to deal with the mentally disturbed. Lawmen, lawyers, and even judges were all completely baffled by what to do with her. If her last name had not been Rea or if she had not been able to afford high-powered lawyers, she would have been shipped off to either Rusk or Terrell state hospital when she first ran afoul of the law. In the end, it was only chance that kept her from killing someone during one of her courthouse tirades. But since she never killed or even seriously injured anyone, she is simply remembered by her descendants as "a corker."[22]

Epilogue:

Sadly, Mary's rampage in 1914 was not the last time gunfire was heard in a Fort Worth courtroom. In other examples, as in Mary's case, domestic disputes rather than great crimes seem to be what drove people to violate the traditional sanctity of the court of law. In 1986 Domingo Velasquez managed to smuggle a pistol into a Fort Worth courtroom during a nasty divorce proceeding and use it to shoot his estranged wife's boyfriend and take her hostage. Court officers overpowered Velasquez before he could do any more damage. In 1989 Deputy Sheriff Manny Cabano took his former girlfriend hostage in a JP's court, then shot himself and her in a case of murder-suicide. The most dramatic and bloody courtroom shooting to date occurred on July 1, 1992, when attorney George Lott smuggled a 9 millimeter semiautomatic pistol into the Second Court of Appeals during his divorce-and-child-custody case. Three appeals judges were working that day when Lott opened fire without warning, wounding two of the judges and killing two attorneys before escaping the courthouse. He was caught, convicted of capital murder, and executed in September 1994. These three cases caused more grief and mayhem, but one could argue it all started with Mary Rea.

CHAPTER 11

Madam Mary Porter: Mary, Mary Quite Contrary

Few people have ever heard of Mary Porter, although many think they have. That is because Mary is usually confused with Fannie Porter, the notorious San Antonio madam who became famous as the consort of Butch Cassidy and the Sundance Kid. In the 1970 documentary "The Making of *Butch Cassidy and the Sundance Kid*," Director George Roy Hill stated that Sundance's beautiful girlfriend, Etta Place, was "one of Fanny [*sic*] Porter's girls in Fort Worth." Wrong. *Mary* Porter was Fort Worth's most notorious madam at the turn of the century, not Fannie Porter; they were not related except for being in the same line of work. And unlike Fannie, Mary Porter's story was not turned into a Hollywood-ready legend; in fact, until now it has never been told.

She was born in Ireland in July 1844. Her family name is unknown at this time, and her time in the country of her birth was short.[1] Ireland at the time was in the grip of *An Gorta Mór*, the Great Hunger, caused by the failure of several successive potato crops. Between 1845 and 1850 more than a million people died of starvation and disease in a country of only eight million. Of the survivors, more than 2.1 million left Ireland for good, 1.5 million of them settling in the United States. Among those who came to America were the infant Mary, her sister Catherine, and her parents. They probably landed in

Canada sometime before 1850, then crossed into the United States over the open U.S.-Canadian border, eventually landing in Rochester, New York. Alternatively, they might have come through the Castle Garden port of entry in New York City and then made their way up to Rochester. The record is not clear. Because New York had a large resident Irish population, the newcomers felt comfortable and entered the workforce as menial laborers, which was still a vast improvement over life back in the old country. As one of their fellow countrymen observed of New York City, "No man or woman ever hungered or ever will and where you will not be seen naked . . . where you would never want or be at a loss for a good breakfast and dinner."[2]

In 1860 the family was living in Rochester, their status much improved through hard work and a bit of Irish luck. Sixteen-year-old Mary was probably working as a laundress (taking in laundry) or a domestic, the most common jobs for young Irish women at this date. Sometime in the next twelve years, Mary met and married George Porter and they settled in Hot Springs, Arkansas. The Irish faced less prejudice out West than back East. With no established social hierarchy and success measured by accomplishment rather than pedigree, the frontier was a place for starting over. Pockets of Irish could be found in cities all over the West about equally represented in politics, law enforcement, and vice. Hot Springs at this time was a popular health resort with a thriving vice district. The marriage may have been either a proper "Boston marriage" or a common-law arrangement; the record is not clear. They were definitely living in Hot Springs in 1880 as Mr. and Mrs. George B. Porter. They ran a "boarding house," which may have been a euphemism for a bordello because Mary was listed as the "head of household." Two other single young women "boarded" with them. Forty-two-year-old George died on March 30, 1882, and was buried in Hot Springs' Hollywood Cemetery. Mary stayed in town for at least another three years before packing up and leaving for greener pastures. There is some indication in local records that she had worn out her welcome, which was normal for women in her line of work, particularly after a turnover in municipal government. The world's oldest profession never really went out of fashion, but the faces changed. Mary never returned to Hot Springs, although she kept her house there and continued to operate it under her name for another five years.[3]

The death of George forced Mary to start life over as a thirtysomething widow with no schooling or marketable skills. If she was not already the breadwinner in the family, being thrown on her own forced her to earn a living any way she could. What she lacked in education and job skills, she more than made up for in business savvy and a talent for old-fashioned Irish blarney.

An indicator of Mary's chosen line of work is that her best friend was a major player in Hot Springs' sex trade: Josie Belmont, who like Mary was living on her own with no stated occupation on record. They became fast friends for the next twenty-five years, drawn together by the fact that they were both working in the world's oldest profession. There is no evidence that either of them was ever a "working girl," but they quickly established themselves as madams. Around 1885, Hot Springs became either too small or too hot for them, so they relocated to Fort Worth, arriving as passengers on a Cotton Belt train with nothing but each other and a small nest egg. Mary and Josie were just part of a "Hot Springs pipeline" to Fort Worth during these years. The Arkansas resort was a jumping-off place and so was Fort Worth. Gamblers, madams, bawds, and sporting men regularly moved back and forth between the two. Gracie Lane, another Fort Worth madam, made the trek down from Hot Springs to Fort Worth around the same time as Mary and Josie, although not in company with them.[4]

By November 1886, Mary and Josie were established in Fort Worth and doing business as proprietors of their own house, to which they gave the grandiose name "Maison de Joie"; others called it what it was, a "cathouse" or "disorderly house." In a matter of months Mary went out on her own, purchasing a place on lower Rusk, which had been one of the original streets when the town was laid out, along with Main, Houston, and Throckmorton. It was also the central axis of the red-light district known as Hell's Half-acre, a collection of dance halls, saloons, and bawdy houses. Her place, 1116 Rusk, was at a prime location on the corner of Rusk and Eleventh. On the other three corners were another bawdy house and two saloons. In bigger cities with more airs, the top-of-the-line places were known as parlor houses, but in Fort Worth they had a more prosaic name, boardinghouses, reflecting their relative lack of refinement. Mary's place may not have had fancy furnishings, drop-dead gorgeous girls, and a well-stocked wine cellar, but it was hers and she was proud of it. In the 1886–87 city directory, she described herself as the "madame" of her establishment. That simple listing was the equivalent to a formal announcement that she was open for business. Pearl Beebe, another recent arrival, went into business as a friendly competitor right across the street. In later years Mary would describe herself in more modest terms as the "owner" of a "boarding house."[5]

Mary prospered in the years that followed, but she had to establish herself first as a reputable operator in a disreputable business. That meant enduring a certain measure of official harassment while building her clientele and forging good relationships with some of the city's prominent men. When first hauled into court in 1885–86, she was slapped with $100 fines for running a "disorderly house," a broad euphemism that covered any troublesome business. In the years that followed she made fewer and fewer appearances in court; her lawyer and her connections took care of that. It also helped that she found benefactors among the most powerful of city fathers, which is not to say they were customers. Her two biggest benefactors from the ranks of polite society were Ephraim B. Daggett and William H. Ward. Daggett was the scion of E. M. Daggett, dubbed the "Father of Fort Worth," although Junior was the black sheep of the family. Ward was the respected proprietor of the upscale White Elephant Saloon, alderman, and member of the City Council's police committee. These were good men to have on one's side if one needed to have bond posted periodically. A madam could not waste time sitting in jail or appearing in police court. Besides, it was bad for her image.[6]

Mary had to endure her share of misfortune, which because of her line of work, got more than the usual press coverage. In November 1886 her establishment was burglarized by a petty thief. Police caught the man easily, but newspapers in both Fort Worth and Dallas reported that "Madam Porter's bagnio" had been hit. There is no record that she pressed charges. Then there were the routine visits to county court to pay the $200 fine for "running a disorderly house."[7]

All her misfortunes were not related to her line of work. In 1891 she was out driving in her buggy when her horse was spooked by the noise of an engine being backed up in the Santa Fe rail yards. The animal bolted, and she was thrown from the buggy, sustaining serious injuries. Never shy about standing up for herself, Mary hired a lawyer and filed suit against the railroad for $5,000. The suit was settled in March 1891 in her favor, but she was only awarded $100 for her pain and suffering.[8]

No matter what was going on in her personal life, Mary always kept her eye on the ball, which was running a first-class operation. She operated openly, paying the occasional fine, which constituted a sort of sin tax that allowed her to keep her doors open. A good madam had to keep both her girls and her customers happy. Quarrelling girls or disgruntled customers were equally bad for business. Many if not most young women in the business were emotional wrecks, irresponsible, and drug addicts. As employees they had to be handled with an iron fist inside a velvet glove. Mary possessed the right combination of no-nonsense toughness and motherly compassion. Her girls and employees were her family, and a close-knit little family it was. In 1900 there were six girls living in the house, ranging in age from fifteen to thirty-one. (At this date, the age of consent in Texas was fifteen.) She also employed an "enforcer" and an African American couple as her porter and housekeeper. The little family living under her roof could number as many as ten.[9]

And business was good. As early as 1894 she had expanded her operation, taking over the house next door at 1106 Rusk, making hers the biggest brothel in Fort Worth. Henceforward she kept her business office at that address using the other house strictly for entertaining. Two years later she had a telephone installed, which was an invaluable business tool in her line of work. It could be used to summon police if necessary or take reservations for preferred clients. Fort Worth's first telephone had been installed in 1877, but Mary still was a trailblazer as attested to by her telephone number, 72, which meant only seventy-one other people in town got a telephone before she did.

Her place was known by a variety of names in the public print: the aforementioned "bagnio," and "disorderly house," but also "hotel" or "boarding house." They all described the same sort of operation. No one was misled by the variety of names for what was known in less polite company as a whorehouse. Just like Eskimos have many different names for snow, Westerners had many different names for whorehouses.

Mary exercised a madam's right to be choosy about which girls she brought into her house. After all, her business reputation depended on them. The residents of Mary's house were polite and polished by the standards of a town not far removed from the frontier. There was, for instance, the English-born Madeline Turner, who was already a veteran of the business when she came to work for Mary. Still, despite a madam's best efforts, occasionally trouble erupted. In 1889, two of her girls laid claim to the same man. The hard feelings escalated into a catfight, then on a Thursday night in June one of them pulled a gun and opened fire, shooting the man at the center of the dispute. It was just the sort of thing that drew the unwelcome attentions of the authorities to a business that operated best in the shadows. But the worst thing a girl could do was rob a customer. If the "gentleman" complained to the police, Mary had to go to court, and if the word got around that her girls did such things, business could be ruined. In 1894 Mary had to appear in police court when Ruth Cameron and Hazel Lamont were accused of fleecing a customer. Her lawyer got them off, and she hustled them back to down to Rusk Street, but they soon found themselves out on the street.[10]

Despite the occasional bad apple, the turnover among Mary's girls was less than normal, largely because she considered it part of her job to be a mother hen. She could be altruistic as well as business-minded, as the case of Velma Banks, *aka* Miss Belknap, showed. Poor Velma was a teenager who landed in Fort Worth after running away from home and went to work in Mary's house. Rather than exploit her youth and innocence, Mary offered to buy the girl a train ticket home, and when that was refused, graciously allowed her to go to work for a rival, Mildred Clifton. That was after providing Velma a home and a job for five months. The amount of goodwill that Velma's story brought Mary both in the profession and the justice system was incalculable but easily worth a slew of well-placed bribes.[11]

The staff of a successful bordello included more than just the madam and a few girls. Besides those already mentioned, there was always a bartender, a boy to run errands, and a resident piano player. The last-named was essential. Music hath charms to soothe the savage beast—or the nervous john. The "professor" as he was sometimes known in big-city establishments played sprightly tunes in the parlor to entertain customers while they waited their turns with one of the girls upstairs. Just like a luxury hotel requires a first-rate staff, so a successful bordello requires people behind the scenes to prepare food, do the laundry, and keep the place clean. Mary relied on Bill and Effie Hamilton, an African American couple, at the turn of the century. There is no record that she kept a lawyer or bookkeeper on retainer, but with no training in either field, she would have had to have someone on call to provide expertise in such matters. She probably also had a policeman or two and maybe even an alderman on payroll.[12]

Mary served liquor and beer at her place, but brooked no drunkenness or rough stuff from her customers. She relied on her formidable reputation to keep an orderly "disorderly house." The police were not called out to break up fights, and customers did not seek out the police to file complaints. As a rule, her clientele were well behaved and her customers satisfied. Over a span of twenty-plus years, there was not a single newspaper report of a shooting or knifing or even an old-fashioned brawl at Mary Porter's, and that was not just because she paid off the authorities. She knew how to walk the thin line between providing a necessary service and openly defying the law.

On occasion, usually around election time, city fathers made a great show of shutting her down and others of her ilk. In the summer of 1890 the grand jury moved to indict property owners in the Acre "for renting places to parties of ill-repute." Mary's house on Rusk was a prime target. She received a notice from the city that she would be evicted effective November 1. She tried to fight it, but when the day arrived, she and her girls found themselves out on the street. The city promptly put the now-empty house up for rent, and the Union Bethel Mission and Women's Industrial Home fought to grab it for their rescue work in the Acre. The Union Bethel Mission won and soon moved in. Undaunted, Mary opened a new place on Rusk Street, right next door to the mission![13]

When pushed, Mary fought back, putting city fathers on notice that she would not meekly submit. But she also knew when to go quietly into the night. After routine police raids, she marched down to Recorder's Court, i.e., municipal court, and paid the nominal fines for herself and her girls. Those seldom amounted to more than ten dollars for herself and five dollars per girl. It was all grand theater because the fines were duly reported in the newspapers, which heartened reformers, but nobody spent any time in jail, which was good for business. Nonetheless, Mary had to go through a learning curve on these things. When she started out in Fort Worth, she had unwisely fought her first conviction in municipal court, which automatically kicked the appeal up to county court. That meant the case had to be put on the higher court's docket, she had to engage a lawyer, and there was always the possibility of losing on appeal, as she did the first time. Appeals cost more time and money than they were worth, so she learned to pay the piddling fines and get back to work. Which is not to say she did not make her share of appearances in county court over the years. In just the four-year span between 1893 and 1897, she was on the docket 130 times charged with a variety of crimes, the most frequent being "keeping a disorderly house," selling beer and liquor without a license, and "vagrancy" (another catchall category used against those engaged in prostitution). Her win-loss record is not known, but her doors were still open and she was bigger than ever at the turn of the century. In one mass roundup of the city's Big Five madams in 1900, she and her sisters were all hauled before the County Judge at the same time to face multiple charges each. They were found guilty, paid their fines, and were open for business as usual that night. [14]

While she tried to run a clean house, she could not always keep out the "bad actors." In 1891, Frank Simmons, a freight conductor for the Fort Worth and Denver City, got drunk and came to see his regular girl, Kittie Clark. He also had a wife, and the stress of trying to keep two women happy had finally gotten to him. As soon as he and Kittie were alone, he pulled out a pistol and shot her in the stomach, then put a bullet into his own brain. The police came and took away Simmons' body and the mortally wounded girl. Whether she survived or not, Kittie's days as a member of Mary's household were over. The negative attention she had brought down on her employer could not be tolerated if Mary wished to continue plying her trade in Fort Worth. It was that kind of business.[15]

Mary recognized the sad fact that there was no long-term future in her line of work, so almost from the beginning she began creating a nest egg for her eventual retirement. She bought real estate, assembling her portfolio a piece at a time, a lot here, a block there, all over the city. Most of it was in the Daggett Addition, an area that included but was not limited to Hell's Half-acre. The centerpiece of her portfolio was the entire east side of the 1100 block of Rusk where her house was located. But she also bought more respectable properties in other parts of the city such as the upscale Tucker Addition. She did not blink at paying as much as $5,000 for a single piece of property.[16]

While her real estate investments were shrewd and farsighted, her business instincts occasionally failed her. She resisted paying property taxes, a bit of stubbornness which left her two years in arrears on some of her properties by 1901. She owed the city $89.25, for instance, on her Rusk Street property.[17]

Mary's chosen line of work did not prevent her from maintaining strong family ties. Being Irish Catholic and having arrived in this country as an immigrant made her always hold family close. She remembered her family even in death, leaving a substantial part of her estate to two nieces she barely knew. During her working years in Fort Worth, she had also provided employment for two family members from her husband's side, Ruby Porter and Annie Porter. Ruby was twelve years old when she took up residence in Mary's boardinghouse. Ruby did not stay long, however, because she fell in love with one of Mary's customers, Slim Harkreader of Johnson County. The happy couple eloped, but before they could tie the knot, Ruby's father had Slim arrested for trying to marry the underage girl.[18] Her line of work may have been disreputable, even debauched, but Mary believed in taking care of family.

It was not family ties but professional connections that smoothed her way in Fort Worth for some twenty years. She enjoyed the protection of certain city fathers. These were highly placed men who looked out for her, occasionally posted bond for her, and saw that police did not harass her unnecessarily. Her biggest protector was Nat Kramer, not an elected official but a well-connected "sporting gentleman" who was part owner of the classy Cattle Exchange Saloon, a rival of the White Elephant, and an organizer of the Saloon Men's Association. He was on a first-name basis with the likes of Jake Johnson, Luke Short, Kleber Van Zandt, and John Peter Smith. Nat never carried a gun or acted in any manner unbecoming a gentleman. His principal vocation was gambling, in all its varied forms, which occasionally earned him a fine that he paid without complaint. In 1890 he was convicted in Recorder's Court of "riding with a prostitute," who may or may not have been one of Mary's girls. Whether he "kept" Mary is impossible to say, but he looked after her interests, even after she died. According to Mary Daggett Lake, the wife of cattleman Will Lake and a chronicler of Fort Worth's wild 'n' woolly days, he may have been secretly married to Mary, but if so, this would have been big news to his wife of many years, Katherine (Kate) Kramer.[19]

As a result of her high-placed connections, her occasional petitions to the City Council received a sympathetic hearing. In 1899, for instance, she asked the Council to make a special exception to the "fire limits" ordinance to exempt her house on Rusk from the fire codes, inspections by the fire marshal, and other bothersome rules. There is no indication that she received her exemption, but the petition was taken up by the Council, and there is no indication that it was denied either.[20]

Late in life Mary decided to get out of the business. It had been good to her, but she wanted to become respectable; she did not want to spend her last days in a whorehouse, even if it was a classy whorehouse. Besides, she was suffering from dementia. In her last five years, there was a series of small strokes that left her briefly "brain paralyzed," as the court documents awkwardly put it, after each one. The effect of those strokes had to be cumulative, too, causing increasing senility. She did not sell out but turned the operation of the business over to her old friend Nat Kramer and moved away from Rusk Street. For a while she roomed on Calhoun, one block east of her former stomping grounds, before buying a small house at 800 East Fifth. She had finally moved uptown.[21]

On Saturday, June 10, 1905, Mary Porter died at her home, probably of heart failure. The death certificate listed cause of death as "senile debility," which meant the doctor's best guess without an autopsy. She was sixty-five years old. Nat Kramer was with her at the end but not just as her longtime friend. For some time he had been her designated heir, the person she left almost everything to in her will. That will, which raised serious questions about the exact nature of their relationship, would be at the center of the legal battle over her estate. But, first things first: her passing had to be publicly announced to the community that she had called home for some nineteen years. The *Fort Worth Star-Telegram*'s obituary treated her as if she had been one of the city's grand dames, never mentioning her occupation. However, the paper could not pass up the opportunity to take some parting shots either, giving her age as seventy-five and emphasizing the point by calling her "an old resident of the city" and giving the cause of death as "old age." Had she been a society matron of similar years she would have received much more respectful treatment. [22]

St. Patrick's Catholic Church at 1206 Throckmorton, a landmark in Fort Worth since 1890. Mary Porter may not have been a regular parishioner, but Father Guyot gave her a proper Catholic send-off here in 1905. There was a delicious irony to the fact that St. Patrick's front door looked right down Twelfth Street (out of picture, right) to the heart of Hell's Half-acre where Mary conducted business for so many years. (Courtesy Fort Worth Public Library, Genealogy, Local History, and Archives Unit.)

Sanctuary of St. Patrick's, n.d., from post card. (Courtesy Fort Worth Public Library, Genealogy, Local History, and Archives Unit.)

She had no family in the city and most of her more respectable friends were not eager to admit that they knew her. But she had made all her own arrangements in advance. No time was wasted putting her into the ground. The funeral service was at St. Patrick's Catholic Church on Sunday afternoon, but holding the service on the Lord's Day was not the biggest surprise, having it in St. Patrick's was. Father Jean Guyot, longtime priest of the Fort Worth parish, allowed the notorious madam to receive last rites on holy ground. Truly, grace was multiplied. There is no record of how many of the church's 2,000 parishioners attended the funeral mass, but probably not many. The only married man there without his wife was Nat Kramer, whose friendship with Mary had flouted convention for many years. As for Father Guyot, he may have been so charitable because of Mary's generous donations to his church over the years. Like the *Star-Telegram*, the Dallas newspapers in reporting her death made no mention of how she had made her living. There was some confusion over the time of the funeral, however; the Dallas newspaper the next day placed it at four thirty, a half-hour later than the Fort Worth paper.[23]

She was laid to rest in Oakwood Cemetery in a lot owned by longtime friend Pearl Beebe beside three prostitutes who had worked for Pearl, constituting what would decades later be dubbed "Soiled Dove's Row." Whether Mary's grave ever had a headstone is open to question, but if so, it disappeared at some point, the victim of vandals or Mother Nature. Today the only way to find her final resting place is with a map of the cemetery. Pearl probably intended to be interred beside Mary and the others, but it never came to pass. She had moved on to El Paso after Fort Worth became too uptight for her type, and there she died. There was no financial reason why Mary was buried in someone else's plot and did not have a headstone grand enough that it could not be carried away or sink into the earth; she had more than enough money to go out in fine style.[24]

Mary Porter proved as controversial in death as she had been in life. It started when her will was filed for probate in county court three days after her death. Her last will named Nat Kramer as executor "without bond," and except for $500 to be split between two nieces, she left the bulk of her estate, approximately $20,000, to him. Kramer had been separated from his wife, Kate, for years, and he and Mary had maintained a close relationship, which is not to say intimate.[25]

When they learned of the arrangements, the two nieces, Anna M. Matthews and Nellie Shaughnessey, raised a howl, arguing that Kramer had exercised "undue influence" on their aunt and was not "akin to the deceased." They said the new will was all Nat's doing, and their aunt was "not of sound mind" when she signed it, and pointed out that Kate Kramer was only Nat's common-law wife, which came as a surprise to many people. For all these reasons, they demanded that the terms of the will be changed to leave them everything, both real and personal property, and hired W. A. Hanger of one of the city's most prestigious law firms, to represent them. It got worse. Kramer himself died less than two months later, before Mary's will could be probated, and there were questions of Kate's competence as well. (She would be judged insane in 1907 and a guardian appointed.) The two nieces redoubled their efforts to lay claim to Mary's estate. They had a strong case since Kate was only the common-law wife and was non compos mentis. Absent all the other complications, this was arguably the first case of palimony, which is the current legal principle that gives legal standing to the relationship between long-term, cohabiting couples. Neither the terminology nor the legal principle existed in that day, but the concept was introduced when Kate Kramer's legal representation argued that as "the wife" she was entitled to inherit Nat's estate.[26]

The court appointed an executor, Sidney L. Samuels, to administer the estates of both Mary and Nat. Since one of the nieces' charges was that Nat was draining their aunt's estate while outstanding debts went unpaid, Samuels had the power to "take charge and manage, control and collect rents from" Mary's Rusk Street property. Meanwhile, Kate Kramer, joined by Nat's sister, Mrs. Hannah Starr of Louisville, Kentucky, hired their own lawyer and prepared to do battle with the nieces.[27]

The contest over Mary's estate dragged on for a year. It was finally settled out of court in September 1906 when the two parties agreed to sell everything of Mary's and divide the proceeds, giving each niece $1,000 with the balance going to Kate Kramer and Hannah Starr. One year into the legal fight, Mary's estate was valued at $10,000 not the $20,000 originally estimated. The most valuable piece was the eight lots comprising the 1100 block of Rusk, which included the houses where she had run her business. When those lots were auctioned off on the courthouse steps on November 6, they brought altogether $33,500, but Judge George Hosey refused to approve the results of the public auction and ordered another sale, this time with privately submitted bids. That second sale brought in $35,000, justifying Hosey's order. On December 2, 1906, Sidney Samuels filed his final report on the disposition of the estate, closing the probate book on Mary Porter. Less court costs and lawyer fees, Katherine Kramer and Hannah Starr split more than $30,000 from Mary's estate and $18,000 from Nat's. Kate Kramer had not been a part of all the legal squabbling except by proxy. When she died in 1920, Mary's nieces reappeared to lay claim to her estate, but they lost out again. The tangled relationship between Nat Kramer, Kate Kramer, and Mary Porter kept Mary's ghost alive for years after her spirit had departed her mortal body.[28]

Even after the nieces' suit against Nat Kramer's estate was settled, county court was not done with Mary Porter yet. It turned out there was a vendor's lien on some of Mary's Rusk Street property for unpaid bills, left over from when Mary had contracted to have major work done on the houses. Some of the contractors and construction workers had never been paid, and now the estate had to settle with them before Mesdames Kramer, Starr, Matthews, and Shaughnessey could get their money. The vendors were finally paid off and the remaining money divided as laid out above.[29]

Mary Porter's life was an object lesson in what happens when a person who has lived most of her life on the wrong side of the law tries to go respectable at the end. She sold her business and relocated, but could not escape her past, and a woman with a past can never run fast enough or far enough to completely escape it. All the goodwill Mary had accumulated over the years as the best at what she did could not redeem her reputation. It was sufficient to get her a proper church funeral and a discreet obituary in the newspaper, but it could not save her estate from probate hell. The yearlong probate fight dragged her reputation through the mud one more time after she had been retired from the business for years and living respectably. The last memory Fort Worth had of Mary Porter was of the old madam who stole Kate Kramer's husband, embarrassed her blood kin, and left a financial mess behind for the courts to sort out. Forgotten was the Irish immigrant survivor who worked her way up from nothing to become a successful businesswoman, triumphed over being widowed and run out of Hot Springs, Arkansas, and ultimately died in her own bed with financial security and a man's love.

For more than a hundred years Mary Porter lay in an unmarked grave in Oakwood Cemetery. If it was ever marked, no one could tell; there was just a grassy spot with five unmarked spaces side by side. That changed in 2009. Mary finally got a measure of respect. On January 16, appropriately a bitterly cold, overcast day, a small group of Fort Worth historians gathered to put down a headstone on Mary's grave and say a few words over her. The headstone is a small, modest one, which besides the basic information, simply says, "Call me Madam," not a direct quote, but a summation of her defiant approach to life. As far as is known, Mary Porter is the only madam in Texas history, maybe all of history, whose final resting place proudly says so.

Oakwood Cemetery, Fort Worth's second public cemetery, is the final resting place of the city's famous and infamous since 1879. It lies on the north side of the Trinity River, almost directly across from the Courthouse. (Author's collection.)

Oakwood Cemetery sign. (Author's Collection.)

One hundred and four years after her death, Mary Porter finally got a headstone on her grave in Oakwood Cemetery. She lies in lonely solitude in what is now known as "Soiled Doves' Row" with three other members of her profession. The stone was emplaced in a small ceremony in January 2009 by modern-day FOMs. (Author's collection.)

CHAPTER 12

James W. Swayne: Straight-arrow Judge

A Southern lawyer who also happened to be a man of high principle. A friend of the black man and defender of black civil rights when doing so was the exception rather than the rule. This could be a description of Atticus Finch, the fictional hero of Harper Lee's bestselling 1960 novel, *To Kill a Mockingbird*, brought to life on the screen by Gregory Peck in 1962. It is also a description of the flesh-and-blood James W. Swayne of Fort Worth. Swayne was a public figure for thirty-five years and set a standard during his years on the bench of the Seventeenth District Court that few have approached, much less equaled since.

James Swayne was born in Lexington, Tennessee, on October 6, 1855, or at least that is the best guess here. His death certificate and an early biographical sketch give two different years, as do the census records.[1] He had a brother, John F. Swayne, five years older, and a sister, Mary W. Swayne, three years older. Although James was the second-born son, he was the one named for his father. The parents, James W. and Amanda Henry Swayne both died prematurely, when James, Jr., was less than two years old. The children, now orphans, lived with their grandfather, Felix W. Henry, for the next nine years, until 1866 when W. C. McHaney of Henderson County became their legal guardian. Mr. and Mrs. Swayne had been prosperous if not wealthy. Papa was an eminent lawyer, who at his death inherited sufficient funds to loan a brother-in-law $2,000 for a business venture, which had to be paid back only "if he succeeded." The estate was kept in trust after Amanda Swayne died, and as the kids came of age, they each received a share. Mary Swayne received $1,499.36 in 1869, and John received $1,771.13 in 1871. James' share, which he received on January 24, 1877, amounted to only $830.56. Still, it would not have been an insignificant bankroll to start the rest of his life with had he not spent it all to pay off debts incurred in getting his education. By the time he arrived in Fort Worth a year later, he was "without a dollar to his name." Years later, Swayne also told his biographer that his parents had left "a fine fortune," but his guardian, i.e., Grandpa Henry, had squandered most of the estate in a series of bad loans that went down the drain along with the Confederate cause in the Civil War. He never attempted to hold the old man legally responsible, but he never forgot his lost inheritance either.[2]

James Swayne set his sights high when it came to his education. Perhaps it was because he came from a family of lawyers, but he could not be content just learning the 3Rs or, when it came to his career choice, merely "reading the law" before hanging out his shingle. His paternal grandfather had been a country lawyer, his uncle Noah Swayne had sat on the U.S. Supreme Court, and a cousin, Wagner Swayne, had been one of the chief solicitors of financier Jay "I don't build railroads, I buy them" Gould. The law was part of his genes. He attended the Kentucky Military Institute before getting a law degree from the Lebanon Law School in Tennessee, launching pad for many prominent Texas lawyers in the days before the University of Texas opened a law school so that the state's sons did not have to go out of state to get a law degree. At the time he graduated, most men still came to the law by "reading" with an established member of the profession. In fact, one version of Swayne's life says that he got his training by "reading law" with unnamed Fort Worth attorneys, but the fact is he went the law school route, graduating in 1877.[3]

Like so many Southerners during Reconstruction, Swayne decided to go west and start over. He followed his brother to Fort Worth, arriving in January 1878 with little more than his law books and the clothes on his back. John had preceded him by seven years and already established his own law practice in the city. They were eventually followed by their sister and her husband and by their cousin John

M. Taylor. James and John joined with Charles M. Crane to open a fire insurance agency, always a good business to go into in frontier towns made almost entirely of wood and lighted with gas and kerosene lamps. John and their cousin also sold real estate and practiced law at 615 Main Street. James opened his own law practice at 501½ Main and resided at El Paso and Ballinger. If the Swayne boys did not exactly have Fort Worth in their pocket, they were definitely making their mark, which was why they had come to town in the first place.[4]

Both Swayne boys were hardworking, unusually well educated, and "determined to push their way to the front." John attended Washington College in Lexington, Virginia, right after the Civil War, when Robert E. Lee was its president, and graduated with a law degree. Both brothers married well and, with cousin John, jumped into politics with both feet. John Taylor was the first to win elective office (the State Legislature), but John and James were not far behind him. John Swayne won his first election in 1873 to become Fort Worth's first city secretary, and seven years later he was elected county clerk. They set the bar high, but James would ultimately surpass them both.[5]

In an age before having boatloads of money was a prerequisite for entering politics, James had all the necessary qualifications: He was likable, articulate, and possessed an insightful mind. He was also highly ambitious. In Fort Worth, making a career in politics meant belonging to the party of Andrew Jackson and the Old South. James was a lifelong Democrat.[6] In 1883 he won his first elected office, as city attorney, and was re-elected in 1884. Since city offices only paid a modest honorarium, he maintained his private law practice to pay the bills and fund his political ambitions. He continued to practice law and keep his hand in politics for the rest of his life.[7]

James Swayne was more than a resident of Fort Worth; he was a proud citizen of the city in the same way that the ancient Greeks defined themselves by their home city, not their national, ethnic, or political group: Leonidas was a Spartan, Socrates was an Athenian. Swayne and his contemporaries considered it their civic duty to support and promote their hometown, even to the extent of digging into their own pockets to fund public works that would make it a better place. In 1881 as an "assistant foreman" of the volunteer fire department, he took the lead in "devising the proper steps" to reorganize the force on a more efficient and professional basis. In 1886 he served as treasurer of the Fort Worth Police Department, and when policeman Dick Townsend was killed in the railroad strike that spring, he represented the Department at Townsend's funeral.[8]

He exemplified civic boosterism although he was not above making a little profit at it. Supporting the community and turning a profit went hand in hand. Fort Worth was still a frontier town in the 1880s with a tax base too small to support grandiose public works. It took men of means and vision to get things done. James Swayne was one of those men. He subscribed to every railroad that came to town, and he was the driving force behind getting a "magnificent" natatorium built in 1889. This combination public swimming hall and hotel at the corner of Third and Rusk was the city's first family entertainment venue. It would stand for many years as a landmark to the city's coming of age. In 1889 he became one of seventeen directors of the Texas Spring Palace, an ambitious project to steal the spotlight from the annual state fair in Dallas. The other men on the list were a Who's Who of the city's movers and shakers, including B. B. Paddock, W. A. Huffman, and John Peter Smith. Despite financial losses, they kept the Texas Spring Palace going for a second season. For the 1890 season he served on the soliciting committee to raise $50,000 by putting the strong arm on the city's business community. In the 1880s he also threw himself into the fight against the Dark Lantern Party, a secretive coalition of left-leaning radicals that posed a serious threat to the political status quo in Texas. Fort Worth was the group's headquarters, from where it mounted a major challenge to the ruling Democrats in 1886.[9]

By the middle of the next decade, Swayne had managed to build a political base and an impressive financial position for himself. He made his money in the insurance business and real estate, not in the law, selling fire, accident, and casualty insurance for years as the junior partner in the firm of Harrison, Barron, and Swayne. His two offices, law and insurance, were a block apart on Main Street. As he was in law and politics, he proved a quick study in business. Fort Worth was booming in the 1880s, so he began buying up real estate, including one bundle of five lots in the Daggett Addition near the railroad station for $15,000 in 1890. He was on his way to becoming one of what he called the "Financial Kings of Fort Worth." Then the Panic of 1893 hit the nation, taking railroads, banks, and even cities down with it. Swayne found himself holding municipal bonds and railroad stocks that had lost 90 percent of their value. He even found himself on the opposite side of the bar, as a defendant trying to recover his losses from the likes of the Union Mutual Life Insurance and H. L. Crowl companies. He narrowly avoided filing for bankruptcy. It would not be the last time his financial instincts would fail him badly. A few years later he partnered with future governor James Hogg to stake a claim in the legendary Spindletop oil field in east Texas. The Hogg-Swayne Syndicate launched a project to build a pipeline to Houston, but there is no evidence that they completed it, and unlike his partner, Swayne cashed out before the really big money began rolling in. Still, he managed to parlay his political influence and business experience into some lucrative opportunities back home, such as becoming a director of the Fort Worth Oil Company in 1902.[10]

Although Lady Luck had deserted him in business, she was definitely on his side in love. He met Josephine B. Latham of Terrell, Texas, in the middle 1880s. Like him, she was an orphan and from a highly educated family. Her grandfather had been president of Madison College in New York and her father, president of Tuscaloosa College in Georgia. Born in Virginia in 1859, she grew up as a ward of the H. W. Dodge family after her father died during the Civil War. When Swayne met her, he was swept away, not only because of her beauty, but also because she had a good head on her shoulders and was financially well fixed. She had attended Vassar, then finished her education at the University of Missouri, where she was honored as the best Latin scholar ever to attend the school, male or female. Not for her the role of simple goodwife and helpmeet. Her own ambitions in many ways matched those of her husband. They made a good team: he, the legal eagle and rising political star; she, the writer, clubwoman, and business entrepreneur. They were married on October 6, 1887. By 1890, she was "one of the most accomplished ladies of Texas." In 1907 she published a book, *The Story of Concord*, which reviewers called "the most notable literary work that has ever been issued by a resident of the city of Fort Worth." And by World War I she was an insurance underwriter with an office in the Burk Burnett Building, a business she probably learned from her husband.[11]

Swayne built a legal career by standing on principle and speaking out whenever the situation demanded. He did not work just the sunny side of the street where wealthy corporations and deep-pocketed clients resided. He paid his civic and moral dues as a criminal defense lawyer taking on the "unwinnable" cases that nobody else wanted, such as Jim Burris, *aka* Jim Toots. Burris was a Negro sporting man who shot white policeman Lee Waller in 1892. A white Fort Worth jury found him guilty and sentenced him to hang, although Waller was a well-known racist and bully who had a personal beef with his murderer. Swayne took the case all the way to the Texas Court of Criminal Appeals, arguing, "Justice should be done an unfortunate Negro who, if he had been a white man, would never have been indicted in the first place." Swayne could not convince the court, but he did not give up. Still battling for his client, in 1895 he went to Austin to make a personal appeal to Governor James Culberson for Burris' life. His passionate appeal got the death sentence commuted to life in prison. Seven years later, Governor Joseph Sayers granted Burris a full pardon. In his proclamation he cited Swayne's opinion first among all those he cited supporting the pardon.[12]

Taking on unpopular causes was what won Swayne the highest respect of his peers, culminating in his appointment to the bench of the Seventeenth District Court in 1909. He was appointed in March to serve out the unexpired term of Judge Mike Smith who had resigned, and was reappointed in his own right the following year.[13] During seven years on the bench he heard a series of headline cases that ensured his place in Fort Worth history. He was the only judge in Fort Worth history to send three defendants to the gallows: Tommy Lee in 1914, C. A. Myers and Clint Williams in 1915. He took no delight in sentencing men to hang, particularly when they were mentally unbalanced (Myers) or poor and black (Lee and Williams), but he never shirked his duty either. That is why the Seventeenth District Court became the court of choice for difficult and controversial cases. More than once he had howling mobs outside his courtroom trying to sway the proceedings.

In modern parlance, James Swayne was an activist judge who was not content just to hear those cases that happened to come his way. He used the bench as a platform to fight for the causes he believed in, such as honest government, Negro civil rights, and wiping out vice in the city. It was his use of the grand jury system to pursue his personal causes that made him a pioneer in jurisprudence locally. He wielded his judicial powers far beyond trial proceedings by charging his grand juries to go after specific criminal activities. On more than one occasion he summoned a grand jury and told them what he expected, then sat back and waited impatiently for them to hand up indictments. Most of his grand juries over the years proved to be quite compliant in this regard. Sometimes his aggressive tactics forced reluctant county attorneys (*aka* district attorneys) to prosecute weak cases. It was these personal crusades against crime and injustice that defined his tenure on the bench.

His first crusade after taking the bench in 1909 was to convene the grand jury and order them to investigate the licensing of saloonkeepers. The barmen had been operating their joints for years in open defiance of both state law and local ordinance. Backroom gambling and Sunday operations were just two of the most blatant examples of criminal behavior that were tolerated. Swayne and his allies were not able to shut the saloons down, but they made a dent in their operations, and thereby reduced their influence in public affairs.

That same year, he took on Hell's Half-acre, the notorious vice district on the south end of town. It began with a "stirring speech" to his grand jury in August calling on them to abolish the district even if it meant taking on "men of power and strength in the city." In taking on the Acre, he took on the city commissioners who favored legalizing it. To them he declared, "The crimes must stop!"[14]

In 1911 he ordered his grand jury to investigate the lax enforcement of the Sunday closing law. There had been a city ordinance on the books since 1889 requiring saloons to be closed on the Lord's Day, and there would be a state law to that effect after 1913. But the city ordinance was a joke and a state prohibition was still being fought out in the legislature. Swayne was willing to use his authority to do what, so far, neither city fathers nor state legislators had been able to do. In his "special charge" to the grand jury he chastised his fellow citizens: "I hear that there is a large proportion of people in Fort Worth encouraging, aiding and abetting in every way they can the people who are violating the Sunday laws." Based on the grand jury's report, he called for moving prosecution of violators of the ordinance from police court where they usually got a slap on the wrist to district court where convictions were more likely to be handed down—particularly in his court.[15]

In 1913, he ordered the grand jury to investigate "graft . . . in the affairs of county and city government." As in his crusade against saloons, the instrument of his righteous justice was not the leading lights of the community but a collection of ordinary citizens empowered to root out evil in their community. Their names were not found on the front page of the newspapers or in the social register but on the voting rolls. Because of the broad latitude allowed grand juries, they could launch an investigation based on nothing more than "rumors current." That was enough for Swayne to rally his troops. As usual, he worded his charge to the gentlemen of the grand jury in provocative language guaranteed to garner newspaper coverage. He characterized the so-called grafters as "leaches" on society. That was just for starters. He went on in that vein:

> The man who deliberately takes his gun and goes out on the highway and robs can be given the death penalty under our laws. . . . The man who has the confidence of the public and uses his office for private gain, who accepts money on the side, who sells his vote for filthy lucre is worse than the criminal, because he has robbed those who have placed their confidence in him.[16]

In the end, the grand jury did not uncover any vast conspiracies of graft among public officials, but it certainly got their attention and made ordinary citizens take a closer look at the men they elected to run their community. And there was more than a little irony to Swayne taking the lead in rooting out graft since it had only been a few years since he himself had been accused of the same thing.

Over a long career in law and politics, he took his share of lumps. In 1903 a group of five citizens brought suit against him for collecting "excess fees" when he was county attorney (1896–1900). County and city officials in those days could earn fees in addition to their regular salaries; it was the system. The malfeasance charged in this instance was about the amount of the fees, not the act of accepting them. The plaintiffs asked that Swayne reimburse the public treasury for $15,000 in excess fees with interest. In addition to the criminal investigation, County Commissioners Court also looked into the accusations. Swayne, who heretofore had enjoyed an unblemished reputation and knew his way around a courtroom, vigorously contested the lawsuit, contending that he had been entitled to the fees under state law for the "many extra duties" he had performed. The case was not finally settled until 1908, but in the end he was vindicated twice—in Forty-eighth District Court and by the Commissioners' investigation.[17]

In his own court, James Swayne always ran a tight ship. He prided himself on keeping his docket clear by moving cases along promptly. Four years into his tenure he said, "It has been my rule and practice since I have been District Judge to never let a criminal case lag, and especially a murder case."[18] And over the years he heard more than his share of murder cases. No matter how explosive the case, he was always in control in his courtroom except once (see below). He did not like continuances or lawyers who used stalling tactics to try to gain an advantage. And he was as well known for his speeches delivered ex cathedra from the bench and in the form of instructions to grand juries as he was for his decisions. He never let pass an opportunity to lecture his fellow citizens about their moral and civic duties. He did not mind whose toes he stepped on either. Klansmen, gamblers, liquor dealers, he blasted them all equally, and never gave a thought to the possibility that some of those he took aim at might come looking for him. His words were always well selected and pointed, and the newspapers made a habit over the years of printing them verbatim. This was the age before sound bites and Judge Swayne spoke in paragraphs more often than not. Since he was usually quite "jovial," his occasional pontificating never failed to get his listeners' attention.[19]

Physically, he was not an imposing man. Just the opposite: he was never in the best of health, although that never seemed to hold him back. In 1884 it was reported in Fort Worth papers that he was "very ill and not expected to live." The specific ailment was not mentioned; he could have been a victim of one of the occasional typhoid or smallpox epidemics that swept through the city, or some more mundane infectious disease. In 1903, while on a business trip to New York City, he was again reported to be "at the point of death" with "a severe attack of pneumonia," and he again seemed to defy the odds by surviving. Then in 1913, at the age of fifty-eight, he was confined to bed for a week with some unspecified illness. His respiratory problems seemed to have been chronic, and he also seemed to have been accident-prone.

In 1886, while attempting to climb onto a wagon while it was in motion, his foot was run over leaving him limping badly for some time afterwards.[20]

Most of the defendants who appeared before Judge Swayne over the years respected him, even if they did not like the sentence he imposed. There were only a few notable exceptions, the first being C. A. Myers, convicted for the murder of A. W. Montague in 1915 and sentenced to hang. Myers was so volatile and difficult a client that the Judge had to appoint a second public defender to represent him after the first one quit. At his sentencing, Myers turned his wrath on Swayne: "You had the jury [so] keyed up they had to give me the extreme penalty or they were likely to get roasted [by your honor]." Swayne, refusing to be intimidated, replied, "My conscience is clear."[21]

A second, much more serious incident occurred when defendant Mary Rea took exception to Judge Swayne's rulings. The mentally unbalanced woman declared on war on Swayne after he granted her long-suffering husband a divorce in 1910 then ruled against her in several civil suits in the years following. Mary was relentless. Not even fines or jail time for contempt made her back off. She was still nursing the original grudge when, in 1914, she came before Swayne in a family dispute. When the verdict did not go her way, she pulled out a pistol and opened fire in his general direction. At the time, Swayne was casually sitting in the jury box addressing her. She managed to empty the pistol before her lawyer could wrestle her out of the courtroom. Fortunately, all of the shots went into the wall or ceiling, but Swayne displayed nerves of steel during the melee. He kept his seat, not even flinching as the bullets flew. The next time Swayne saw Mary was when he was called as a material witness at her trial for attempted murder. She was found guilty but served no time and, insofar as the record shows, never bothered Swayne again. Besides being a cool customer, the remarkable thing about the Judge was the consideration he had extended to Mary over the years that she stalked him. He had lectured her about her behavior a few times, fined her for contempt of court, and even ordered her to jail for two nights, but he had never used the full weight of the law against her. He let the contempt fine slide and refused to instigate commitment proceedings even after she disrupted his courtroom and confronted him on the street. In the end, his compassion nearly got him killed, but it was part of his character.[22]

Barely a year after Crazy Mary nearly killed him, another irate woman confronted the Judge in his courtroom. Pea Howard was the wife of police officer Peter Howard, who was murdered by Luis Flores and an accomplice on August 16, 1915. Flores was tried for first-degree murder in Forty-eighth District Court in April 1916. He was convicted and the jury sentenced him to life in prison, but Mrs. Howard took exception to the conduct of the trial and to the sentence; she wanted Flores to go to the gallows. After the verdict was read, she "bitterly attacked" Swayne who, with the Mary Rea episode in mind, ignored her tirade and quickly exited the courtroom.[23]

Swayne faced some "bad actors" during his years on the bench, but he never lost his humanity. He felt compassion for the unfortunate and powerless members of the community who were likely to be steamrolled by the justice system because they had public defenders or no defenders at all. It is his record with minorities that makes him stand out as a jurist of the first rank. When the Negro Tommy Lee murdered officer John Ogletree and another man and wounded four others in 1913, a white lynch mob formed outside the jail to break him out and string him up. Frustrated in that objective, they turned their wrath on the "Negro quarter" on the south end of town, looting and pillaging until the authorities finally drove them away. Sheriff William Rea and Police Chief Oscar Montgomery did their jobs and kept Lee out of the mob's hands even at great personal risk to themselves. But it was James Swayne's finest hour. Ordinarily, it is not a judge's job to interpose himself between a lynch mob and its intended victim. Yet Swayne did not hesitate. With the county jail under siege, he stood on the steps and ordered the howling mob to disperse. As he explained his stand the next day,

> It became my duty as one of the Magistrates of this State to call upon them to disperse and tell them what the law is, and I did this in no uncertain terms; and after they failed to disperse each and every one of them was guilty of the conduct of the other, whether he participated in it or not.[24]

He instructed Sheriff Rea and Chief Montgomery to order their men to fire into the crowd if they could not control the situation any other way. He was determined not to let a mob break into the jail.

On May 16, while a large swath of south Fort Worth was still smoldering and talk of lynching was still in the air, Swayne showed that he was just getting started. He had a murder defendant to bring to trial and a riot to deal with. He did not wait for others to step forward; instead he pushed and prodded the legal system into action, appointing "able and distinguished" counsel from among the city's white legal fraternity to defend Tommy Lee. Then he dispensed with any idea that he was just going through the motions when he added, "I will not excuse any of the lawyers I have appointed to defend Lee [for any reason]."[25]

He did not let his grand jury off the hook either, urging them to indict each and every rioter. He appealed to the better natures of the all-white jury members but was also shrewd enough to put the issue in terms of community pride and the bedrock American faith in property rights:

> The Negroes of Fort Worth and their property are entitled to as much protection as the white people and theirs. Thousands of dollars have been lost through the outrage and shame of last night, and I shall expect you to return, not a few, but hundreds of indictments.[26]

And so, he thundered, "Gentlemen, investigate it! Investigate it thoroughly! It matters not who is guilty, return a bill against them. Each and every man . . . is guilty of an unlawful assembly and guilty of riot." He succeeded in putting enough backbone into the Seventeenth District Court's grand jury to secure a handful of indictments, but he was less successful getting all-white trial juries to convict the accused.[27]

More than any other city father, Swayne took the lead in the days following on two fronts: bringing the rioters to justice and seeing that Tom Lee got a fair trial. He was the conscience of the city and the voice of reason, even visiting Lee in jail to see for himself that the prisoner was being treated right by his jailors. Some might have considered such unconventional behavior on the part of a jurist going too far, but it was typical of Swayne. "Our city has been disgraced!" he thundered more than once. But he did more than chastise; he urged Fort Worth businessmen to dig into their own pockets and pay for the damages to the black neighborhood, estimated at more than $14,000. In the end, he made it his personal mission to see that his city did the right thing while he tried to keep a lid on an explosive situation. The fact that there was no more rioting and no more killing shows how well he succeeded.[28]

Two years later, when Mexican aliens Luis Flores and Joe Estapa stabbed police officer Peter Howard, Flores' trial was held in Swayne's Seventeenth District Court. Just as he had done for Tommy Lee, Swayne assigned first-rate lawyers as public defenders although many in the city were ready to execute summary justice on the only one of the two cop killers in custody.

None of which is to say that Swayne was a bleeding-heart liberal; he was not. He simply believed in equal justice for all. Plus, he also counted among his friends members of the city's black community, which made defending their rights a matter of conscience that extended beyond his courtroom to the community at large. After the 1913 riot, he said of one of the black businessmen whose property had been heavily damaged, "I have known him since I was a boy. He and I were children together in the old State of Tennessee." For Swayne, black members of the community were more than mere plaintiffs or defendants in his court; they were in some cases personal friends. He vouched for his unnamed friend (it may have been Bill McDonald) in another statement to the press, calling him "a good Negro, respectful to white people, honest and saving his money. He is a good citizen." These were the sort of words calculated to prick the consciences of Fort Worth's white majority and encourage them to do the right thing. On another occasion, a legless, elderly black man appeared before him charged with assault to commit murder with a gun. Swayne recognized the defendant as his shoeshine man for many years and a harmless character at heart. There was no question, however, that the man was guilty. After the verdict was delivered, Swayne exercised his judicial discretion to suspend the sentence, admonishing the oldtimer to stick to shoeshining. The grateful defendant never appeared in court again.[29]

And Fort Worth's black community respected Swayne's integrity and his efforts in their behalf. Starting in 1896, Swayne was invited to speak at the annual Juneteenth celebration in (Frederick) Douglass Park. Some whites, like the Mayor, were invited to speak because

James W. Swayne as state senator representing the Thirtieth District, which included Tarrant County. Taken about 1891 or '92, this is his formal portrait on the wall of the State Senate Chamber, Austin. (Author's collection.)

it was expedient. Swayne was always invited because he was welcome.[30]

James Swayne's political career soared along with his legal career. After winning his first city office, he set his sights higher. In 1886 he ran for mayor against Henry S. Broiles. John Peter Smith had just retired after four successive terms in office, so the way was wide open for a fresh face. Swayne squared off against Dr. Broiles, and the race quickly became "quite warm." He lost out to Broiles and never ran for city office again, but his ambition for public office burned just as brightly, and he would enter the lists again.[31]

He subsequently won county office, but that did not satisfy him either, unlike his brother John who was content to serve two terms as county clerk. In 1890 Swayne ran for representative from Tarrant County in the Twenty-second State Legislature. He won and held that seat from January 13, 1891, until April 12, 1892. In 1892 he mounted a vigorous campaign for the State Senate. While the race was going on that fall, he turned over his judicial duties to R. E. Beckham. After he lost the race he returned to the bench. Two years later, when state elections rolled around again, "the Honorable James W. Swayne" was asked by a newspaper reporter if the rumors were true that he would be running for the State Senate again. It was the cagey politician, not the judge who replied the rumors were untrue: "his aspirations did not stop short of the United States Congress!"[32]

In so saying, he was being more playful than seriously testing the political waters. But running for political office was never far from his mind. He ran for county attorney and won in 1896. He won re-election in 1898 but left office under a cloud in 1900 when the graft accusations began flying. The case was in litigation for five years (1903–1908), but that did not prevent him from making another run for public office while it was pending. In 1907 he made his first run for national office, challenging Oscar W. Gillespie for the District Twelve seat in the House of Representatives. At the time, Gillespie had held the seat since 1903 so there was no shame when Swayne lost to the man who held the record as the longest-serving congressman from Fort Worth (four terms) until Fritz G. Lanham laid claim to that title (fourteen terms, 1919–1947).[33]

Judge James Swayne presided over the Seventeenth District Court for the State of Texas on the second floor of the Tarrant County Courthouse, pictured here as it would have appeared in the 1920s. This is the same courthouse where Jeff Daggett took his fatal elevator ride and Mary Rea sneaked in a gun and opened fire on Swayne in his courtroom. (Post card image. Courtesy Fort Worth Public Library, Genealogy, Local History, and Archives Unit.)

In 1914 he launched another run at the U.S. House of Representatives, kicking off his campaign for the Sixty-fourth Congress on July 1 with a big rally on the west lawn of the courthouse, although the election was not until November 1915. His opponent this time, Oscar Callaway of Comanche, was not as formidable as Oscar Gillespie, but he was still running for his third term representing District Twelve. Swayne had a number of heavyweights present the night he kicked off his campaign to endorse his candidacy, including an aged Sam Woody, Fort Worth's oldest living pioneer. The candidate also announced that women would be welcome at the rally although at this date they were still denied the right to vote. Swayne was a "happy warrior," but he still lost to the incumbent in November 1915.[34]

Whether running for office, ruling from the bench, or holding a surprise party for the sheriff, James Swayne was always newsworthy. The Fort Worth and Dallas newspapers reported regularly on what he said and did. His long public career is a testament to the high esteem in which his fellow citizens held him, but his poor record running for high elected office shows that he was more admired as jurist of principle than as a politician. That he never made it onto the national stage does not diminish what he did for Fort Worth. The surprising part is that he was so quickly forgotten after his death.

When Swayne died on February 11, 1929, a Monday, at the age of seventy-four, he was still in harness serving as chairman of the State Industrial Accident Board. At the time of his death he was in Austin fulfilling the duties of his office despite being in poor health for some time. His remains were returned to Fort Worth for the funeral service five days later followed by interment in Greenwood Cemetery. Cemetery records have his name wrong (as James M. Swayne), and he is buried in a lot with no other immediate family members around him, more alone in death than he ever was in life. His had been a forty-six-year career in public service, most of it spent serving Fort Worth. He had always been a defender of law and order but also social justice. Today, if you listen hard you may still be able to hear his footsteps walking the hallways of the Tarrant County Courthouse or see his ghost looking over the shoulders of a new generation of district court judges.[35]

ENDNOTES

Introduction

1. Quoted in Kasey S. Pipes, *Ike's Final Battle* (Los Angeles: World Ahead Publishing, 2007), p. xv of Preface.

Chapter 1

1. Ella Hazel Atterbury Spraker, *The Boone Family: A Genealogical History of the Descendants of George and Mary Boone Who Came to America in 1717* (privately printed, 1922).

2. The words of New York newspaper editor John L. O'Sullivan, written in the *Democratic Review* in the summer of 1845, which perfectly captured the attitude of millions of Americans in that era.

3. Any attempt to describe Arnold's physical characteristics cannot be anything more than an educated guess because neither the Army nor those who knew him best left us a description. A handwritten note by an anonymous researcher in his vertical file at the Fort Worth Public Library describes him as "6 feet tall, gray eyes, auburn hair." Until recently, there was not even a photograph to go by. Now that we have a photographic image, it does not seem to show a man six feet tall.

4. Ripley Arnold's complete military record is found in George W. Cullum, *Biographical Register of the Officers and Graduates of the U.S. Military Academy at West Point, New York* (Boston: Houghton, Mifflin and Company / Riverside Press, 1891, 3rd ed.), pp. 722–23.

5. There is more than one version of the "Benny Havens, Oh!" story. An alternative version credits the song solely to O'Brien. Regardless of who is credited with writing the lyrics, the tune was not original; it was the Irish standard, "The Wearing o' the Green." James S. Robbins, *Last in Their Class: Custer, Pickett and the Goats of West Point* (New York: Encounter Books, 2006), pp. 73, 426 n. 20; "Major Arnold's Life Adventurous; He Fought Duel at West Point," *Fort Worth Star-Telegram*, October 30, 1949; Clay Perkins, *Fort in Fort Worth* (Keller, TX: Cross-Timbers Heritage Publishing Co., 2001), p. 36.

6. Records of the Office of the Judge Advocate General (Army), Record Group 153, Registers of the Records of the Proceedings of the U.S. Army General Courts-Martial, 1809–1890, Records CC-225 and 243, Washington, DC.: National Archives and Records Administration. Also cited in Perkins, *Fort in Fort Worth*, pp. 36–37.

7. Historian Clay Perkins characterizes Arnold as "gregarious and good-natured." He was neither. Perkins, *Fort in Fort Worth*, p. 35; "Major Arnold's Life Adventurous"; Robbins, *Last in Their Class*, p. 426.

8. Perkins, *Fort in Fort Worth*, p. 38; Robbins, *Last in Their Class*, p. xii.

9. Ripley and Catherine Arnold had five children—Willis, Florida Belle, Kate, Sophia, and Nannie—between 1838 and 1851. Pinning down the birth date and birthplace of each is extremely frustrating because records are either lacking or contradictory. The 1850 census and the work of Mary Bruner, genealogist with the Fort Worth Museum of Science and History, provide the best information. See "Ripley Arnold" in Seventh United States Federal Census (1850), Navarro County, Tarrant County, TX, Microfilm Roll No. M-432_910 (available on-line at http://AncestryLibrary.com); and Bruner, "Descendants of Ripley Allen Arnold," MS in vertical files, Genealogy, Local History, and Archives Unit, Fort Worth Public Library, Central Library.

10. Arnold's drinking first becomes an issue while he was a cadet. It continued to plague him throughout his military career although his problems must be inferred rather than being documented. Right up to his death at Fort Graham in 1853, his propensity for drinking is strongly suggested by contemporary accounts. The effect of alcohol on his military career is chronicled in Perkins, *Fort in Fort Worth*, p. 40 passion.

11. Bruner, "Descendants of Ripley Allen Arnold," p. 1.

12. John K. Mahon, *History of the Second Seminole War, 1835–1842* (Gainesville: University of Florida Press, 1967), p. 315; Cullum, *Biographical Register*, p. 722; Perkins, *Fort in Fort Worth*, p. 41; Robbins, *Last in Their Class*, p. 52; "Major Arnold's Life Adventurous"; Richard Selcer, *The Fort That Became a City* (Fort Worth: Texas Christian University Press, 1995).

13. Willis H. Arnold to the Hon. J. Henderson, June 1, 1840; and Sec. of War to Hon. J. Henderson, July 1, 1840, in Ripley Arnold's Consolidated Correspondence File, National Archives, Record Group 92, Records of the Office of the Quartermaster General, Consolidated Correspondence File, 1794-1815, Box 57, Entry No. 225.

14. Ninth United States Federal Census (1870), Marlin, Falls County, Texas, Microfilm M-593, Roll 1584. Cf. Bruner, "Descendants of Ripley Allen Arnold," who says incorrectly that Kate was born in Indiana. She probably got her information from the 1850 census, which for some reason is also incorrect. Perkins, *Fort in Fort Worth*, pp. 41–42.

15. Court-martial record of R. A. Arnold (No. EE-16), December 2, 1844. U.S. Army Court-Martial Records, Record Group 153, Records of the Office of the Judge Advocate General, National Archives and Records Administration, Washington, DC.

16. Described in scathing terms by one who was present in Ethan Allen Hitchcock, *Fifty Years in Camp and Field: The Diary of Major General Ethan Allen Hitchcock*, ed. by W. A. Croffut (New York: G. P. Putnam's Sons, 1909).

17. Some sources say Thornton commanded eighty men that day, of whom eleven were killed and six wounded. See letter to the editor from Dr. Dan Lawrence in "Response" section, *Blue & Gray Magazine*, vol. 23, no. 1 (Spring 2006), p. 43. Cf. John S. D. Eisenhower, *So Far from God: The U.S. War with Mexico, 1846–48* (New York: Random House, 1989), p. 65. Perkins, p. 26.

18. Arnold to Henry Foote, December 16, 1848, Letters Received, Secretary of War, National Archives; Cullum, *Biographical Register*, p. 722.

19. Perkins, *The Fort in Fort Worth*, pp. 44–45, 101.

20. Cullum, *Biographical Register*, p. 723; Perkins, *Fort in Fort Worth*, pp. 40, 45; Bruner, "Descendants of Ripley Allen Arnold," p. 1; Ninth United States Federal Census (1870) for Marlin, Falls County, TX.

21. Perkins, *Fort in Fort Worth*, pp. 49, 52.

22. Perkins, *ibid.*, p. 24.

23. Ray Miller, *Ray Miller's Texas Forts: A History and Guide* (Houston: Gulf Publishing Company, 1985), p. 42; Perkins, p. 28.

24. Captain R. A. Arnold to Major General Roger Jones, June 2, 1849, Letters Received, Adjutant General's Office, 1822–1860, RG 94, National Archives.

25. Selcer, *Fort That Became a City*, p. 39.

26. Perkins, *Fort in Fort Worth*, p. 61.

27. Ibid., p. 77.

28. Ibid., p. 101.

29. *Austin Telegraph and Texas Register*, November 6, 1850.

30. Perkins, *Fort in Fort Worth,* p. 69.

31. Ninth United States Federal Census (1870) for Marlin, Falls County, TX.

32. Perkins, *Fort in Fort Worth,* p. 158; Selcer, *Fort That Became a City,* p. 123; Bruner, "Descendants of Ripley Allen Arnold," p. 1. Willis Arnold does not appear in the 1850 Census as a member of Major Arnold's household, but Sophie does. The data was gathered during the first week of November 1850.

33. *Austin Texas State Gazette*, June 30, 1855.

34. *Daily Missouri Republican*, October 7, 1853.

35. Samuel H. Starr to Eliza K. Starr, May 19, 1853, Starr Papers, Center for American History, University of Texas at Austin; Harold B. Simpson, *Hill County (Texas) Trilogy* (Hillsboro, TX: Hill College Press, 1986), pp. 4–5; Diary of Josephus M. Steiner, May 3, 1849, Steiner Papers, Center for American History, University of Texas at Austin.

36. Report of R. H. Anderson, September 7, 1853, in Senate Docs., 33rd Congress, 2nd Session, Doc. No. 395, pp. 2–3.

37. The dialogue comes from the testimony of Corporal Joseph Stewart, September 10, 1853, recorded by C. Brooks, Justice of the Peace, Hill County, TX, on microfilm, Confederate Research Center, Hill College, Hillsboro, TX. He is also cited, along with other witnesses, in *Austin Texas State Gazette*, November 15, 1853, *Daily Missouri Republican*, October 7, 1853.

38. Slade's testimony in civil court is quoted in *Austin Texas State Gazette,* November 15, 1853. Cf. his deposition, dated September 10, 1853, contained in Senate Doc., 33rd Congress, 2nd Session, Report of Committee No. 395, pp. 2–3.

39. East coast newspapers picked up their reports of events in Texas from the *New Orleans Picayune*. See *New Orleans Picayune*, September 22, 1853; see also *New York Times*, September 22 and December 6, 1853; and *Baltimore Sun*, September 23 and October 17, 1853.

40. Sam Kinch, "Slayer of Fort Worth Founder Became Prominent Citizen, State Official," *Fort Worth Star-Telegram*, October 30, 1949, Historical Section, p. 4; "Major Arnold's Life Adventurous"; Perkins, *Fort in Fort Worth*, p. 158.

41. The reinterment is first reported in the *Dallas Herald*, n.d., then picked up by the *Austin Texas State Gazette*, June 30, 1855. See also *Fort Worth Telegram*, March 15, 1903, and *Fort Worth Star-Telegram*, Special Centennial Edition, October 30, 1949, Community Life section, p. 10. Note: The *Fort Worth Telegram* was one of the predecessors of the *Fort Worth Star-Telegram*.

42. Because it was specifically granted to her, the pension is filed under Catherine Arnold's name, not Captain Arnold's in War Department records. See Catherine B. Arnold (widow), Pension Application Files, Misc. Service, Certificate No. 5317, File No. 9705, State of Mississippi, Record Group 15, Old Wars Series, National Archives and Records Administration, Washington, DC. (henceforward cited as "Arnold pension file'). Catherine Arnold's forty-year fight for an army pension is told in Richard Selcer, "The Widow vs. the Bureaucrats: The Strange Case of Mrs. Captain Ripley Arnold," *Southwestern Historical Quarterly*, vol. 107, no. 3 (January 2004), pp. 361–87.

43. Kate Arnold to President Roosevelt, July 2, 1902, in Arnold pension file.

44. Selcer, "Widow vs. the Bureaucrats."

45. *Fort Worth Telegram*, March 15, 1903.

46. *Fort Worth Star-Telegram*, October 7, 1936.

47. John L. Clum, Deputy Quartermaster General, U.S.A., to Mr. Abraham Harris of Fort Worth, September 7, 1901, in Records of the City of Fort Worth, Series I, Mayor and Council Proceedings, September 20, 1901, Genealogy, Local History, and Archives Unit, Fort Worth Public Library, Central Library.

48. The former RadioShack headquarters is now occupied by the downtown campus of Tarrant County College. There is no indication on the property that the site ever memorialized Major Arnold. *Fort Worth Star-Telegram*, January 9, 2003, p. 7B.

49. Mrs. Kate (Arnold) Parker to "U.S. Pension Agent" (i.e., Bureau of Pensions, Dept. of the Interior), July 28, 1894, and same to "U.S. Auditor," August 16, 1895, in Arnold pension file.

Chapter 2

1. *Fort Worth Daily Gazette*, February 10, 1887.

2. See Robert DeArment, *Jim Courtright of Fort Worth: His Life and Legend* (Fort Worth: Texas Christian University Press, 2004); and F. Stanley, *Longhair Jim Courtright: Two-Gun Marshal of Fort Worth* (Denver, CO: World Press, 1957).

3. DeArment, *Jim Courtright of Fort Worth*, pp. 11–14, 109.

4. *Fort Worth Daily Democrat*, March 30, 1879.

5. See *Galveston Daily News*, December 19, 1875, and *Fort Worth Democrat*, January 15, 1876.

6. C. F. Colcord, *Autobiography of Charles Francis Colcord* (Tulsa, OK: privately printed, 1970), p. 45. W. F. Oglesby, quoted in Jim Lanning and Judy Lanning, eds.,

Texas Cowboys: Memories of the Early Days (College Station, TX: A&M University Press, 1984), p. 8.

7. *Fort Worth Daily Democrat*, March 30, 1879.

8. Various positive comments on Courtright come from W. H. King, Adjutant-General of Texas (quoted in DeArment, p. 45) and *Fort Worth Daily Democrat*, March 30, 1879. "Free-and-easy" comes from the *Democrat*, ibid.

9. Owens' reputation has more solid evidence to back up his reputed skills with a six-gun than Courtright's. Jack Burrows, "Commodore Perry Owens Had Plenty of Nerve and He Backed It up by Wielding a Winchester [as] Well," *Wild West Magazine*, vol. 18, no. 4 (December 2005), pp. 12–14ff.

10. DeArment quotes a secondhand reference that Texas Ranger legend Jim Gillett once said Courtright "handled his Colts as a sleight of hand performer juggled glass ball on the stage." The fact of Courtright's "crippled hand" comes from Oliver Knight, *Fort Worth: Outpost on the Trinity* (Norman: University of Oklahoma Press), p. 80. DeArment also speculates that Courtright got his handicap from an encounter with a wild bear cub in 1877, *Jim Courtright of Fort Worth*, p. 262 n. 49.

11. The five confrontations where gunplay was involved were with Bingham Field, N. H. Wilson, O. F. Cheney, John C. Morris, and Bud Davis. See DeArment, *Jim Courtright of Fort Worth*, pp. 18–19 (Field), 38–41 (Wilson), 65–67 (Cheney), 86–90 (Morris), and 111–12 (Davis).

12. Presumably, this meant that he did not follow the popular practice of taking his beer with a whiskey chaser. *Fort Worth Daily Democrat*, March 8, 1879.

13. *Fort Worth Democrat*, June 19, 1877. A full account of the Wilson affair is given in DeArment, *Jim Courtright of Fort Worth*, pp. 38–41.

14. See *State of Texas v. T. I. Courtright*, Case No. 1476 (filed 03/20/77); Case No. 1568 (filed 08/21/77); Case No. 2193 (filed 10/28/80); and Case No. 2230 (filed 02/14/81) in Tarrant County District Court Records, Criminal Index to Felony Cases, January 15, 1876–September 30, 1932, Volume A–Z, Tarrant County Justice Center, County Clerk's Office, Criminal Section.

15. *Dallas Daily Herald*, February 11, 1880.

16. The Mayor, with the Council's approval, had the final say in choosing members of the police force. The Marshal could only recommend officers. DeArment, *Jim Courtright of Fort Worth*, p. 47; *Fort Worth Democrat*, May 22, 1878.

17. *Fort Worth Democrat*, March 7, and April 2, 1879. The five other candidates for Courtright's job were S. M Farmer, James M. Williams, W. P. Thomas, B. M. Melton, and H. P. Shiel.

18. The two men went from mentor-protégé to political rivals to bitter enemies in a matter of months. For the unraveling of the friendship, see *Dallas Morning News*, December 3 and 4, 1878.

19. Sheriff John M. Henderson appointed Courtright to the deputy sheriff's job in November 1877; U.S. Marshal Thomas F. Purnell gave him his deputy U.S. Marshal commission in December. See *Dallas Daily Herald*, February 11, 1880 (quoted in DeArment, *Jim Courtright of Fort Worth*, pp. 67–68.) For bloodhounds, see *Fort Worth Daily Democrat*, May 19, 20, 22, and 25, 1881.

20. *State of Texas v. T. I. Courtright*, Case No. 1001C, November 3, and December 1, 1880, Tarrant County Criminal Docket, County Court, 1878–79, one volume, Special Collections, University of Texas at Arlington Library. (Also cited in Selcer, *Hell's Half Acre*, pp. 114–115.)

21. *Fort Worth Democrat*, January 15 and April 6, 1881.

22. G. D. Freeman, *Midnight and Noonday* (Norman: University of Oklahoma Press, 1984), p. 207.

23. DeArment, *Jim Courtright of Fort Worth*, p. 114.

24. Ibid., pp. 120–21.

25. Jim McIntire, *Early Days in Texas: A Trip to Hell and Heaven* (Norman: University of Oklahoma Press, 1992 reprint of 1902 ed.), p. 78.

26. The *Fort Worth Gazette* says they were indicted on May 5, which is impossible, but it also mentions only one of the victims and even then misspells the name as "Grosstel." *Fort Worth Daily Gazette*, April 30, 1885, p. 5.

27. *Santa Fe Daily New Mexican*, May 25, 1883.

28. An account of the murders is contained in "American Valley Murders: An Overview," no author given, an unpublished MS in History File No. 21, State Records Center & Archives, Santa Fe, New Mexico.

29. The exact date of Courtright's appointment is unknown, but new hirings tended to come just after municipal elections in April every year. What is known is that by the end of June, Courtright had his commission as a deputy marshal. *Fort Worth Gazette*, June 29, 1884.

30. To Anglo Texans, *New* Mexico was nothing more than an extension of Old Mexico, populated by the same detestable Hispanics, popularly referred to in the Lone Star state as "greasers." If Ireland had any future political ambitions in Texas, it behooved him to go along with public opinion in any conflict between Texans and New Mexicans. Besides, he could always hope that no extradition papers would ever be served. *Dallas Herald*, October 19, 1884.

31. J. A. Gooch, "100 Years: Cantey, Hanger, Gooch, Munn & Collins" (Fort Worth: privately printed, n.d.), p. 3. Gooch was the in-house historian of longtime Fort Worth law firm Cantey, Hanger, Gooch, Munn & Collins. The story is also repeated in Ann Arnold, *History of the Fort Worth Legal Community* (Austin, TX: Eakin Press, 2000), p. 154; and Bill Fairley, "Lawyer was Fast Thinker," *Fort Worth Star-Telegram*, July 13, 2005.

32. *Dallas Daily Herald*, October 20, 1884.

33. Maddox's lie is exposed in the City Council minutes. On October 4, they granted Marshal Rea's request for a two-week leave of absence to go to Mississippi and join the search for W. T. Wise's murderer. For Maddox's interview, see *Dallas Morning News*, January 22, 1886. For Maddox's lie, see minutes of the meeting of October 7, 1884, in Records of the City of Fort Worth, Series I, Mayor and Council Proceedings, Genealogy, Local History and Archives Unit, Fort Worth Public Library, Central Library.

34. Merchant's Restaurant was an institution in 1880s Fort Worth. It was owned and operated by Christopher C. Lawson. Tracing its history reveals the changeover in 1885 to a new system of numbering addresses on the main down-

town streets. Heretofore, buildings had been numbered consecutively going south from the courthouse. Starting in 1885, city blocks were numbered 100, 200, etc., and an address was based on which hundred block it was on and where it was located on the block. Thus, Merchant's Restaurant appears in the 1883–84 city directory with its address at 41 Main St., while in the 1885–86 directory it appears at 303 Main. Fort Worth City Directories, 1883–84 and 1885–86, on microfiche in the Genealogy, Local History, and Archives Unit, Fort Worth Public Library, Central Library.

35. *Dallas Daily Herald*, October 20, 1884.

36. *Dallas Morning News*, January 21, 1886. None of this came out until after Courtright returned from exile, and then the Dallas newspaper got the dates wrong, placing the events in October rather than November. Texas Rangers' Monthly Report for November 1884, by Captain Schmitt, Company C, "Frontier Battalion," Texas State Library and Archives, Austin.

37. Report of the Adjutant General of the State of Texas, Texas Rangers Service Reports, Frontier Battalion, pension file for A. C. Grimes, Record No. 401-154; and mustering out document for H. L. Hays, Frontier Battalion Muster Rolls, Company C., Folder 36, Record No. 401-750, Texas State Library, Austin.

38. *Dallas Morning News*, January 21, 1886.

39. *Albuquerque Morning Journal*, October 16, 1885.

40. *Dallas Morning News*, February 16, 1886.

41. It is not generally known that the ex-Marshal went to work for the Sheriff's Department upon his return, but during the strike he clearly had more authority than that of a mere private security guard for the railroad. A newspaper article two years later describing the arrest of the last of the Fort Worth strike leaders gives Courtright his due. *New York Times*, March 14, 1888.

42. Richard O'Connor, *Iron Wheels and Broken Men* (New York: G. P. Putnam's Sons, 1973), pp. 285–86; Robert Edgar Riegel, *The Story of the Western Railroads* (Lincoln: University of Nebraska Press, Bison ed., 1967), pp. 249–51; Report of the Adjutant General of the State of Texas, re: mobilizing the state militia, December, 1886 (Austin: Triplett & Hutchings, 1886), pp. 8–9, Texas State Library, Austin.

43. From Courtright's own testimony in *H. Henning v. State of Texas*, Case No. 2616, Court of Appeals of Texas, 24 Tex. Ct. App. 315, 6 S.W. 137, 1887 Tex. Crim. App. A slightly different version is given in the newspaper account: "For God's sake, don't shoot!" *Fort Worth Daily Gazette*, April 4, 1886.

44. In the early days of law enforcement, officers supplied their own weapons. The Fort Worth Police Department did not purchase a supply of long guns until the World War I era. The only other source the sheriff and marshal had for long guns in an emergency was to clean out the local gunshops, which was done in 1913 when a mob threatened to take a prisoner from the county jail.

45. From their testimony at the habeas corpus hearing for Henry Henning on January 15, 1887, reported in the *Dallas Morning News*, January 18, 1887.

46. *Dallas Morning News*, April 24, 1886.

47. *Dallas Morning News*, May 7, 1886.

48. Ibid.

49. *H. Henning v. State of Texas*, Case No. 2616. Excerpts of trial testimony were also reported in the *Fort Worth Gazette*, December 22, 1887. See also DeArment, *Jim Courtright of Fort Worth*, p. 199.

50. Testimony of J. H. Walker for the State, in *H. Henning v. State of Texas*, Case No. 2616.

51.. *H. Henning v. State of Texas*, Case No. 2616. Opinion delivered by Trial Judge R. E. Beckham.

52. *San Antonio Light*, April 10, 1886.

53. Ibid.; Dallas Morning News, April 17, 1891; *Atlanta Constitution*, April 9, 1886. Also quoted in DeArment, *Jim Courtright of Fort Worth*, pp. 201–02.

54. "Money matters" comes from Rea interview with *Fort Worth Star-Telegram*, April 7, 1918. "Hired assassin" story comes from *Texas State Gazette*, February 10, 1887.

55. Short habitually carried his pistol in a leather-lined, inside breast pocket of his coat, but on this occasion he was carrying it in a more accessible pocket, perhaps because he had been anticipating trouble that evening. From Jake Johnson's testimony at the coroner's inquest the next day, cited in the *Dallas Morning News*, February 10, 1887.

56. *Texas State Gazette*, February 10, 1886.

57. Last words from Officer Fulford's testimony at the coroner's inquest the next day, *Fort Worth Gazette*, February 10, 1887. Mary Ellen's reaction from *Texas State Gazette*, February 10, 1887.

58. *Dallas Morning News*, February 10, 1887.

59. Ibid.

60. *Galveston Daily News*, October 20, 1884.

61. In reporting the capture of the last Fort Worth fugitive wanted for the strike of 1886, the *New York Times*, March 14, 1888, identified Courtright as a deputy sheriff.

62. Pendleton quotation from DeArment, *Jim Courtright of Fort Worth*, p. 90. Maddox quotation from interview in *Dallas Morning News*, January 22, 1886. Such ringing endorsements from a public official and a respected, veteran peace officer are impressive, but must be taken with a grain of salt. Pendleton was Jim's lawyer in several scrapes before becoming a prosecutor, and this is the same Maddox whom Courtright called a "warm personal friend." From Report of Texas Ranger Captain George Schmitt to Adjutant General William H. King, October 30, 1884, in Report of the Adjutant General of the State of Texas, December 1884 (Austin: Triplett & Hutchings, 1884).

63. Another part of the mystery is the presence in Decatur, Texas (just north of Fort Worth), of another lawman named "Jim Cartwright." Cartwright was also a town marshal who got his name in the newspapers occasionally for one scrape or another. Nothing is known of Cartwright except he was a contemporary of Courtright. It is possible that Timothy Isaiah adopted the name Longhair Jim to distinguish himself from just-plain Jim Cartwright. See *Galveston Daily News*, December 26, 1882, p. 1. "Farewell" comes from *Fort Worth Daily Gazette*, February 10, 1887.

Chapter 3

1. The tragic story of how slaves were systematically limited to a single given name is well told by Henry Louis Gates, Jr., using modern African Americans as case studies. See Gates, *In Search of Our Roots: How 19 Extraordinary African Americans Reclaimed Their Past* (New York: Crown Publishing Group, 2009). Hagar Tucker's illiteracy is inferred from the fact that he did not sign his name to his own will but only "made his sign," which was then witnessed by others. Last will and testament of Hager [*sic*] Tucker, Texas Probate Records, 1876–1927 for Tarrant County, Instrument No. 1199, Tarrant County District Clerk's Office (Civil), Tarrant County Justice Building.

2. The Tarrant County website ("History of the Tarrant County Sheriff's Office") says William B. Tucker arrived in Tarrant County "while Fort Worth was still an Army garrison," probably not true. Cf. Tarrant County voter rolls for 1867, which show that Hager [*sic*] had been living in the county for ten years at that point and hailed from Kentucky. This date can only be accepted as a rough approximation because these rolls were not notarized and also because the William B. Tucker family arrived in Fort Worth earlier in the decade. Betty Coburn Winchester, compiler, "A List of Registered Voters of Tarrant County, Texas, for the Year 1867," in *Footprints: The Quarterly of the Fort Worth Genealogical Society*, vol. 13, no.1 (February 1970), pp. 105, 107. These voter rolls are compiled from original lists in the Archives Division of the Texas State Library, vol. 2-1/170, Austin.

3. Cf. Ninth United States Federal Census (1870) for Fort Worth, Tarrant County, TX, Microfilm Roll No. M593_1605, and Tenth United States Federal Census (1880) for Fort Worth, Tarrant County, TX, Microfilm Roll No. T9_1328.

4. Information derived from 1870 and 1880 census records, and from Fort Worth city directories, 1878. The 1870 census lists offspring, but only by single initial, not full name. Curiously, none of the city directories lists Amy Tucker with Hagar, though they do list various children residing at different addresses. This is not completely surprising because Amy was African American and a spouse who did not work outside the home.

5. Reminiscences of Charles Ellis Mitchell, "When Every Man Carried a Six-Shooter," in Mack Williams, ed., *In Old Fort Worth*, Sesquicentennial Edition (Fort Worth: privately printed, 1986), p. 46.

6. Winchester, "A List of Registered Voters of Tarrant County, Texas, for the Year 1867," pp. 105, 107.

7. Mitchell, "When Every Man Carried."

8. Mayor and Council Proceedings, Minutes of the City Council, April 23, 1873, Box A, Genealogy, Local History, and Archives Unit, Fort Worth Public Library, Central Library.

9. Julia Kathryn Garrett, typed MS notes for "Fort Worth: A Frontier Triumph," University of Texas at Arlington Library, Special Collections.

10. Interview with J. L. Terry, June 2, 1938, in Federal Writers' Project, "Research Data," vol. 2, pp. 535–36, Genealogy, Local History, and Archives Unit, Fort Worth Public Library, Central Library.

11. These highly detailed maps of Fort Worth were produced by the Sanborn Fire Insurance Company and updated every few years, starting in the 1880s. The earliest two editions, 1885 and 1889, show the city's "Negro tenements" on Calhoun and Jones streets. Sanborn Fire Maps for Fort Worth (New York: Sanborn Map & Publishing Co., Ltd., 1885 and 1889), original copies at Center for American History, University of Texas at Austin; also available through ProQuest Information and Learning's Digital Sanborn Maps, 1867–1970, on-line at Environmental Data Resources website, http://www.erdnet.com/.

12. Fort Worth city directories, 1882–1890.

13. For Tucker's role as a charter member of Lodge no. 148, see Charles R. Perkins, *History of Fort Worth Lodge No. 148, A.F.&A.M., 1855–1955* (Fort Worth: privately published, 1957), pp. 18 ff (originally a Master of Arts thesis for the Department of History, Texas Christian University, 1956). The Ancient and Accepted Scottish Rite of Freemasonry, Prince Hall Affiliation, Local History, existed in a close but uneasy relationship with the Grand Lodge Masons. White members of the Grand Lodge of Texas have never accepted their black brethren as complete equals or formally affiliated with them, but this does not mean they have not assisted and encouraged them over the years. The exact date and circumstances of the founding of the first black Masonic lodge in Fort Worth is not known. For a general history of the movement in Texas, see Robert L. Uzzel, *Prince Hall Freemasonry in the Lone Star State: From Cuney to Curtis, 1875–2003* (Fort Worth: privately printed, n.d.).

14. Tucker Hill was not part of the silk-stocking district that included A. B. Wharton's Thistle Hill and the other mansions on Pennsylvania, Summit, and Penn streets, yet it was every bit their equal. For Thistle Hill and the other surviving mansions, see Ruby Schmidt, ed., *Fort Worth & Tarrant County: A Historical Guide* (Fort Worth: Texas Christian University Press, 1984), p. 78.

15. "Mattie" must have been Martha who was born in 1879. The other two daughters cannot be identified in the census records, and "Doña's" name is a guess from a barely legible directory listing. Fort Worth city directory, 1890.

16. Tarrant County Tax Rolls, 1850–1910, Microfilm Roll No. 1: 1876 and 1877, Precinct No. 1, available in Genealogy, Local History and Archives Unit, Fort Worth Public Library, Central Library.

17. Last will and testament of Hager [*sic*] Tucker, Texas Probate Records, 1876–1927 for Tarrant County, Instrument No. 1199, Tarrant County District Clerk's Office (Civil), Tarrant County Justice Building.

18. Sometimes called "Old Trinity Cemetery" even though strictly speaking, it is not a separate cemetery. There is also a Trinity ("New Trinity") Cemetery in Fort Worth at NE 28th and Beach streets, and it, too was designated as a "Negro Cemetery."

19. This is nineteenth century Masonic funeralogy. It is the only firm historical evidence we have that Hagar Tucker was a Mason, but since the Masonic symbols would never have been used indiscriminately by those who buried him or who put up the marker, then the man buried beneath the marker must have been a Mason, *ipso facto*. And since that man was black, he could only have been a Prince

Hall Mason. Identification of the symbols from e-mail correspondence with current Masons Robert P. Holmes, Jr., Past Master of Lodge no. 148, Kevin Foster of Cooke Peavey Lodge no. 1162, and Bryce A. Hardin, Right Worshipful Grand Tiler of the Prince Hall Grand Lodge of Texas, July 2, 3, and 5, 2006.

20. Twelfth United States Federal Census (1900) for Fort Worth, Tarrant County, TX, Precinct 1, Microfilm Roll No. T623_1671.

21. From debate at City Council meeting in August 1891 where white officers declare they will not "work with a nigger" under any circumstances. Quoted in *Dallas Morning News*, August 13, 1891, p. 5.

22. Bob Ray Sanders, "Black Officer Paved the Way for Others," *Fort Worth Star-Telegram*, March 2 and 5, 2003, p. 1B*ff* (both).

Chapter 4

1. *Fort Worth Daily Democrat*, December 3, 1878, and March 8, 1879.

2. *Fort Worth Daily Democrat*, February 21, March 1, and May 22, 1878.

3. See "Samuel M. Fanner" [*sic*] in Seventh United States Federal Census (1850), Cole County, MO, Microfilm Roll No. M432_397; and "Saml Faimer" [*sic*] in Eighth United States Federal Census (1860), Cole County, MO, Microfilm Roll No. M653_615. (All census records cited available on-line at http://AncestryLibrary.com.)

4. Family lore comes from descendant J. R. Taggert of Lohman, Missouri, interviewed by Fort Worth Public Library librarian-genealogist Shirley Apley over the telephone, January 8, 2008. Notes from interview provided to this author (hereafter cited as "Taggert interview"). For background on Quantrill, see Albert E. Castel, *William Clarke Quantrill: His Life and Times* (New York: F. Fell Publishers, 1962).

5. Like many Civil War veterans, including E. M. Daggett, the Father of Fort Worth, Sam continued to wear his wartime rank proudly long after the Civil War, turning it into political advantage come election time. See, for example, *Fort Worth Democrat*, November 6, 1881.

6. Sam's activities back in Missouri did not become an issue in Fort Worth until his first political campaign. B. B. Paddock's *Fort Worth Democrat* provided a forum for both the candidate and his critics. See *Fort Worth Daily Democrat*, March 25 and 27, 1879.

7. Taggert interview.

8. *Fort Worth Daily Democrat*, March 27, 1879.

9. For his work as a fireman, see *Fort Worth Daily Democrat*, August 3, and December 17, 1878, also cited in "Federal Writers' Project, Research Data: Fort Worth and Tarrant County, TX" (Fort Worth: Fort Worth Library Unit, 1941), vol. 27, p. 10531. For Masonic connection, see Sandy Clark, historian and secretary of the Grand Lodge of Missouri, Columbia, MO, to Ms. Clara Ruddell via e-mail, January 14, 2008, and Bruce Mercer, librarian, Masonic Grand Lodge of Texas, Waco, Texas, to Clara Ruddell, October 2005 (copies of both communications in this author's files). The Grand Lodge of Texas does not list Farmer until 1880, leaving an unexplained three-year gap in his membership records.

10. *Fort Worth Daily Democrat*, December 3, 1878; March 26, 27, and 30, 1879.

11. Ibid., May 2, 1879.

12. Ibid., April 8, 1879.

13. Ibid., April 27, 1879.

14. *Dallas Morning News*, September 3, 1887.

15. Ibid., September 29, 1887.

16. *Galveston Daily News*, May 24, 1879.

17. Sam's real estate transactions are found in the Grantor and Grantee Indexes to Deeds, Tarrant County, TX, County Clerk, Deeds Records Office, Tarrant County Courthouse. Sam's misadventures in civil court are reported in the newspaper, various dates spanning several years (e.g., *Dallas Morning News*, March 27, 1890); and in District Court civil records, Tarrant County, Texas, Family Law Center, Disposed Records, Civil and Family, 200 E. Weatherford, Ft. Worth, TX. (See Index to Minutes, Defendants E to K, 1879–April 30, 1930).

18. *Fort Worth Democrat*, January 15, 1881. (Note: By 1880, the *Democrat* no longer put out a weekly edition, so "Daily"/"Weekly" had been dropped from the masthead.)

19. *Dallas Daily Herald*, February 11, 1880.

20. Quoted in *Fort Worth Democrat*, November 6, 1881.

21. *Dallas Herald*, November 6, 1881; *Dallas Morning News*, June 24, 1888; *Fort Worth Daily Democrat*, November 27, 1881.

22. Family background on Martha Farmer comes from Twelfth United States Federal Census (1900), Fort Worth, Tarrant County, TX, Microfilm Roll No. T623_1671; and Fourteenth United States Federal Census (1920), Fort Worth, Tarrant County, TX, Microfilm Roll No. T625 1848; from her obituary in the *Fort Worth Star-Telegram*, August 22, 1932, a.m. ed.; and from testimony of Mrs. Mary Johnson in Mattie Farmer v. Sam Farmer divorce suit, Case No. 12590, Forty-eighth Judicial District Court, January 12, 1897, District Court civil records (hereafter cited as "Farmer v. Farmer"). Mattie Johnson's occupation and celebrity status are well documented in Fort Worth newspapers during these years. See, for instance, *Fort Worth Daily Democrat*, April 27, 1879, and December 22, 1881. For Martha Johnson to S. M. Farmer, see Weldon I. Hudson, compiler, *Tarrant County Texas Marriage Records* (Fort Worth: privately printed, 1984), vol. I (1876–1885), p. 65.

23. *Fort Worth Daily Gazette*, July 30, 1883; *Fort Worth Democrat*, May 9, 1882; Johnson testimony, Farmer v. Farmer. For Sam's residence at the jail, see "Sam M. Farener" [*sic*] in Tenth United States Federal Census (1880), Fort Worth, Tarrant, TX, Microfilm Roll No. T9_1328.

24. *Fort Worth Daily Gazette*, July 30, 1883; Johnson testimony, Farmer v. Farmer.

25. Divorce petition, Farmer v. Farmer; Johnson testimony, ibid.; testimony of Mrs. Maggie Young, ibid.; testimony of R.Y. Prigmore, ibid.

26. *Dallas Morning News*, November 27, 1886; Johnson testimony, Farmer v. Farmer.

27. Testimony of Dan Dearing, Farmer v. Farmer.

28. Testimony of Dr. H. C. Whitehead, Farmer v. Farmer, and divorce petition, ibid.

29. *Dallas Morning News*, September 10, 1895.

30. Johnson testimony, Farmer v. Farmer; testimony of Mrs. Maggie Young, ibid.

31. She is buried in Fort Worth's Greenwood Cemetery beside Russell Prigmore. *Fort Worth Star-Telegram*, January 15, 1919, and August 22, 1932, a.m. ed.

32. *Fort Worth Democrat-Advance*, January 27, 1882, cited in Nyle H. Miller and Joseph W. Snell, *Why the West Was Wild* (Norman: University of Oklahoma Press, 2003), p. 453; Bill O'Neal, *Encyclopedia of Western Gunfighters* (Norman: University of Oklahoma Press, 1979), pp. 222–23; Jack DeMattos, *Mysterious Gunfighter: The Story of Dave Mather* (College Station, TX: Creative Publishing Company, 1992).

33. *Fort Worth Democrat*, September 21, 1878.

34. For Sam and Courtright, see *Fort Worth Democrat*, December 3, 1878. For Sam and Garrett, see ibid., December 27, 1881.

35. *Dallas Morning News*, June 24, 1888, p. 14.

36. *Fort Worth Democrat*, May 19, 1881.

37. For telephone, see Harold Wayne Rich, "Twenty-Five Years of Struggle and Progress: The Fort Worth Police Department, 1873–1897 (Master of Arts thesis submitted to AddRan College, Texas Christian University, 1999), p. 64 (hereafter cited as "Rich thesis").

38. For Maddox v. Farmer, see Glenn Shirley, *Heck Thomas: Frontier Marshal* (Norman: University of Oklahoma Press, 1981), pp. 35–36. See also Rich thesis, p. 78; and *Dallas Morning News*, March 13, 1887. For Negro assassins, see *Dallas Daily Herald*, September 11, 1884.

39. *Fort Worth Democrat*, August 16, 1881.

40. A velocipede was a human-powered, one-man cycle that rode on the railroad tracks and was used primarily by track inspectors to cover long distances swiftly. *Fort Worth Democrat*, May 9, 1882.

41. *Fort Worth Democrat*, August 11, 1881.

42. *Fort Worth Daily Democrat*, August 11, 1881; February 25, 1882; and *Dallas Morning News*, September 4, 1890. For deputy U.S. marshal errands, see *Dallas Daily Herald*, February 11, 1880.

43. *Dallas Daily Herald*, February 11, 1880.

44. Ibid.

45. *Fort Worth Gazette*, October 1, 1888.

46. *Dallas Morning News*, March 27, 1890.

47. Ibid., March 13, 1887.

48. U.S. Marshal accounts for the Northern District of Texas, ending December 31, 1894, National Archives, Washington, DC; *Dallas Morning News*, February 25, 1892, and September 10, 1895.

49. Taggert interview; *Fort Worth Morning Register*, December 20, 1899.

Chapter 5

1. Details of his life come from Hayne family tree provided by Major Tony Gaite, a descendant, Durrington, New Salisbury, Wiltshire, England, 1993; from Alfred Hayne to Georgianna (sister) from Fort Worth, December 16, 1880, copy provided by Major Gaite; from "Al Hayne's Room Remains as He Left It . . . ,"*Fort Worth Gazette*, typescript copy of undated 1895 article in "Al Hayne" vertical files, Tarrant County Historical Commission (hereafter cited as *Fort Worth Gazette* typescript). For Al Hayne's and Eugene Hayne's arrivals, see "Alfred S. Hayne" and "E. A. Hayne" on "Passenger and Crew Lists of Vessels Arriving at New York, 1820–1957," Record Group 36, National Archives Microfilm Roll No. M237_363 (available on-line at http://www.AncestryLibrary.com).

2. For T&P employment record, see *Fort Worth Daily Gazette*, June 24, 1882, and June 9, 1890; and *Dallas Morning News*, June 1, 1890. Masonic connection comes from the files of the Masonic Grand Lodge Library and Museum of Texas, Waco, TX, Grand Secretary Harvey C. Byrd to Mrs. Mickey Dowdy, June 24, 1987 (copy in this author's files). References to "Captain Al Hayne" come from *Fort Worth Daily Gazette,* June 24, 1882; "Eugene Hayne" in Tenth United States Federal Census (1880), Marshall, Harrison County, TX, Microfilm Roll No. T9_1309. (All census records cited available on-line at http://www.AncestryLibrary.com.)

3. Hayne to Georgianna, December 16, 1880; Fort Worth city directory, 1882, on microfiche in Genealogy, Local History, and Archives Unit, Fort Worth Public Library, Central Library.

4. Fort Worth city directories, 1882 and 1885–86.

5. Major John B. Hawley to Thomas J. Powell, August 20, 1931, copies of Hawley-Powell correspondence from Deborah Sizemore of Crowley, Texas, 1992. *Fort Worth Daily Gazette*, June 5, 1890. *Dallas Morning News*, June 1,1890. For lawsuit, see *Dallas Morning News*, August 25, 1887.

6. George C. Werner, "Gulf, Colorado and Santa Fe Railroad," *The New Handbook of Texas*, Ron Tyler et al., eds. (Austin: Texas State Historical Association, 1996), vol. 3, pp. 376–77; Vernon Gladden Spence, *Colonel Morgan Jones: Grand Old Man of Texas Railroading* (Norman: University of Oklahoma Press, 1971), pp. 49–53; *Dallas Morning News*, September 21, 1886, p. 5.

7. The original photograph belongs to his descendants in England who graciously provided a copy to this author.

8. Fort Worth city directory, 1885–86.

9. Hawley to Powell, August 17 and August 20, 1931.

10. For rumors of return, see *Fort Worth Weekly Gazette*, May 31, 1890. At the time of his death, sources differed over how long he had been in the country—ten or fifteen years. Cf. *Dallas Morning News*, June 1, 1890. For "most beautiful structure . . .," see Mary Daggett Lake, quoting unnamed contemporary source in photocopy of one of her columns (undated) in "Texas Spring Palace News Clippings" vertical file, Mary Daggett Lake Papers, Genealogy, Local History, and Archives Unit, Fort Worth Public Library, Central Library (hereafter cited as "Mary Daggett Lake clipping"). For "pleasant evening" and "best of health," see recollections of T. J. (Hugh)

Powell in "Al Hayne, Hero of 1893 [*sic*] Fire...," *Fort Worth Star-Telegram*, photocopy of undated 1930s article in "Al Hayne" vertical file in Genealogy, Local History, and Archives Unit, Fort Worth Public Library, Central Library (hereafter cited as "Al Hayne, Hero of Fire"). This explanation of why he was there that night ("for pleasure") is supported in "Eulogy to Al Hayne . . ." in *Fort Worth Star-Telegram*, September 18, 1934. For a brief history of "Decoration Day," first celebrated in 1868, see Richard F. Selcer, *Civil War America, 1850 to 1875* (New York: Facts on File, 2006), p. 65. The "decorations" refer to the flowers and garlands placed on the graves of Union soldiers killed in the Civil War, a complementary image to the karporama that was the Spring Palace. (Karporama is an archaic, nineteenth-century term for any grand exhibit of the products of field, forest, orchard, and garden. The official name of the Texas Spring Palace was "Karporama: The Fruits of the Earth," but it went down in history as simply the "Spring Palace.")

11. Details of the distance to the ground, the numbers saved, the extent of Hayne's injuries, and the identities of the men who rescued him are not in agreement in the various accounts. As a rule, greater credence has been given to accounts closer to the event. *Fort Worth Star-Telegram*, September 18, 1934, October 30, 1949, and June 4, 1950; *Fort Worth Press*, May 30, 1946, and September 20, 1959; *Fort Worth Telegram*, April 8, 1905; *Fort Worth News-Tribune*, December 5, 1980. (Note: The *Fort Worth Telegram* was one of the predecessors of the *Fort Worth Star-Telegram*.)

12. *Dallas Morning News*, June 2, 1890.

13. The "Day Book" is quoted in Jean Wysatta, "Nuns Led a Tough Life at Fort Worth's Frontier Hospital," *Fort Worth Press*, February 25, 1973. Journalist and local historian Mack Williams placed Hayne's death "an hour later." See "Spring Palace Blaze Recalled by Pioneer," *Fort Worth Press*, May 27, 1957. The massive Centennial edition of the *Fort Worth Star-Telegram* placed it "four hours" later. *Fort Worth Star-Telegram*, October 30, 1949. Other details of Hayne's rescue come from D. E. Claypool, one of the men who pulled Hayne to safety, interviewed for *Fort Worth Star-Telegram*, June 4, 1950.

14. *Dallas Morning News*, June 2, 1890.

15. *Fort Worth Star-Telegram*, October 9, 1947.

16. *Fort Worth Daily Gazette*, June 1, 1890.

17. One of those invitations measuring 5x8 inches is in the Bill Jary Collection, University of Texas at Arlington Library, Special Collections. Pallbearers were G. H. Day, T. P. Martin, J. P. Nicks, J. F. Clements, W. J. Bailey, and W. L. Rail. *Fort Worth Daily Gazette*, June 1, 1890.

18. *Dallas Morning News*, November 9, 1890. See also recollections of Clay Sandidge, a volunteer fireman on the night of the Spring Palace fire. *Fort Worth Press*, May 27, 1957. See also *Fort Worth Star-Telegram*, September 18, 1934. One historical account says the funeral cortege was "half a mile long." Duane Gage, "Hero Gave His Life During Palace Fire," *Fort Worth Star-Telegram*, undated newspaper clipping (ca. 1986) in vertical files, Genealogy, Local History, and Archives Unit, Fort Worth Public Library, Central Library.

19. *Dallas Morning News*, November 9, 1890.

20. *Fort Worth Gazette* undated article, typed copy of original, in "Texas Spring Palace" vertical file in Genealogy, Local History, and Archives Unit, Fort Worth Public Library, Central Library (hereafter cited as "*Fort Worth Gazette* typescript"); "Al Hayne, Hero of Fire."

21. "Eugene Haynes [*sic*]" in Twelfth United States Federal Census (1900), Liberty, TX, Microfilm Roll T623_1655; and "E. A. Hayne" in Fifteenth United States Federal Census (1930), Houston, Harris County, TX, Microfilm Roll No. T626_ 2352.

22. *Fort Worth Gazette* typescript; Tarrant County Scrapbook No. 1, "Letters to the Editor" vertical file, Center for American History, Eugene Barker Library, University of Texas at Austin; *Dallas Morning News*, June 2, 1890; T. J. Powell to Maj. John B. Hawley, August 19, 1931, in Hawley-Powell correspondence provided by Deborah Sizemore, Crowley, TX, 1992; *Fort Worth Daily Gazette*, June 5, 1890.

23. Attributed to "Shawmut," reprinted in part in *Fort Worth Star-Telegram*, September 18, 1934.

24. The ultimate cost of the monument was $2,500, all raised by popular subscription. The organization behind the drive is sometimes inaccurately known as the "Women's Humane Society." *Dallas Morning News*, September 26, 1891, and June 2, 1890; *Fort Worth Daily Gazette*, June 9 and 22, 1890; *Fort Worth Telegram*, April 8, 1905.

25. Mary Daggett Lake clipping; *Fort Worth Press*, September 20, 1959.

26. *Dallas Morning News*, February 1, 1893.

27. "Al Hayne, Hero of Fire"; *Fort Worth Telegram*, April 8, 1905.

28. Powell to Hawley, August 17, 1931.

29. *Fort Worth Daily Gazette*, June 1, 1890; *Dallas Morning News*, May 16, 1891.

30. *Dallas Morning News*, May 13, 1892.

31. *Fort Worth Gazette*, May 11 and 12, 1893; *Dallas Morning News*, May 13, 1892, July 8, 1896, and May 14, 1903.

32. *Dallas Morning News*, August 1, 1911.

33. *Fort Worth Register*, January 18, 1902; *Fort Worth Mail-Telegram*, September 9, 1902.

34. *Fort Worth Star-Telegram*, May 12, 1920.

Chapter 6

1. This description is pieced together from a variety of newspaper accounts and court testimony plus the Fort Worth city directories, 1892–93 and 1894–95, and the February 1893 Sanborn Fire Map of Fort Worth. The city directory is available on microfiche in the Genealogy, Local History, and Archives Unit, Fort Worth Public Library, Central Library. The Sanborn map is available in original form at the Center for American History, University of Texas at Austin; and through ProQuest Information and Learning's Digital Sanborn Maps, 1867–1970, on-line at Environmental Data Resources website, http://www.erdnet.com/. The Dallas newspaper is also available on-line at the *Dallas Morning News* Historical Archive. The Fort Worth newspaper is only available currently on microfilm. See *Dallas*

Morning News, October 13, 1893; May 1 and 2, 1894; and *Fort Worth Gazette*, May 1 and 2, 1894. Dallas coverage of the crime and the subsequent judicial proceedings was much more thorough than the leading Fort Worth newspaper of the day, which seemed to be less fascinated by the crime right from the beginning. Unfortunately, surviving microfilmed copies of the *Gazette* are virtually unreadable in many places.

Margaret lived with her niece and niece's husband in an apartment in the old Huffman Building. For some reason the Dodds are not listed in the city directory. For information on the niece, see Francis A. Dodd in Twelfth United States Federal Census, Fort Worth, Tarrant County, TX, Microfilm Roll No. T623_1671 (viz., 37 years old and widowed in 1900).

2. For Maggie's physical description, see *Dallas Morning News*, May 2, 1894, testimony of Louis Reiney and Annie Edmonds. For the ring, see ibid., October 19, 1893. This ring, which seemed to be such a crucial element in the investigation early on, proved ultimately to have no bearing on the case.

3. *Dallas Morning News*, October 13, 1893.

4. Testimony of Dr. Stevens and Deputy Gunnells, *Dallas Morning News*, May 1, 1894; and *Fort Worth Gazette*, May 1, 1894. Their testimony, virtually identical, was also taken at the "preliminary hearing," cited in *Dallas Morning News*, October 19, 1893. The address where the body was found was given at the trial as 714 West Weatherford. At the time of the crime, no address was given. See *Dallas Morning News* and *Fort Worth Gazette*, January 25–27, 1893; cf. *Fort Worth Gazette*, May 1, 1894.

5. Elizabeth Stride, an East End of London prostitute long past her prime, found murdered and mutilated in 1888, was the third of the Ripper's five victims. Randle's official actions and his conclusions come from his trial testimony, cited in *Fort Worth Gazette*, May 1, 1894; and *Dallas Morning News*, May 1, 1894.

6. From Harden Gunnells' testimony under oath. *Fort Worth Gazette*, May 1, 1894.

7. The nature and contents of the bottle subsequently became a matter of some dispute, being variously described as "a flask" or "bottle of medicine" in newspaper reports and trial testimony. It was clearly a bottle of private-label wine. *Dallas Morning News*, May 1, 1894; cf. *Fort Worth Gazette*, May 1, 1894.

8. *Fort Worth Gazette*, May 1, 1894; *Dallas Morning News*, May 1, 1894.

9. See Maddox's trial testimony, *Dallas Morning News*, May 1, 1894. Anton Happy's saloon-residence was at 509 West Weatherford. Fort Worth city directory, 1892–93. The crime scene investigation is described in the *Dallas Morning News*, January 26 and October 13, 1893, and May 1 and 2, 1894; also in the *Fort Worth Gazette*, January 26 and 27, 1893. Sketches of the crime scene were printed in the *Dallas Morning News*, January 26, 1893, and May 2, 1894.

10. *Dallas Morning News*, October 13, 1893; and May 1, 1894.

11. There is not even agreement on the spelling of her last name, "Tewmey" or "Twomy." Both variations appeared in the newspapers, with the *Dallas Morning News* preferring the second spelling while the *Fort Worth Gazette* consistently used

the former. "Tewmey" gets the benefit of the doubt here because that is the spelling found in Oakwood Cemetery records and because Maggie's family lived in Fort Worth and had plenty of opportunity to correct it during the seventeen months of the investigation and trial.

12. Maggie's personal history emerged in bits and pieces during the investigation, provided by a variety of sources. Most of what is given here comes from court testimony as reported in the *Dallas Morning News*, October 19, 1893, and May 2, 1894. (No official court transcript survives.) Since much of this testimony was given by family members under oath, more credence is given to it than to simple newspaper accounts. Additional information, uncredited, is taken from the *Dallas Morning News*, October 13, 1893. Information on Mary E. Shanahan comes from 1892–93 Fort Worth city directory and from Twelfth United States Federal Census (1900), Fort Worth, Tarrant County, TX, Microfilm Roll No. T623_1671.

13. *Dallas Morning News*, May 1, 1894; *Fort Worth Gazette*, May 1, 1894.

14. *Dallas Morning News*, May 1, 1894. *Fort Worth Gazette*, January 25, 1893.

15. *Fort Worth Gazette*, January 25 and 26, 1893; *Dallas Morning News*, January 25 and 27, 1893.

16. *Dallas Morning News*, January 26 and October 14, 1893.

17. Ibid., January 26 and October 19, 1893, and May 1, 1894.

18. *Fort Worth Gazette*, January 29, 1893.

19. According to cemetery records eleven Tewmeys are buried in the Calvary section of Oakwood, in two different plots dating from the 1880s through the early twentieth century. *Dallas Morning News*, January 26, 1893.

20. *Dallas Morning News*, January 26, 27, and 28, 1893.

21. Ibid., January 28, 1893.

22. Ibid., January 29, 1893.

23. There are two distinct versions of Annie's story, the one that was reported in the newspaper in October 1893 and the one that was told some six months later at the trial. The original version sounds less coached, more spontaneous, but for that very reason, it is far less detailed. See *Dallas Morning News*, October 13, 1893, and May 2, 1894.

24. Ibid., October 13, 1893.

25. For Lola's other legal troubles, see *Dallas Morning News*, October 13 and 21, 1893, August 1 and 3, 1893, and February 10, 1895. See also Annie Edmonds' testimony reported in ibid., May 2, 1894.

26. The first time the veil comes up in testimony is at the trial in May 1894. *Dallas Morning News*, October 14, 19, and 20, 1893, and May 2, 1894.

27. Ibid., October 21, 1893.

28. Ibid., November 28, 1893, and January 30, 1894.

29. No person named "Prickett," either black or white, appears in the Fort Worth city directory for 1892–93, nor for the years immediately preceding or following it. *Dallas Morning News*, October 28 and November 2, 1893, January 25, 1894.

30. *Dallas Morning News*, January 30, 1894.

31. *Dallas Morning News*, May 2 and 3, 1894. See Anton Happy in Fort Worth city directory, 1892–93; and Tenth United States Federal Census (1880), for Fort Worth, Tarrant County, Texas, Microfilm Roll No. T9_1328. (Available on-line at http://www.AncestryLibrary.com.)

32. *Fort Worth Gazette*, May 1 and 2, 1894; *Dallas Morning News*, May 2, 1894.

33. *Fort Worth Gazette*, May 2, 1894; *Dallas Morning News*, May 2, 1894.

34. *Fort Worth Gazette*, May 2, 1894; *Dallas Morning News*, May 2, 1894.

35. *Dallas Morning News*, May 2, 1894.

36. Ibid.

37. Ibid.

38. Ibid.

39. Ibid., May 3 and September 20, 1894.

40. Ibid., February 10, 1895.

41. *Fort Worth Telegram*, February 10, 1907. (Note: the *Telegram* was one of the predecessors to the *Fort Worth Star-Telegram*.)

42. *Fort Worth Telegram*, February 10, 1907.

43. Oliver Knight, *Fort Worth: Outpost on the Trinity* (Norman: University of Oklahoma Press, 1953), p. 136.

Chapter 7

1. The only history to date of the Fort Worth Daggetts is Julia Kathryn Garrett, *Fort Worth: A Frontier Triumph* (Austin, TX: Encino Press, 1972, reprinted Texas Christian University Press, 1996), pp. 125–28. Garrett incorrectly states that E. B. Daggett's mother was Faribo Hayes Daggett (p. 127). For information on Fort Worth's antebellum plantations, see Charles Ellis Mitchell memoir in "Federal Writers' Project, Research Data: Fort Worth and Tarrant County, TX." (Fort Worth: Fort Worth Library Unit, 1941), vol. 5, p. 2000.

2. Daggett family history comes from longtime Fort Worth historian Ruby Schmidt, in conversations with this author in 1987. Copies of E. M. Daggett's last will and testament, both the 1876 and 1882 versions, are in Mrs. Schmidt's possession. The tangled relationship between Daggett senior and his son is detailed in Selcer, *Hell's Half Acre*, pp. 141–42. Jeff Daggett, alias "Jeff Smith," was listed as a "mulatto" in Huntsville prison records when he entered in 1892, with a Texas-born father and a Virginia-born mother. See Jeff Daggett, Convict No. 7888, Convict Record Ledgers, 1849–1970, Texas Department of Criminal Justice (on microfilm, roll no. 3) (hereafter cited as Daggett convict record).

3. When processed into Huntsville penitentiary on April 5, 1892, Daggett gave his birth date as July 3, 1864. Cf. the information his wife provided for his death certificate in 1917, giving his birth date as 1863. I have chosen to go with the former date since it came from Daggett himself. Daggett convict record; Death Certificate for Jeff Daggett (No. 29347), filed October 27, 1917, in Texas Death Records, 1890–1976, Texas State Board of Health, Bureau of Vital Statistics (available on-line at http://www.pilot.familysearch.org) (hereafter cited as Daggett death certificate).

4. Up through 1920, the U.S. Census Bureau used "mulatto" as a racial category. Thereafter, after determining that no fewer than three-quarters of the American Negro population had white ancestors, the Bureau dropped the designation from its official categories. Jeff Daggett's death certificate shows his mother's name but contains no entry under "father." See Daggett death certificate.

5. Biographical sketch of E. M. Daggett in Fort Worth City Directory, 1877, on microfiche in Genealogy, Local History, and Archives Unit, Fort Worth Public Library, Central Library.

6. See "Jeff Smith" (*aka* Jeff Daggett) in Twelfth United States Federal Census (1900), Fort Worth, Tarrant County, TX, Microfilm Roll No. T623 1671; and "Jeff Daggett Smith" in Thirteenth United States Federal Census (1910), Fort Worth, Tarrant County, TX, Microfilm Roll No. T624_1590 (available on-line at http://www.AncestryLibrary.com). The tattoo is described in his Huntsville admission record, Daggett convict record.

7. *Dallas Morning News*, January 20, 1889.

8. For comparisons to grandfather, see Garrett, *Fort Worth*, pp. 126 and 128. For Jeff's physical description, habits, and lack of education, see Daggett convict record. *Dallas Morning News*, November 24, 1885.

9. The Dallas newspapers on occasion reported Bud Daggett's business activities and Jeff Daggett's latest brush with the law in the same column ("The News from Fort Worth") without connecting father and son. *Dallas Morning News*, August 11, 1888, December 8, 1888, February 23, 1889, and April 9, 1889.

10. *Dallas Morning News*, January 20, 1889; *Fort Worth Telegram*, May 12, 1904. Note: *Fort Worth Telegram* was one of the predecessors of the *Fort Worth Star-Telegram*.

11. The "Zip Coon" stereotype was the fast-talking, conniving, flashy urban black as opposed to the more benign "Uncle Tom" stereotype. Fort Worth newspapers, as opposed to the Dallas papers, tended to describe him in less derogatory terms, probably out of consideration for his white family. *Dallas Morning News*, January 20 and February 23, 1889.

12. Jeff's married life must be pieced together from census records. See "Jeff Smith" [*sic*] in Twelfth (1900) and Thirteenth (1910) United States Federal Censuses. For insult, see *Dallas Morning News*, August 9, 1888.

13. *Dallas Morning News*, June 19 and January 20, 1889.

14. Ibid., June 19, 1889; and *Rockdale (Texas) Messenger*, June 27, 1889.

15. *Dallas Morning News*, June 20 and September 11, 1889.

16. Ibid., September 17 and October 6, 1889; Daggett convict record.

17. *Dallas Morning News*, March 13, 1904.

18. Fort Worth city directory, 1916.

19. As African Americans or mulattos, it did not matter—Jeff and Hester had only two choices of where to live at this time in Fort Worth history: either on the east side of the Third Ward or in Battercake Flats (Franklin Hill) between the bluff and the river, where African Americans lived. For second residence, see Daggett death certificate.

20. Described as "a resort for Negroes," Douglass Park, named for Fredrick Douglass, was actually an unappealing piece of land in the Trinity River bottoms. It was where African Americans celebrated Emancipation Day every June 19 with parades, speeches, and sporting contests. They were prohibited from using the city's other public parks. For Daggett, see *Dallas Morning News*, May 5, 1909. For Douglass Park, see *Dallas Morning News*, June 20, 1900, June 20, 1901, June 16 and 19, 1907.

21. *Fort Worth Star-Telegram*, July 6, 1909.

22. *Fort Worth Record*, October 24, 1917.

23. Quoting County Attorney Marshall Spoonts with a Fort Worth dateline, *Weatherford Daily Herald*, October 24, 1917.

24. See "Jas. B. Legett" [*sic*] in Twelfth United States Federal Census (1900), Portales, Chaves County, NM, Microfilm Roll No. T623_999; "James B. Legett" in Thirteenth United States Federal Census (1910), Fort Worth Ward 2, Tarrant County, TX, Microfilm Roll No. T624_1590; and "James Legett" in Fourteenth United States Federal Census (1920), Justice Precinct 1, Tarrant County, TX, Microfilm Roll No. T625_1848. For "Legett's" career, see *Fort Worth Star-Telegram*, April 6, 1917. For background on Rusk, see Christopher Long, "Rusk, Texas," in Ron Tyler et al., eds., *New Handbook of Texas* (Austin: Texas State Historical Association, 1996), vol. 5, pp 722–23; and Paul M. Lucko, "Rusk Penitentiary," in Tyler et al., *New Handbook of Texas,* vol. 5, pp. 726–27. For murder of Peter Howard and Flores trial, see *Fort Worth Star-Telegram* and *Fort Worth Record*, August 17–18, 1915, and April 13–16, 1916.

25. For Anna, see "Jas. B. Legett" in Twelfth United States Federal Census (1900); and "James B. Legett" in Thirteenth United States Federal Census (1910); and "Anna Legett" in Thirteenth United States Federal Census (1910), Tulsa Ward 3, Tulsa County, OK, Microfilm Roll No. T624_1274.

26. *Fort Worth Record*, October 24, 1917.

27. The press accounts of the affair are alike on all major points, only differing on small details. The Weatherford newspaper seems to have gotten its facts from Fort Worth reporters. The Dallas newspaper maintained an office in Fort Worth, and its reporters filed their own stories. Because of the historic rivalry between the two cities. Dallas reporting was always more critical, i.e., more embarrassing, than Fort Worth reporting. *Fort Worth Star-Telegram*, October 24, 1917; *Dallas Morning News,* October 24, 1917; *Weatherford Daily Herald,* October 24, 1917.

28. *Dallas Morning News*, October 24, 1917; *Fort Worth Star-Telegram,* October 24, 1917.

29. *Fort Worth Star-Telegram*, October 24, 1917.

30. *State of Texas v. J. Ben LeGett*, Case No. 23714, Tarrant County District Court Criminal Records, Index to Felony Cases, January 15, 1876–September 30, 1932, County Clerk's Office, Criminal Section. Tarrant County Justice Center.

31. In 1917 the Legislature had created the Criminal District Court for Tarrant County to relieve some of the case overload of the existing District Courts (the Seventeenth, Forty-eighth, and Sixty-seventh).

32. See Marshall Spoonts' comments, quoted in *Dallas Morning News* and *Weatherford Daily Herald*, October 24, 1917.

33. See "James D. Legett" [*sic*] in Fifteenth United States Federal Census (1930), Riverside, Clackamas County, OR, Microfilm Roll No. 1940, p. 2A, Enumeration District 85; and "James Legett" (Certificate No. 278) in Oregon Death index, 1903–98, Oregon State Archives and Records Center, Salem, OR.

Chapter 8

1. See Quanah Parker to Charles Goodnight, undated, in Chas. Goodnight Papers, Research Center, Panhandle-Plains Historical Museum, Canyon, Texas; also cited in Bill Neeley, *The Last Comanche Chief: The Life and Times of Quanah Parker* (New York: John Wiley & Sons, 1995), p. 32. Cf. Brian C. Hosmer opts for 1845 in "Quanah Parker," in *The New Handbook of Texas* (Austin: Texas State Historical Association, 1996), vol. 5, p. 61; William T. Hagan opts for 1852 in *Quanah Parker: Comanche Chief* (Norman: University of Oklahoma Press, 1993), p. 7. Cf. historical novelist Charles Brashear, *Killing Cynthia Ann: A Novel* (Fort Worth: Texas Christian University Press, 1999), "Historical and Bibliographic Notes," p. 204, prefers 1847, based on the "fact" that Quanah was "about thirteen" when his mother was repatriated in 1860. Finally, there is Quanah Parker's tombstone, which says he was sixty-four when he died February 21, 1911, likewise putting his birth date at 1847.

2. The Comanches had no written language, so their names must be transliterated into the proximate English spelling based on pronunciation. Usually, the names are written as a series of syllables divided by hyphens, thus "Qua-ha-de" or "Qua-ha-di." Sometimes the name of Quanah's group is spelled "Quahada," reflecting a different pronunciation. For simplicity's sake, this work will use "Quahade." A quick tutorial on Comanche names was provided by William Voelker, *aka* Wahathuweeka, of SIA: The Comanche Nation Ethno-Ornithological Initiative, in a series of e-mails, February 3–6, 2009 (henceforward cited as "Voelker correspondence").

3. The exact year of birth is not known for either child. The best approximation for Pee-nah is "about 1850," making him anywhere from three to five years younger than Quanah. See Brashear, p. 204. Cf. Garrett, *Fort Worth*, p. 191, who says Pee-nah was nine years old in 1860. Margaret Schmidt Hacker, author of the "Cynthia Ann Parker" biography in *The New Handbook of Texas* (vol. 5, p. 58), takes the safe path, offering no date whatsoever. (The *Handbook* entry is a good summary of the same author's biography, *Cynthia Ann Parker: The Life and Legend* [El Paso: Texas Western Press,1990]). Native American names are notoriously difficult to translate into English, both because the meaning is not always clear and because the spelling on the printed page winds up being a phonetic approximation. Case in point is the Comanche meaning of Quanah, which in numerous sources is incorrectly translated as "Fragrant" or "Fragrance," or even "Son of Fragrant," versus "The Eagle." Likewise, his sister's Comanche name is sometimes spelled out as "Toposannah" and sometimes Toh-Tsee-Ah. Voelker correspondence and the Smithsonian Institution Research Information System website of the Smithsonian Institution, National Anthropological Archives.

4. Howard R. Lamar, ed., *The Reader's Encyclopedia of the American West* (New York: Thomas Y. Crowell, 1977), p. 250.

5. Years later, Quanah stated that none of the three were present that day. Cf. memoirs of Sul Ross in Judith Ann Benner, *Sul Ross: Soldier, Statesman, Educator* (College Station, TX: Texas A&M University Press, 1983), p. 54. This same mistake is perpetuated by Fort Worth historian Julia Kathryn Garrett who says that the three escaped the massacre by fleeing. See Garrett, *Fort Worth: A Frontier Triumph* (Fort Worth: Texas Christian University Press, 1996, reprint of 1972 ed.), pp. 188. The Quanah version is endorsed by Neeley, *Last Comanche Chief*, pp. 47–48, 53.

6. Ross's specious claim was publicized when he ran for governor for the first time in 1887, and was subsequently repeated both by himself and others many times. It was part of his obituary in 1898 and was still being told as "fact" more than forty years later. See obituary in *Dallas Morning News*, January 4, 1898, p. 1, and "Hand-to-Hand Battle Kills Indian Chief" in *Dallas Morning News*, April 11, 1942. Quanah's scornful response was proclaimed from the lecture platform on at least two occasions (see *Dallas Morning News*, October 27, 1909, and October 25, 1910), and later endorsed by folklorist-historian Frank X. Tolbert in "Tolbert's Texas" column, *Dallas Morning News*, June 28, 1964, p. 23. See also Benner, *Sul Ross*, pp. 54–56, and Neeley, *Last Comanche Chief*, p. 62.

7. The picture is probably a daguerreotype. The photographer is identified in Mildred P. Mayhall, *Indian Wars of Texas* (Waco: Texian Press, 1965), p. 121. Garrett, *Fort Worth*, pp. 190–92.

8. Hacker, *Handbook of Texas*, vol. 5, p. 58. The date 1870 is verified by the 1870 Census report. It is also cited by historian William T. Hagan and historian-novelist Charles Brashear. See Hagan, *Quanah Parker: Comanche Chief* (Norman: University of Oklahoma Press, 1993), p. 7; and Brashear, *Killing Cynthia Ann,* "Historical and Bibliographic Notes," p. 206. Cf. historians Neeley, *Last Comanche Chief*, p. 52, and Garrett, *Fort Worth*, p. 192, who both cite the conventional but incorrect date, 1864. For burial, see Paul I. Wellman, "Cynthia Ann Parker," *Chronicles of Oklahoma*, vol. 12, no. 2 (June, 1934), pp. 163–171; and Mayhall, *Indian Wars*, p. 121.

9. From eulogy given at Cynthia Ann's reinterment at the Post Oak Mission Church Cemetery, near Cache, Oklahoma, in 1910. Quoted in *Dallas Morning News*, December 5, 1910.

10. Brashear, *Killing Cynthia Ann*, "Historical and Bibliographic Notes," p. 208.

11. Birdsong story comes from a signed affidavit in possession of Parker family and cited in Mayhall, *Indian Wars*, p. 121. For additional information on Cynthia Ann's fate, see Brashear, *Killing Cynthia Ann*, pp. 208–09.

12. Comanche oral tradition is not in agreement on exactly when and how Quanah became aware of his mother's true identity. Peta's deathbed confession is affirmed in Neeley, *Last Comanche Chief*, p. 53.

13. For physical description of Quanah, see Neeley, *Last Comanche Chief*, pp. 59 and 230; Lamar, *Reader's Encyclopedia*, p. 249; and Douglas C. Jones, *The Trea-*

ty of Medicine Lodge: The Story of the Great Treaty Council as Told by Eyewitnesses (Norman: University of Oklahoma Press, 1966). See same for character traits of Comanche.

14. Based largely on the testimony of pioneer Texan Olive King Dixon, "Fearless and Effective Foe, He Spared Women and Children Always," MS in O. K. D Papers, Research Center, Panhandle-Plains Historical Museum, Canyon, Texas.

15. Whether To-nar-cy was his first wife or not is yet another matter of dispute in Comanche oral tradition. Affirming her as the first of numerous wives are Neeley, *Last Comanche Chief*, pp. 79–80; and Zoe A. Tilghman, *Quanah: The Eagle of the Comanches* (Oklahoma City, OK: Harlow Publishing Corporation, 1938), p. 195.

16. Lamar, *Reader's Encyclopedia*, p. 719. See also Jones, *Treaty of Medicine Lodge*.

17. Richard Selcer, *Fort Worth: A Texas Original!* (Austin: Texas State Historical Association, 2004), p. 6.

18. William T. Hagan, *United States-Comanche Relations* (New Haven, CT: Yale University Press, 1976), p. 154, cited in Neeley, *Last Comanche Chief*, p. 175.

19. Col. Ranald Mackenzie to Col. E. J. Strange, quoted in Brashear, *Killing Cynthia Ann*, p. 207.

20. Tilghman, *Quanah*, p. 194; Hosmer, "Quanah Parker," *New Handbook of Texas*, vol. 5, p. 62.

21. The two-story, twelve-room house, with one of the first telephones in the Indian Territory, was distinguished by the large white stars painted on the roof. The name reportedly was bestowed after an army general out of Fort Sill came to visit Quanah dressed in full military panoply, including stars on his shoulders. For gift of house, see Voelker correspondence, February 4, 2009.

22. For Quanah, Texas, see, "Dallas and Texas 50 Years Ago," *Dallas Morning News*, November 19, 1936, p. 7. The town of Nocona in Montague County, Texas, is named for his father, Peta Nocona, just as Parker County is named for his mother's family, showing that the universal goodwill extended to all branches of his family. Neeley, *Last Comanche Chief*, pp. 228–29.

23. Lamar, *Reader's Encyclopedia*, p. 251.

24. Mack Williams, "Burk Burnett: Giant of the Frontier," in Mack Williams, ed., *In Old Fort Worth: The Story of a City and Its People as published in* The News-Tribune *in 1976 and 1977* (Fort Worth: privately printed by Mack H. Williams and Madeline C. Williams, 1986), pp. 68–69. "Quanah Parker in Town [Fort Worth]," *Dallas Morning News*, March 10, 1904. For Quanah's description of his friendship with Burnett, see *Dallas Morning News*, October 25, 1910.

25. From interview with Hugh Hannah, one of the old railroad men, August 19, 1937, vol. 38, p. 219, Indian-Pioneer Papers, Western History Collection, University of Oklahoma Library, Norman, OK, cited in Neeley, *Last Comanche Chief*, pp. 228–29. *Dallas Morning News*, March 10, 1904.

26. Lamar, *Reader's Encyclopedia*, p. 989; Neeley, *Last Comanche Chief*, pp. 154–55, 165.

27. Brashear, *Killing Cynthia Ann*, pp. 207–08.

28. The Smithsonian's National Anthropological Archives says six (ca. 1892). Brashear, in *Killing Cynthia Ann*, p. 207, says seven. The *Fort Worth Star-Telegram*, July 31, 1960, says nine. The *Fort Worth Chronicle*, July 31, 1994, says eight. After the numbers got up there, nobody knew for sure, perhaps not even Quanah himself.

29. *Dallas Morning News*, August 9, 1897.

30. Neeley, *Last Comanche Chief*, pp. 79–80.

31. Hagan, *Quanah Parker*, pp. 48–49.

32. Lamar, *Reader's Encyclopedia*, p. 251. The numbers come from an interview with Captain Lee Hall, Indian agent on the Comanche-Kiowa-Wichita Reservation in 1885. *Fort Worth Gazette*, December 22, 1885.

33. *Dallas Morning News*, May 23 and November 1, 1906.

34. Quoted in Neeley, *Last Comanche Chief*, p. 161.

35. For Theodore Roosevelt and Quanah, see *Dallas Morning News*, October 25, 1910. Quanah being quoted by Red River store owner Corwin Doan about leaving Indian Territory in Bill Fairley, "Tarrant Chronicles" column ("Parker Was Deft in Whites' Ways"), *Fort Worth Star-Telegram*, July 7, 1999. For the high regard in which he was held by locals, see *Fort Worth Gazette*, December 22, 1885.

36. *Dallas Morning News*, October 25, 1910.

37. Ibid., December 21, 1885, March 10, 1904, and March 12, 1909. For Wild West Shows, see ibid., June 22, 1908.

38. Ibid., March 10, 1904; Brashear, *Killing Cynthia Ann*, pp. 208–09.

39. *Fort Worth Gazette*, December 21, 1885. Some newspapers claimed (incorrectly) that this was a Christmas-gift-buying trip.

40. *Fort Worth Gazette*, December 21 and 22, 1885.

41. *Dallas Morning News*, November 2, 1885, December 21 and 22, 1885. A firsthand recollection of the episode was related for the Federal Writers' Project in 1938 by early Fort Worth resident C. J. E. Kellner. He got the date and the name of the hotel wrong, putting the incident in 1882 at the El Paso, but otherwise his recollections are reliable. Reprinted as Kellner, "Getting Started in Fort Worth in 1881," in Mack Williams, ed., *In Old Fort Worth*, p. 49. The newspapers and Parker biographer William T. Hagan (*Quanah Parker*, p. 49) correctly identify the hotel as the Pickwick, which was the successor to the El Paso, at the same location.

42. *Fort Worth Gazette*, December 22, 1885.

43. *Wheeling (WV) Register*, December 21, 1885. *Washington (DC) Critic Record*, December 21, 1885. Both the Wheeling and the Washington, DC, newspapers call Chief Yellow Bear "Yellow Bag," and neither one mentions Quanah at all. Quanah's memory of the date was fuzzy in later years, placing it some ten years later. *Dallas Morning News*, March 10, 1904.

44. *Dallas Morning News*, March 10, 1904, and March 27, 1909.

45. Ibid., August 29, 1897.

46. Pneumonia is the cause cited by his modern biographers based on the symptoms that were described. For the rheumatism-and-arthritis theory attributed to some doctors at the time and the equally preposterous conspiracy theory, see *Dallas Morn-*

ing News, February 28, 1911. The "got-drunk-and-fell-off-his-horse" legend was related to this author by an old Texas friend who is part Anglo and part Comanche and could offer no source for it other than popular lore he had always heard.

47. Neeley, *Last Comanche Chief*, p. 235.

48. For background to Cynthia Ann's marker, see Bud Kennedy, "In My Opinion" ("Twice-abducted Woman Should Get a Marker"), *Fort Worth Star-Telegram*, November 30, 2006. For first public recognition of Quanah's Comanche descendants in Fort Worth, see Barbara Cannon, "Cynthia Parker Descendants Living Here," *Fort Worth Press*, June 2, 1968.

49. Pekka Hämäläinen, *The Comanche Empire* (New Haven, CT: Yale University Press, 2008). Not about Quanah personally, this is, however, a groundbreaking study of the culture and society of one of the great Indian nations of American history. As such, it provides insight into Quanah's place in Comanche history.

50. The story of how his name came to be mistranslated is related in the *Dallas Morning News*, October 25, 1910. As told by J. Collin George, who introduced Quanah that day, the story was unsubstantiated "legend," but Quanah did not repudiate it in his remarks immediately following.

51. The film was produced and directed by legendary Western lawman Bill Tilghman and "starred" his pal and fellow lawman, Heck Thomas, who was also a Fort Worth resident for a while. A single copy of *A Bank Robbery* survives today in the Library of Congress. "Letters to the Editor," *Wild West*, vol. 21, no. 3 (October 2008), p. 7.

52. *Fort Worth Star-Telegram*, July 31, 1960.

Chapter 9

1. The Finch family can be followed through the census records. See "Amos Finch" in Tenth United States Federal Census (1880), Precinct 5, Wise County, TX, Microfilm Roll No. T9_1333; "Thomas E. Finch" in Twelfth United States Federal Census (1900), Precinct 5, Wise County, TX, Microfilm Roll No.T623_1680; and "Thomas E. Finch" in Thirteenth United States Federal Census (1910), 2nd Ward, Decatur, Wise County, TX, Microfilm Roll No. T624_1600.

2. Historic information on Decatur and Wise County from the city's website http://www.decaturtx.org/history, and http://www.texasescapes.com.

3. See "Thomas E. Finch" in Wise County census records, 1900 and 1910; and "Leona Finch" in Fourteenth United States Federal Census (1920), Fort Worth, Tarrant County, TX, Microfilm Roll No. T625_1848.

4. See "Drew Finch" and "Jessie Finch" in Thirteenth United States Federal Census (1910), Wise County, TX, Microfilm Roll No. T624_1600; and Fourteenth United States Federal Census (1920), Fort Worth, Tarrant County, TX, Microfilm Roll No. T625_1848. For residence and employment, see Fort Worth city directories, 1916–1918.

5. *Dallas Morning News*, November 28, 1917.

6. Fostepco Heights was a residential addition whose name derived from its developers, Robert H. Foster and Elmer L. Stevens. They started a construction com-

pany around 1910, and Fostepco Heights was the result. Personal background on the Jobes comes from *Fort Worth Star-Telegram*, September 5, 1918, and for Thomas E. Finch, the Thirteenth United States Federal Census (1910) for Decatur.

7. *Fort Worth Star-Telegram*, February 18 and September 5, 1918.

8. The shooting is described in the *Fort Worth Star-Telegram*, September 5, 1918; and the *Fort Worth Record*, November 29, 1917. Typically, the *Record* is the more sensationalist account.

9. The City-County Hospital opened at East Fourth and Jones streets as Fort Worth's first emergency-care facility in 1914.

10. At this time in the city's history, ambulances were operated by the major funeral homes. To summon an ambulance and transport the victim to the hospital probably took twenty to thirty minutes. *Fort Worth Star-Telegram*, September 5, 1918; and *Fort Worth Record*, November 29, 1917.

11. *Fort Worth Record*, November 29, 1917.

12. Ibid.

13. Ibid., December 1, 1917.

14. Ibid.

15. The history of Tarrant County's Criminal District Court, from its origins through its initial proceedings, can be traced in *Dallas Morning News*, January 12, June 13, 22–24; and 29, 1917.

16. *State of Texas v. W. A. Jobe*, Criminal District Court, Case No. 23306, Records of the Tarrant County District Clerk, Criminal Section, Tarrant County Justice Center.

17. *Fort Worth Star-Telegram*, December 15, 1917; *Dallas Morning News*, December 16, 1917.

18. *Fort Worth Star-Telegram*, December 15, 1917.

19. *State of Texas v. W. A. Jobe*, Case No. 23306.

20. *Fort Worth Star-Telegram*, February 18, 1918, pp. 3 and 7.

21. Ibid., September 3, 1918.

22. *State of Texas v. W. A. Jobe*, Case No. 23306; *Dallas Morning News*, February 8, 15, 18, and 19, 1918, and September 5 and 6, 1918; *Fort Worth Star-Telegram*, September 5, 1918.

23. *Fort Worth Star-Telegram*, September 5, 1918.

24. Ibid.

25. Ibid.

26. *State of Texas v. W. A. Jobe*, Case No. 23306.

27. Fort Worth city directory, 1920; "Leona Finch" in Fourteenth United States Federal Census (1920), Niles, Tarrant County, TX, Microfilm Roll No. T625_1848; and "Drew Finch" in Fifteenth United States Federal Census (1930), Fort Worth, Tarrant County, TX, Microfilm Roll No. 2393.

Chapter 10

1. See, for example, the case of Julia Chitwood, dropped off at the county jail in 1893. *Dallas Morning News*, February 28, 1893.

2. For John Rea's personal background, see "John Rea" in Twelfth United States Census (190), Fort Worth, Tarrant County, TX, Microfilm Roll T623_1671; and death certificate for John Thomas Rea, Texas Department of Health, Texas Death Indexes, 1903–2000, Certificate No. 1239, on microfilm. There is some confusion in the public records between John W. (the father) and John T. (the son). For John W. Rea's law enforcement career, see *Fort Worth Telegram*, April 7, 1905; January 8, 1906. Note: the *Fort Worth Telegram* was one of the predecessors of the *Fort Worth Star-Telegram.*

3. *John Rea v. Mary S. Rea*, divorce decree, February 18, 1910 in Seventeenth District Court, Case No. 29579, Book A-7, pp. 289–90, District Court civil records, Tarrant County, TX, Family Law Center, Disposed Records, Civil and Family, 200 E. Weatherford, Ft. Worth, TX. (See Index to Minutes, Plaintiffs L to R, 1879–Apr. 30, 1930). Additional details of the divorce come from *Fort Worth Star-Telegram*, May 15, 1909, February 18, and May 28, 1910. For property settlement, see also e-mail correspondence between Sergeant Kevin Foster of the FWPD and Mary Rea's granddaughter, Marian Rea, July 14 and 15, 2005, which Sergeant Foster graciously shared with this author.

4. Mary S. Rea v. John Rea and Drs. J. A. Kelly and E. P. Hall, May 28, 1910, Seventeenth District Court, Case No. 29989, Index to Civil Minutes, Plaintiffs, L to R, 1879–April 30, 1930, District Court, Tarrant County, TX, on microfilm in Tarrant County Family Law Center. Additional details on the case of Roy Rea come from *Fort Worth Star-Telegram*, May 28, 1910, p. 14; and February 20, 1912, p. 10. For property dispute, see *Fort Worth Star-Telegram*, May 28, 1911, p. 14, and February 20, 1912, p. 10. For John W. Rea's death, see *Fort Worth Star-Telegram*, October 2, 1913, p. 5.

5. For lawsuit, see *Fort Worth Star-Telegram*, March 21, 1911, p. 12, and April 18, 1911, p. 3. Family opinions of Mary come from e-mail correspondence between Foster and Rea, July 14 and 15, 2005. Membership in the "City Federation of Women's Clubs" comes from *Fort Worth Star-Telegram*, August 26, 1914, p. 1.

6. *Fort Worth Star-Telegram*, February 20, 1912, p. 10, and June 28, 1912, p. 9.

7. *Fort Worth Star-Telegram*, February 20, 1912, p. 10, June 28, 1912, p. 9, and July 9, 1912, p. 2; *Dallas Morning News*, July 10, 1912.

8. *Fort Worth Star-Telegram*, July 2, 1914, p. 2.

9. From court testimony of Durward McDonald cited in *Fort Worth Star-Telegram*, March 19, 1915.

10. *Dallas Morning News*, September 23, 1914.

11. Ibid.

12. Sheriff's Rea's quote comes from family stories handed down for years, related by Marian Rea to Kevin Foster via e-mail, July 14 and 15, 2005.

13. *Fort Worth Star-Telegram*, September 24 (p. 11), October 18 (p. 20), and October 20, 1914, p 10.

14. *Fort Worth Star-Telegram*, March 14 and 19, 1915. Statistic comes from *Fort Worth Star-Telegram*, July 29, 2006.

15. *State of Texas v. Mrs. M. S. Rea*, Case No. 21057, Sixty-seventh District

Court, Tarrant County, TX, March 18, 1915, Records of the Tarrant County District Clerk, Criminal Section, Tarrant County Justice Center.

16. For "suspended sentence," see *Fort Worth Star-Telegram*, March 19 and 21, 1915. For weapon search, see ibid., March 19, 1915.

17. Ibid., March 19 and 20, 1915.

18. Ibid., March 21, 1915.

19. For jury's verdict, see *State of Texas v. Mrs. M. S. Rea*, Case No. 21057. For post-verdict remarks, see *Fort Worth Star-Telegram*, March 21, 1915.

20. For Mary's legal battles, see *Fort Worth Star-Telegram*, January 2, 1917, p. 3, and August 13, 1922, p. 13. For Robert Moore case, see ibid., February 24, 1916, p. 16.

21. Foster-Rea e-mail correspondence.

22. Ibid.

Chapter 11

1. There is considerable confusion today about her background before she landed in Fort Worth, some of that confusion created by Mary herself. The most reliable information comes from the 1900 census enumeration. The 1880 census, her death certificate, and the obituaries in the Fort Worth and Dallas newspapers at the time of her death muddy the waters and cannot be taken as reliable. See "Mary Porter" in Twelfth United States Federal Census (1900), Fort Worth, Ward 3, Tarrant County, TX, Microfilm Roll No. T623_1671 (hereafter cited as "1900 census"). Cf. "Mary Porter" in Tenth United States Federal Census (1880), Hot Springs, Garland County, AR, Microfilm Roll No. T9_45. Death Certificate for Mary Porter (No. 240), City of Fort Worth, Vital Statistics Division, date of record June 10, 1905; *Fort Worth Star-Telegram*, June 11, 1905; *Dallas Morning News*, June 11, 1905. These sources variously give her birthplace as Canada [*sic*] and birth date as 1820, 1830, and 1845 [*sic*].

2. The best one-volume history of nineteenth-century Irish migration to America is Jay P. Dolan, *The Irish Americans: A History* (London: Bloomsbury Press, 2008). Quotation from David Goldfield, Carl Abbott et al., *The American Journey: A History of the United States*, 4th ed. (Upper Saddle River, NJ: Pearson Education / Prentice Hall, 2007), pp. 343–44.

3. According to the 1900 census, they were married for ten years before he passed away. Mary's tenure in Hot Springs can be gauged by the fact that her name appears in the *Hot Springs City Directory* in 1880 and makes its last appearance in the 1883–84 edition of the directory. George Porter's death is recorded in the Hollywood Cemetery records, Hot Springs, Arkansas, and his impressive tombstone can still be seen in the cemetery. No marriage certificate can be located for George and Mary, and he left behind no death certificate and no will on record. *Hot Springs City Directory*, 1883–84 and 1887, Garland County Historical Society, Hot Springs, AR. For the Irish presence in the West, see Kevin J. Mullen, *The Toughest Gang in Town* (Novato, CA: Noir Publications, 2005), pp. 143–44.

4. Mary and Josie may have arrived as late as 1885—the record is not clear—

but Mary was here in time to get into the 1886–87 Fort Worth city directory (on microfiche in Genealogy, Local History, and Archives Unit, Fort Worth Public Library, Central Library). Mary's obituary in the *Dallas Morning News*, June 11, 1905, suggests that she arrived in Fort Worth in 1887, but her name appears in that same newspaper on November 26, 1886. Fort Worth genealogist and historian Donna Donnell has done a great deal of work on the Hot Springs connection and Fort Worth's demimonde.

5. *Dallas Morning News*, November 26, 1886. Fort Worth city directory, on microfiche in Genealogy, Local History, and Archives Unit, Fort Worth Public Library, Central library; 1900 census.

6. *City of Fort Worth v. Madame Porter*, October 26, 1887, Case No. 4299, Criminal Minutes, County Court, 1886–87, Special Collections, University of Texas at Arlington. Richard Selcer, *Hell's Half Acre: The Life and Legend of a Red-light District* (Fort Worth: Texas Christian University Press, 1991), p. 88.

7. *Dallas Morning News*, November 26, 1886, and August 3, 1894.

8. Ibid., March 25, 1891.

9. 1900 census.

10. *Dallas Morning News*, June 8, 1889, and August 23, 1894.

11. *Fort Worth Morning Register*, October 18, 1900.

12. 1900 census.

13. *Fort Worth Daily Gazette*, September 30 and November 2, 1890.

14. One hundred and thirty is the total number of times her name appears on the court register, which may include postponements and continuations. Since the registers are all that remain today, and even these are incomplete, it is impossible to know the details of the cases, how they were resolved, or how many times she appeared in court over the course of her career. Tarrant County Index to Criminal minutes, 1893–1897, Special Collections, University of Texas at Arlington. For Big Five's Big Day in court, see *Fort Worth Register*, November 8, 1900.

15. *Dallas Morning News*, November 4, 1891.

16. See "Real Estate Transactions" in *Dallas Morning News*, April 14, 1899, and September 20, 1900; and "Real Estate Transfers" in *Fort Worth Morning Register*, September 21, 1900.

17. Taxes Delinquent to the City of Fort Worth on Real Estate, 1898, vol. 49, p. 85, Receipts Nos. 2015 and 1096, Records Office, Tarrant County Courthouse, Fort Worth, TX.

18. *Dallas Morning News*, June 25, 1895.

19. Mary Daggett Lake Papers, Series II, "State and Local History," Box 5, Folder 3, Genealogy, Local History, and Archives Unit, Fort Worth Public Library, Central Library.

20. Records of the City of Fort Worth, Series I, Mayor and Council Proceedings, August 4, 1899, Meeting, Box 3 of 3, Genealogy, Local History, and Archives Unit, Fort Worth Public Library, Central Library.

21. Mary Porter's probate records (Case No. 2640), Tarrant County Clerk, Probate Office, Tarrant County Courthouse, Fort Worth, TX; Fort Worth city direc-

tory, 1904–05, on microfiche in Genealogy, Local History, and Archives Unit, Fort Worth Public Library, Central Library; *Dallas Morning News*, June 11, 1905.

22. Death Certificate for Mary Porter (No. 240), City of Fort Worth, Vital Statistics Division, date of record June 10, 1905; Porter Probate record (Case No. 2640); *Fort Worth Star-Telegram*, June 11, 1905.

23. Ann Arnold, *Camp Meeting to Cathedral: Fort Worth's Historic Congregations* (Arlington, TX: Landa Press, 2004), pp. 44–46. "Last rites" comes from research by Donna Donnell, sent to this author via e-mail correspondence, March 16, 2008. *Fort Worth Telegram*, June 11, 1905. (Note: the *Fort Worth Telegram* was one of the predecessors of the *Fort Worth Star-Telegram*. It is archived on microfilm with the *Fort Worth Star-Telegram*.) *Dallas Morning News*, June 11, 1905.

24. Mary is buried in block 32.5, lot no. 4, at Oakwood. There are five spaces in that lot and no way of knowing for sure which space she is in. Information on Mary's relationship with Pearl Beebe comes from e-mail correspondence with Donna Donnell to this author, July 5, 2008. Donnell is the historian-genealogist who has kept the name "Soiled Dove's Row" alive. The origins of the name are unknown.

25. *Fort Worth Telegram*, June 13, 1905; *Dallas Morning News*, June 14, 1905.

26. Porter Probate records (Cases No. 2640 and 2667).

27. *Fort Worth Telegram*, August 9, 1905.

28. Ibid., September 4, November 4, December 2, and December 4, 1906; *Dallas Morning News*, November 7, 1906.

29. *Fort Worth Telegram*, February 12, 1907; Porter Probate records (Case Nos. 2640 and 2667).

Chapter 12

1. The death certificate, filled out by his wife, gives 1854. The biographical sketch by John Henry Brown gives 1855. See Brown, *Indian Wars and Pioneers of Texas* (Austin: L. E. Daniell, 1880 [*sic*]), p. 626. (1880 is a printing mistake; the book was published no earlier than 1891.) Different census reports give 1855, 1856, 1857, and "about 1856." At least the biographical sketch and death certificate agree on the month and day if not the year. Texas State Department of Health, Bureau of Vital Statistics, Certificate No. 12857, available on microfilm in Genealogy, Local History, and Archives Unit, Fort Worth Public Library, Central Library. John Henry Brown, *Indian Wars and Pioneers of Texas* (Austin: L. E. Daniell, 1880 [*sic*]), p. 626. (1880 is a printing mistake; the book was published no earlier than 1891.) "J. W. Swayne" in Eighth United States Federal Census (1860), Henderson, TN, Microfilm Roll No. M653_1256; "James W. Swayne" in Ninth United States Federal Census (1870), Henderson, TN, Microfilm Roll No. M593_1537; "James Swayne" in Twelfth United States Federal Census (1900), Fort Worth, Ward 4, Tarrant, TX, Microfilm Roll No. T623 1671; "James W. Swayne" in Fourteenth United States Federal Census (1920), Fort Worth, Ward 2, Tarrant, TX, Microfilm Roll No. T625_1848.

2. For personal and family history, see "J. W. Swayne" in Eighth United States

Federal Census (1860), Henderson, TN, Microfilm Roll No. M653_1256; "James W. Swayne" in Ninth United States Federal Census (1870), Henderson, TN, Microfilm Roll No. M593_1537; "James W. Swayne," in Tenth United States Federal Census (1880), District 88, Ward 1, p. 1, line 4, Fort Worth, Tarrant County, TX, Microfilm Roll No. T9_1328; "James Swayne" in Twelfth United States Federal Census (1900), Fort Worth, Ward 4, Tarrant County, TX, Microfilm Roll No. T623 1671; "James W. Swayne" in Fourteenth United States Federal Census (1920), Fort Worth, Ward 2, Tarrant County, TX, Microfilm Roll No. T625_1848. The 1880 census for Fort Worth is so heavily damaged that Swayne cannot be found by an on-line search, thus the additional details provided here for the entry.

Additional family history comes from Jonathan Kennon Thompson Smith, *A Genealogical Miscellany: Henderson County, Tennessee* (privately printed by Jonathan K. T. Smith, 2001), 5 vols., available on-line at TNGenWeb.org genealogy website, http://www.tngenweb.org/records/henderson/misc. See specifically, vol. I: "Administrators, Executors Settlement Book No. 1, 1867–1881"; vol. II: "Bits and Pieces"; and vol. V: "Henderson County Guardian (Bond) Record, 1861–1892. Brown, *Indian Wars*, pp. 626–27. Cf. Mack Williams' biographical sketch of the Swaynes, in which he says (incorrectly) that James Swayne, Sr., was a Tarrant County farmer and that the boys, James, Jr., and John, grew up in Fort Worth. Mack Williams, "In Old Fort Worth: He Found Adventure in His Home Town," in Mack Williams, ed., *In Old Fort Worth* (Fort Worth: privately printed, 1986), pp. 74–75.

3. *Dallas Morning News*, March 25, 1909; Brown, *Indian Wars*, pp. 626-27. Cf. Williams, "In Old Fort Worth," p. 74.

4. Brown, *Indian Wars*, p. 627; Works Progress Administration, "Federal Writers' Project" (Fort Worth: Fort Worth Public Library Unit, 1941), Consolidated Chronologies, p. 539 (Hereafter referred to as "Federal Writers' Project"). Other details from biographical sketch of Mrs. John Swayne, *Fort Worth Press*, September 2, 1932, and from Williams, "In Old Fort Worth," p. 75.

5. *Fort Worth Press*, September 2, 1932, and April 17, 1946; "Federal Writers' Project," vol. 6, pp. 2,168 and 2,293; and vol. 50, pp. 19, 621.

6. Brown, *Indian Wars*, p. 627.

7. Ibid.

8. *Fort Worth Democrat*, May 19, 1881; *Fort Worth Gazette*, April 5, 1886.

9. *Fort Worth Gazette*, July 2, 1886; *Austin Daily Statesman*, July 2, 1886; *Dallas Morning News*, February 10, 1889, and January 14, 1890.

10. The self-styled title comes from Swayne's testimony in the case of *Joella Sealy v. the Mutual Land Company*, to which he was not a party, in 1913. *Fort Worth Star-Telegram*, October 16, 1913; *Dallas Morning News*, January 23, 1890, and November 19, 1897; *Fort Worth Register*, February 15 and May 13, 1902; Williams, "In Old Fort Worth," p. 75. Brown, *Indian Wars*, p. 627.

11. "J. B. Latham" in Tenth United States Census (1880), Columbia, Boone County, MO, Microfilm Roll No. T9_676. Brown, *Indian Wars*, p. 627; *Fort Worth Telegram*, May 22, 1907; *Fort Worth Star-Telegram*, November 18, 1917. (Note: the *Fort Worth Telegram* was one of the predecessors of the *Fort Worth Star-Telegram*.)

12. *Dallas Morning News*, November 22 and 23, 1895 (p. 9 both), and December 22, 1895 (p. 4). Governor Joseph Sayers, "Proclamation by the Governor of the State of Texas . . ." December 18, 1902, Executive Record Books, Secretary of State, Archives and Information Services Division, Texas State Library and Archives Commission, Austin.

13. *Dallas Morning News*, March 25, 1909.

14. *Fort Worth Star-Telegram*, August 23, 1909.

15. For a discussion of Sunday closing laws, see Richard Selcer, ed., *Legendary Watering Holes: The Saloons That Made Texas Famous* (College Station: Texas A&M University Press, 2004), pp. 274–75. For Swayne's personal crusade, see *Dallas Morning News*, November 22, 1911.

16. *Dallas Morning News*, May 6, 1913.

17. *Fort Worth Telegram*, February 14, 1908.

18. *Dallas Morning News*, May 17, 1913.

19. *Fort Worth Telegram*, January 8, 1903.

20. *Dallas Weekly Herald*, March 13, 1884; *Fort Worth Telegram*, January 8, 1903; *Fort Worth Star-Telegram*, November 16, 1913; Richard Selcer, *Fort Worth: A Texas Original!* (Austin: Texas State Historical Association, 2004), p. 31; *Dallas Morning News*, April 27, 1886.

21. *Dallas Morning News*, January 23, 1915; *Fort Worth Star-Telegram*, June 29, 1915.

22. Mary Rea's case is discussed at length in a series of newspaper stories in the *Dallas Morning News*, September 23, 25, and 26, 1914; and *Fort Worth Star-Telegram*, March 19 and 21, 1915.

23. *Fort Worth Star-Telegram*, April 15, 1916.

24. *Dallas Morning News*, May 17, 1913.

25. *Fort Worth (Weekly) Citizen Star*, May 16, 1913.

26. *Fort Worth Star-Telegram*, May 16, 1913.

27. *Dallas Morning News*, May 17, 1917.

28. *Fort Worth Star-Telegram*, May 16, 1913.

29. *Dallas Morning* News, May 17, 1913; Fort *Worth Star-Telegram*, May 16, 1913.

30. *Dallas Morning News*, June 20, 1896.

31. Ibid., March 23 and 28, 1886.

32. Ibid., May 7 and October 11, 1892.

33. Oliver Knight, *Fort Worth: Outpost on the Trinity* (Norman: University of Oklahoma Press, 1953), pp. 259–60, 263.

34. "Happy warrior," used to describe Alfred Smith, an inveterate campaigner and unsuccessful Democratic candidate for President in 1928, is applied to anyone who truly enjoys the give and take of political campaigning. *Fort Worth Star-Telegram*, July 1, 1914. Knight, *Fort Worth*, p. 259.

35. *Dallas Morning News*, February 12, 1929. Texas Department of Health, Bureau of Vital Statistics, Death Certificate No. 12857; Greenwood Cemetery record of J. M. Swayne, interred February 16, 1929, Sec. 14D, Lot 140.

BIBLIOGRAPHY

Primary Sources and Unpublished Works

"American Valley Murders: An Overview." No author given. Unpublished MS in History Files. State Records Center and Archives. Santa Fe, NM.

Colcord, D. F. *Autobiography of Charles Francis Colcord*. Tulsa, OK: privately printed, 1970.

Convict Record Ledgers, 1849–1970. Texas Department of Criminal Justice, Austin, TX (on microfilm).

Department of the Army. Records of the Adjutant General's Office, 1780s–1917. Record Group 94. Letters Received, 1822–1860 (Main Series), and Records Relating to the U.S. Military Academy, 1812–1867. National Archives and Records Administration, Washington, DC.

Department of the Army. Records of the Office of the Judge Advocate General (Army). Record Group 153. Registers of the Records of the Proceedings of the U.S. Army General Courts-Martial, 1809–1890. National Archives and Records Administration, Washington, DC.

Department of the Army. Records of the Office of the Quartermaster General. Record Group 92. Consolidated Correspondence File, 1794–1815. Letters Sent and Letters Received. File Box No. 30. National Archives and Records Administration, Washington, DC.

Department of the Army. Records of the Office of the Secretary of War. Record Group 107. Letters Received by the Secretary of War, Registered Series, 1801–1870. National Archives and Records Administration, Washington, DC.

Dixon, Olive King. Collected Papers. Research Center. Panhandle-Plains Historical Museum. Canyon, TX.

"Federal Writers' Project, Research Data: Fort Worth and Tarrant County, Texas." 77 bound typescript vols. and 8 index vols. Fort Worth: Texas Writers' Project, Fort Worth Library Unit, 1941. Genealogy, Local History, and Archives Unit, Fort Worth Public Library, Central Library.

Fort Worth, City of. Records of the City of Fort Worth, Series I, Mayor and Council Proceedings. Genealogy, Local History, and Archives Unit, Fort Worth Public Library, Central Library.

Fort Worth city directories, 1877 forward (on microfiche in Genealogy, Local History, and Archives Unit, Fort Worth Public Library, Central Library).

Garrett, Julia Kathryn. MS and notes for "Fort Worth: A Frontier Triumph." Special Collections, University of Texas at Arlington.

Gooch, J. A. "100 Years: Cantey, Hanger, Gooch, Munn & Collins." Fort Worth, TX: privately printed, n.d.

Goodnight, Charles. Collected Papers. Research Center. Panhandle-Plains Historical Museum. Canyon, TX.

Hitchcock, Ethan Allen. *Fifty Years in Camp and Field: The Diary of Major General Ethan Allen Hitchcock*. Edited by W. A. Croffut. New York: G. P. Putnam's Sons, 1909.

Hot Springs, Arkansas, City Directory, 1883–1887. Garland County Historical Society. Hot Springs, AR.

Hudson, Weldon I., compiler. *Tarrant County Texas Marriage Records*. 2 vols.: I (1876–1885) and II (1885–1984). Fort Worth, TX: privately printed, 1984.

Indian-Pioneer Papers. Western History Collection, University of Oklahoma Library, Norman, OK.

Jary, Bill. Collected Papers. Special Collections, University of Texas at Arlington Library

Lake, Mary Daggett. Collected Papers. Genealogy, Local History, and Archives Unit, Fort Worth Public Library, Central Library.

Masonic Grand Lodge Library and Museum of Texas, Archives, Waco, TX.

McIntire, Jim. *Early Days in Texas: A Trip to Hell and Heaven*. Norman: University of Oklahoma Press, 1992 (reprint of 1902 ed.).

Oakwood Cemetery Records. Oakwood Cemetery Association, 701 Grand Avenue, Fort Worth, TX.

Oregon Death Index, 1903–1998. Oregon State Archives and Records Center, Salem, OR.

Passenger and Crew Lists of Vessels Arriving at New York, 1820–1957. National Archives Microfilm Publication T715, 892. Record Group 36. National Archives and Records Administration, Washington, DC.

Reports of the Adjutant Generals of the State of Texas. Texas State Library, Austin, TX.

Rich, Harold Wayne. "Twenty-Five Years of Struggle and Progress: The Fort Worth Police Department, 1873–1897. Master of Arts thesis submitted to AddRan College, Texas Christian University, 1999.

Sanborn Fire Insurance Co. Maps (various years for Fort Worth). New York: Sanborn Map & Publishing Co., Ltd. Hard copies at the Center for American History, University of Texas at Austin. Also available on-line at ProQuest Information and Learning. Digital Sanborn Maps, 1867–1970. Environmental Data Resources website, http://www.edrnet.com/.

SIA: The Comanche Nation Ethno-Ornithological Initiative. Cyril, OK.

Tarrant County Criminal Docket. County Court, 1878–79. One volume. Special Collections, University of Texas at Arlington Library.

Tarrant County Deeds Records. Grantor and Grantee Indexes to Deeds. Tarrant County, Texas. County Clerk. Deeds Records Office. Tarrant County Courthouse, Fort Worth, TX.

Tarrant County District Court Civil Records. Minutes and Indexes to Minutes.

Plaintiffs and Defendants. Family Law Center. Disposed Records. Civil and Family. 200 E. Weatherford Street, Fort Worth, TX.

Tarrant County District Court Criminal Records. Index to Felony Cases, January 15, 1876–September 30, 1932. Vols. A–Z. County Clerk's Office, Criminal Section. Tarrant County Justice Center, 401 West Belknap, Fort Worth, TX.

Tarrant County Index to Criminal Minutes, 1893–1897. Special Collections, University of Texas at Arlington Library.

Tarrant County Probate Records. Tarrant County Clerk. Probate Office. Tarrant County Courthouse, Fort Worth, TX.

Tarrant County Scrapbook No. 1. Center for American History, Eugene Barker Library, University of Texas at Austin.

Taxes Delinquent to the City of Fort Worth on Real Estate. Records Office. Tarrant County Courthouse, Fort Worth, TX.

Texas, State of. Birth Indexes, 1903–1976. Texas State Board of Health. Bureau of Vital Statistics (on microfilm and on-line at http://www.pilot.familysearch.org).

Texas, State of. Convict Record Ledgers, with Indexes, 1849–1954. "A" and "B" series. Department of Criminal Justice. 2002. On microfilm, 20 reels. Texas State Library, State Records Center, Records Management Division, Austin, TX.

Texas, State of. Court of Appeals records (available on-line at http://www.LexisNexis.com law database).

Texas, State of. Death Records, 1890–1976. Texas State Board of Health. Bureau of Vital Statistics (on microfilm and on-line at http://www.pilot.familysearch.org).

Texas, State of. Probate Records, 1876–1927, for Tarrant County. Tarrant County District Clerk's Office (Civil). Tarrant County Justice Building, Fort Worth, TX.

Texas, State of. Reports of the Adjutant General's Office. Texas State Library, Austin, TX.

Thirty-third United States Congress. 2d Session. Senate Docs. Report [on the murder of Ripley Arnold], of R. H. Anderson, September 7, 1853, Doc. No. 395, pp. 2–3.

United States Census Records (available on-line at http://AncestryLibrary.com).
Sixth United States Federal Census (1840).
Seventh United States Federal Census (1850).
Eighth United States Federal Census (1860).
Ninth United States Federal Census (1870).
Tenth United States Federal Census (1880).
Note: Eleventh United States Federal Census (1890) is not available in any form; it was destroyed by fire.
Twelfth United States Federal Census (1900).
Thirteenth United States Federal Census (1910).
Fourteenth United States Federal Census (1920).

Fifteenth United States Federal Census (1930).
University of Texas at Arlington Library. Special Collections.
War Department records. Pension Application Files, Misc. Service. Record Group 15, Old Wars Series, National Archives and Records Administration, Washington, DC.
Winchester, Betty Coburn, compiler. "A List of Registered Voters of Tarrant County, Texas for the Year 1867." *Footprints: The Quarterly of the Fort Worth Genealogical Society* vol. 13, no. 1 (February 1970): pp. 105–107.

Secondary Works

Arnold, Ann. *Camp Meeting to Cathedral: Fort Worth's Historic Congregations*. Arlington, TX: Landa Press, 2004.
———. *History of the Fort Worth Legal Community*. Austin, TX: Eakin Press, 2000.
Benner, Judith Ann. *Sul Ross: Soldier, Statesman, Educator*. College Station, TX: Texas A&M University Press, 1983.
Brashear, Charles. *Killing Cynthia Ann: A Novel*. Fort Worth, TX: Texas Christian University Press, 1999.
Capps, Benjamin, and the editors of Time-Life Books. *The Great Chiefs*. A volume in "The Old West" series. Alexandria, VA: Time-Life Books, Inc., 1975.
Castel, Albert E. *William Clarke Quantrill: His Life and Times*. New York: F. Fell, 1962.
Cullum, George W. *Biographical Register of the Officers and Graduates of the U.S. Military Academy at West Point, New York*. Boston: Houghton, Mifflin and Company: The Riverside Press, 1891 (3rd ed.).
DeArment, Robert. *Jim Courtright of Fort Worth: His Life and Legend*. Fort Worth: Texas Christian University Press, 2004.
DeMattos, Jack. *Mysterious Gunfighter: The Story of Dave Mather*. College Station, TX: Creative Publishing Company, 1992.
Dolan, Jay P. *The Irish Americans: A History*. London, England: Bloomsbury Press, 2008.
Eddins, Evyonne Andrews, Betty Porter, and David Voorhees. *Birdville, Texas: Frontier Wilderness, County Seat & Beyond*. Privately printed, 2005.
Eisenhower, John S. D. *So Far from God: The U.S. War with Mexico, 1846–48*. New York: Random House, 1989.
Exley, Jo Ella Powell. *Frontier Blood: The Saga of the Parker Family*. College Station: Texas A&M University Press, 2009.
Freeman, G. D. *Midnight and Noonday*. Norman: University of Oklahoma Press, 1984.
Garrett, Julia Kathryn. *Fort Worth: A Frontier Triumph*. Texas Christian University Press, 1996 (reprint of 1966 ed.).
Gates, Henry Louis, Jr. *In Search of Our Roots: How 19 Extraordinary African*

Americans Reclaimed Their Past. New York: Crown Publishing Group, 2009.

Goldfield, David, Carl Abbott et al., eds. *The American Journey: A History of the United States*, 4th ed. Upper Saddle River, NJ: Pearson Education Division / Prentice Hall, 2007.

Hacker, Margaret Schmidt. *Cynthia Ann Parker: The Life and the Legend.* El Paso: Texas Western Press, 1990.

Hagan, William T. *United States-Comanche Relations.* New Haven, CT: Yale University Press, 1976.

Hämäläinen, Pekka. *The Comanche Empire.* New Haven, CT: Yale University Press, 2008.

Knight, Oliver. *Fort Worth: Outpost on the Trinity.* Norman: University of Oklahoma Press, 1953.

Lamar, Howard, ed. *The Reader's Encyclopedia of the American West.* New York: Thomas Y. Crowell Company, 1977.

Lanning, Judy, and Jim Lanning, eds. *Texas Cowboys: Memories of the Early Days.* College Station: Texas A&M University Press, 1984.

Lindsley, Philip. *A History of Greater Dallas and Vicinity.* 2 vols. Chicago, IL: Lewis Publishing Co., 1909.

Mahon, John K. *History of the Second Seminole War, 1835–1842.* Gainesville, FL: University of Florida Press, 1967.

Mayhall, Mildred P. *Indian Wars of Texas.* Waco: Texian Press, 1965.

Miller, Nyle H., and Joseph W. Snell. *Why the West Was Wild.* Norman: University of Oklahoma Press, 2003.

Miller, Ray. *Ray Miller's Texas Forts: A History and Guide.* Houston: Gulf Publishing Company, 1985.

Mullen, Kevin J. *The Toughest Gang in Town: Police Stories from Old San Francisco.* Novato, CA: Noir Publications, 2005.

Neeley, Bill. *The Last Comanche Chief: The Life and Times of Quanah Parker.* New York: John Wiley & Sons, 1995.

O'Connor, Richard. *Iron Wheels and Broken Men.* New York: G. P. Putnam's Sons, 1973.

O' Neal, Bill. *Encyclopedia of Western Gunfighters.* Norman: University of Oklahoma Press, 1979.

Packard, Jerrold M. *American Nightmare: The History of Jim Crow.* New York: St. Martin's Press, 2002.

Perkins, Charles R. *History of Fort Worth Lodge No. 148, A.F.& A.M., 1855–1955.* Fort Worth: privately printed, 1957.

Perkins, Clay. *The Fort in Fort Worth.* Keller, TX: privately printed by Cross-Timbers Heritage Publishing Company, 2001.

Riegel, Robert Edgar. *The Story of the Western Railroads.* Lincoln: University of Nebraska Press, Bison Ed., 1967.

Robbins, James S. *Last in Their Class: Custer, Pickett and the Goats of West Point.* New York: Encounter Books, 2006.

Rodenbough, Theophilus F. *From Everglade to Cañon with the Second Dragoons.*

New York: Van Nostrand, 1875 (reprinted).
Schmidt, Ruby, ed. *Fort Worth & Tarrant County, A Historical Guide*. Fort Worth: Texas Christian University Press, 1984.
Selcer, Richard. *Civil War America, 1850 to 1875*. New York: Facts on File, 2006.
———. *The Fort That Became a City*. Fort Worth: Texas Christian University Press, 1995.
———. *Hell's Half Acre: The Life and Legend of a Red-light District*. Fort Worth: Texas Christian University Press, 1991.
———, ed. *Legendary Watering Holes: The Saloons That Made Texas Famous*. College Station: Texas A&M University Press, 2004.
Shirley, Glenn. *Heck Thomas: Frontier Marshal*. Norman: University of Oklahoma Press, 1981 (reprint of 1962 ed.).
Spence, Vernon Gladden. *Colonel Morgan Jones: Grand Old Man of Texas Railroading*. Norman: University of Oklahoma Press, 1971.
Spraker, Ella Hazel Atterbury. *The Boone Family: A Genealogical History of the Descendants of George and Mary Boone Who Came to America in 1717*. Privately printed, 1922.
Stanley, F. *Longhair Jim Courtright: Two-Gun Marshal of Fort Worth*. Denver, CO: World Press, 1957.
Stephens, Robert W. *Texas Ranger Sketches*. Dallas, TX: privately printed, 1972.
Tilghman, Zoe A. *Quanah: The Eagle of the Comanches*. Oklahoma City, OK: Harlow Publishing Company, 1938.
Tyler, Ron et al., eds. *The New Handbook of Texas*. 6 vols. Austin: Texas State Historical Association, 1996
Uzzel, Robert L. *Prince Hall Freemasonry in the Lone Star State from Cuney to Curtis, 1875–2003*. Fort Worth: privately printed, n.d.
Wilbarger, J. W., ed. *Indian Depredations in Texas* (Austin, TX: Eakin Press, 1991.
Williams, Mack, ed. *In Old Fort Worth: The Story of a City and Its People as Published in* The News-Tribune *in 1976 and 1977*. Fort Worth: privately printed by Mack H. Williams and Madeline C. Williams, 1986.

Periodical and On-line Sources

Burrows, Jack. "Commodore Perry Owens Had Plenty of Nerve and He Backed It up by Wielding a Winchester [as] Well." *Wild West* vol. 18, no. 4 (December, 2005): pp. 12–14ff.
Albuquerque (NM) Morning Journal.
Atlanta (GA) Constitution.
Austin Telegraph and Register. (See Selected America's Historical Newspapers on-line at http://infoweb.newsbank.com/iw-search/we/HistArchive.)
Austin Texas State Gazette. (See Selected America's Historical Newspapers on-line at http://infoweb.newsbank.com/iw-search/we/HistArchive).
Baltimore (MD) Sun.

Daily Missouri Republican.

Dallas Herald (Daily and Weekly) (on microfilm).

Dallas Morning News History Archive, 1885–1977 (on-line at http://www.fortworthgov.org/library).

Footprints: The Quarterly of the Fort Worth Genealogical Society. Genealogy, Local History, and Archives Unit, Fort Worth Public Library, Central Library.

Fort Worth Democrat (Daily).

Fort Worth Democrat-Advance.

Fort Worth Gazette (Daily and Weekly editions)

Fort Worth Mail-Telegram (catalogued with *Fort Worth Star-Telegram* on microfilm).

Fort Worth News-Tribune.

Fort Worth Press (on microfilm).

Fort Worth Record.

Fort Worth Register (Morning).

Fort Worth Star-Telegram. (See in particular "Special Centennial Edition," October 30, 1949).

Fort Worth Telegram (catalogued with *Fort Worth Star-Telegram* on microfilm).

Galveston News (Daily).

New Orleans Picayune.

New York Times Backfile, 1851–2001 (historical data base available on-line at ProQuest Historical Newspapers, http://proquest.umi.com/pdqweb?RQT = 302&cfc = 1).

"Quanah Parker, Last War Chief of the Quahadie Comanche." Author unknown. *Fort Worth Chronicle* vol. 2, no. 5 (1994): pp. 3–7ff.

Selcer, Richard. "Quanah Parker: Man of Two Worlds." *Wild West* vol. 20, no. 4 (December 2007): pp. 28–35.

———. "The Widow vs. the Bureaucrats: The Strange Case of Mrs. Captain Ripley Arnold." *Southwestern Historical Quarterly* vol. CVII, no. 3 (January 2004): pp. 361–87.

Rockdale (TX) Messenger.

San Antonio (TX) Light. (See Selected America's Historical Newspapers on-line at http://infoweb.newsbank.com/iw-search/we/HistArchive.)

Santa Fe Daily New Mexican. (See Selected America's Historical Newspapers on-line at http://infoweb.newsbank.com/iw-search/we/HistArchive.)

Washington (DC) Critic Record. (See Selected America's Historical Newspapers on-line at http://infoweb.newsbank.com/iw-search/we/HistArchive).

Wheeling (WVA) Register. (See Selected America's Historical Newspapers on-line at http://infoweb.newsbank.com/iw-search/we/HistArchive).

Williams, Mack, ed. "In Old Fort Worth" (various columns). *Fort Worth Tribune.*

INDEX

F